GOD AND HIS IMAGE

DOMINIQUE BARTHÉLEMY, O.P.

GOD AND HIS IMAGE

An Outline of Biblical Theology

Translated by

DOM ALDHELM DEAN, O.S.B.

Revised Edition and Foreword by

STEPHEN D. RYAN, O.P.

IGNATIUS PRESS SAN FRANCISCO

Original French edition © 1963 by Éditions du Cerf, Paris
New edition © 2004 by Éditions du Cerf, Paris
Dieu et son image: Ébauche d'une théologie biblique
English translation © 1966 by Geoffrey Chapman, Ltd.
Published in 1966 by Sheed and Ward, New York
Published with ecclesiastical approval

Revised edition published by permission of
Continuum International Book Publishing, London

Cover art:
Moses before the Burning Bush
Raphael (1483–1520)
Logge, Vatican Palace, Vatican City
© Scala / Art Resource, New York

Cover design by Roxanne Mei Lum

Published in 2007 Ignatius Press, San Francisco
ISBN 978-1-58617-082-0
Library of Congress Control Number 2005938823
Printed in the United States of America ♾

CONTENTS

FOREWORD TO THE REVISED EDITION

The Word of God is a privileged means by which the Church is constantly renewed and rejuvenated, Pope Benedict XVI has said recently. The book you are holding in your hands is an introduction to the spiritual teaching of the Bible, particularly the Old Testament, and can help believers to hear that renewing and rejuvenating Word of God with deepened understanding. It was first published in 1963. Its author, Jean-Dominique Barthélemy, a French Dominican priest, died in 2002. He was an internationally recognized expert in Old Testament studies, a member of the Pontifical Biblical Commission, and the author of a number of highly specialized works on the Greek and Hebrew texts of the Old Testament. This book is unlike his other publications. In it Fr. Barthélemy dispenses with the technical vocabulary of exegesis and linguistics and speaks theologically, as a priest and a believer. He once compared this book to an oxygen tank used by a scuba diver. Writing this book allowed Fr. Barthélemy to breathe at a time when he was so deeply submerged in the technical study of the textual history of the biblical manuscripts from Qumran that he had begun to lose sight of the larger message of the Bible. With this work, based on lectures given to graduate students at the University of Fribourg (Switzerland) and then published as a series of articles in the French journal *La Vie Spirituelle*, Fr. Barthélemy returned to the heart of the biblical message.

This is a book about God and man. It is also a book about the long history of God's search for man and the difficulty man had in keeping intact the divine image in which he was created. The purpose of the book is to present what God says about himself and about his image in the inspired text of Scripture. Fr. Barthélemy reads the Bible as a Christian, which is to say, as a whole. The Old and New Testaments together unfold the divine plan to redeem man with the aid of the people he chose and formed for freedom, including Moses, David and the prophets, and culminating in the gift of his own Son and the new covenant in the Spirit. This book thus helps us to see the profound unity between the Old and New Testaments and shows that the Old Testament is not only a record of the past addressed to Israel but also a light for men and women of faith today. It is little wonder then that this work was Fr. Barthélemy's most widely circulated publication, having been translated from the original French into a number of modern languages, including German, English, Italian and Russian. From its first appearance in 1963 to its most recent French edition in 2004 (in the Treasures of Christianity series), *God and His Image* has provided a profound entry into the spirituality of the Old Testament for Catholic readers.

Fr. Barthélemy has written a book that both enkindles the heart and enlightens the mind. One of his fundamental insights is that the Old Testament can help modern Christians to see more clearly the ways in which the "old man", the old Adam, is still very much with us. It can help us to see our own idolatries, our misery, our poverty, our ways of trying to escape the freedom and the dignity that God calls us to experience. It is precisely when we see ourselves truly in the mirror of Scripture that we recognize the full extent of our need for God—the God who sent his own Son to redeem us and make us sons with a right of inheritance, heirs of the Kingdom. Fr. Barthélemy's insights about the pedagogical nature and abiding significance of the Old Testament are rooted in the teaching of St. Paul. John Paul II's Encyclical Letter *Veritatis Splendor* (no. 23) summarizes this teaching in a powerful way:

> "The law of the Spirit of life in Christ Jesus has set me free from the law of sin and death" (Rom 8:2). With these words the Apostle Paul invites us to consider in the perspective of the history of salvation, which reaches its fulfillment in Christ, *the relationship between the* (Old) *Law and grace* (the New Law). He recognizes the pedagogic function of the Law, which, by enabling sinful man to take stock of his own powerlessness and by stripping him of the presumption of his self-sufficiency, leads him to ask for and to receive "life in the Spirit." Only in this new life is it possible to carry out God's commandments. Indeed, it is through faith in Christ that we have been made righteous (cf. Rom 3:28): the "righteousness" which the Law demands, but is unable to give, is found by every believer to be revealed and granted by the Lord Jesus.

God and His Image traces this same movement from the Old to the New Law, from the incomplete understandings of God exposed in Scripture to the indwelling of the trinitarian God in the hearts of believers. Fr. Barthélemy thus begins with a consideration of Job's incorrect view of God and concludes with a discussion of the Holy Spirit's regeneration of the image of God in the soul of the believer. In the spiritual itinerary envisioned here it is Scripture, the Word of God, that reveals to us where we are in our journey, the road we still have to travel, and God's plan to bring us to our destination. In this most important journey the Word of God serves as a lamp for our feet and a light for our path.[1]

Fr. Stephen D. Ryan, O.P.
Pontifical Faculty of the Immaculate Conception
Dominican House of Studies
Washington, D.C.

[1] This edition of *God and His Image* generally uses the chapter and verse numbers used in the Jerusalem Bible (Garden City, N.Y.: Doubleday, 1966). However, the translations vary in order to reflect Father Barthélemy's sources and wording. —Ed.

PREFACE

This book is the work of an amateur. An "amateur", from the Latin *amare*, is one who hastens toward the things he loves, without constantly checking that the ground he treads on is solid, recovering by his next step the balance he lost in the last, uncertain one. Yet in spite of this too simple apology, the pages that I now offer for publication cause me a little misgiving. I am afraid that in writing them I have succeeded only too well in forgetting what I know about textual or literary criticism. When I set forth certain precepts of the law, the Elohistic and Deuteronomic codes intermingle without the least constraint. Traits in the character of Moses are gathered from Yahwistic, Elohistic and sometimes priestly traditions as though it were quite in order to unite their witness without learned preliminary discussions. The Books of Exodus, Ezekiel and Revelation converse together like old friends, without any introduction. I am therefore afraid that those who peruse these pages may be shocked to find me regarding the Bible as the work of a single author. I am aware that a work cannot be called serious—in the critical sense—if it springs from such an old-fashioned idea. So it must be clearly understood that in this sense the present work is not serious.

However, I bring myself to publish it because I have come to the conclusion that reams written in an overcritical spirit run the risk of concealing the fundamental nature of Holy Scripture: a word of God spoken to his people today, spoken to you and me. Just before writing the ten chapters of this book, I spent ten whole years studying the Palestinian recensions of the Greek Bible made during the first century of the Christian era. This work is now in the hands of printers in Holland.[1] I do not belittle it, but I confess it brought me no new light whatsoever on the impact that the Word of God must have on my life. One could take a painting and write the story of the successive varnishings and cleanings it has undergone and discuss the changes of emphasis these have led to. One might write the history of the progress of the cracks in the *Mona Lisa* and seek to discover when it was that the crack joining the inner corner of the right eye to the right nostril first appeared, or the slightly winding one a little to the right of it. This has importance, for these two cracks make it difficult to perceive the transition from the nose to the cheek, both of which are equally clear, and yet are placed on two different planes. Since the Bible is the word of God, it is only right that much time and trouble should be given to the study of the various transformations undergone by its text. But the enlarged photographic effect thus produced has little connection with the viewpoint of *lectio divina*.

To take another example, the meaning of that strange figure nowadays called the Winged Victory of Samothrace is not revealed by the story of its mutilations or the remaking of its right wing and the left side of its torso. In its mutilated and half-restored form, the Winged Victory "exists" for us much more—though in quite a different way—than it did for those who contemplated it new in the temple of the Cabiri during the second century B.C. The rediscovery

[1] Fr. Barthélemy refers to his study of the early history of the transmission of the text of the Old Testament, a study that made use of the recently discovered Dead Sea Scrolls. It appeared as *Les Devanciers d'Aquila* (Supplements to Vetus Testamentum, 10; Leiden: Brill, 1963).—ED.

in 1950 of the palm of its right hand and the comparison of this with the fragments of fingers preserved in the museum of Vienne shed no light on the significance of *our* Winged Victory, whose unique characteristic suggests a bursting into the future, her headless bust borne up by wings to which the absence of arms gives true meaning. If the sculptor had produced his statue with neither arms nor a head, we should be shocked by so harsh a surrealistic conception. But the hazards of its decay have stripped it with impunity of all that detracted from its true meaning as a bastion of Greek civilization in our ageless Western culture. To grasp the idea of its flight, our attention must be fixed on the left wing, the only authentic one; but it is the mass of the restored right wing alone that enables the left wing to suggest soaring flight instead of want of balance.

Our Bible also, as the Churches of Antioch, Rome and Alexandria inherited it at the time of their foundation, is something unique, heir of a thousand transformations. Some books have been lost, others considerably altered. Centuries overlap, voices intermingle. Yet in this precise form it is for us the word of God. The Holy Spirit has willed to give it to us in this state; and if critical research is useful in helping us understand the steps by which it reached this state, its object should not be to replace it by a more primitive version. We must recognize that the form of the Christian Bible toward the end of the first century is its mature form, and that it possesses an internal coherence willed by the Holy Spirit, whose inspiration brought it to that maturity in which it was to become the sacred library of the people of the new and eternal covenant. And the kind of reading properly suited to this Holy Scripture is *lectio divina*, that is, a reading that looks upon the Bible as the work of a *single author*: God.

A work of "biblical theology", therefore, can be attempted only on two conditions:

1. The refusal to isolate a book, or even a Testament, since the *Bible as a whole* is as vitally integrated as a drama in five acts.

2. To keep the mind fixed on *what God tells us of himself.* If we fail to observe the first condition, we have no right to call our theology biblical; if we fail to observe the second, our biblical study cannot be called theology.

I will not insist on this paradox to the extent of saying that it would be better to ignore the literary prehistory of the sacred texts. But at all events, we must not be led astray into shifting and uncertain criticism. It is enough for the biblical theologian to know on which of the Victory's wings he prefers to concentrate; but I think little is to be gained by talking about it. Criticism can only help us to keep the relationship between the various texts in due perspective; occasionally this will set the synthesis of the whole in higher relief. On other occasions, however, nothing is to be gained by emphasizing the "relief" element, and a more telescopic perspective will bring out the fundamental unity of God's word. Whereas criticism comes near to certainty only by means of the precision of its minute analyses, biblical theology depends on the ability to form certain broad views, whether it is a matter of integrating ideas that are apparently opposed to one another, or of unifying what seem to be the heterogeneous stages of some development.

To distinguish the theologian's point of view from that of the critic, let us take another comparison. A newspaper reproduction of a photograph consists of a number of black-and-white dots. Imagine a reproduction that can scarcely be made out because it is blotchy, uneven and far too dark. The critic will make an analysis of the reproduction, carefully counting the black dots in one section after another. The theologian will hold the reproduction at arm's length in a good light and half close his eyes in the hope of making out some image. Since we are looking for an image to give meaning to the whole reproduction, the second method is the only sound one. Similarly, the way we should read the Bible will depend on whether or not the Bible has a meaning as a whole. If it has no meaning, the critic's analysis will be able to set down the bewildering heterogeneous details only where the darker shades predominate. But if the Bible does have an all-embracing meaning, analysis will have to give way to a general view, which implies that one must step back and bring both eyelid and iris into play. A keener look will be given only to certain details to check, in a particular case, the probability of an interpretation suggested by the more general effect. The texts used by the theologian in support of his general views will benefit by being presented in translations of varying degrees of literalness, depending on whether the intention is to show the tone of a whole passage at a glance, or to bring out some characteristic detail by a kind of photographic enlargement.

But it is by no means easy to take a sufficiently synthetic view of the fifteen hundred pages that make up the average Bible. To achieve such an end, one must begin by tirelessly delving into the whole Bible, so that it becomes engraved on the memory in broad, distinct outlines. When one is examining a particular text, the general outline must always remain in one's mind, so that a particular intuition may find its appropriate echo in some verse several hundred pages away. To take up a concordance and study a word analytically may help in giving precision to certain data, but it can never replace that casual conversation that goes on in the memory between the voice I am listening to today and another voice that I was listening to in a different part of the Bible several months ago, which I did not understand at the time. Moreover, if the verse that I am reading today—and which I have often read before, thinking I understood it—now speaks with a new voice, it is because several months ago I was struck by the tone of the other verse that I did not then understand. Now I become aware of a dialogue between the two, which previously I did not suspect.

It is not enough just to read and reread the Bible if we want it to speak to us. Let us go back to our comparison of a newspaper photograph that is hard to decipher. It would be easier for me to make out the meaning of this image if I already knew the reality it represents. In a way, one can even say that it is only possible to make out something one is capable of recognizing. I could recognize, even in a very bad reproduction, the features of a face well known to me, because these features are already engraved in my mind. The smallest shadows and reflections will have meaning if the object represented already dwells in my memory. But realities that are of no real interest to me do not remain as faithful guests of memory. For a voice to be recognized, it is not enough that we should have already *heard* it; it is at least necessary that it should have *spoken* to us in its normal tone. The man who has not yet identified the tone of God's word in his life will not be able to decipher the word of God in Holy Scripture. I shall never succeed in getting on to the wavelength where his voice can be recognized unless my loving silence is already at home on that wavelength.

Now that these principles have been put forward I cannot pretend to have applied them in the present work. It was only in the course of the work that they progressively came home to me, and I have tried to state them only now that this book is finished. I did not start out on these chapters with a preconceived plan, but here is the order they have ended up by taking: after briefly introducing the Christian to the Bible, and more particularly to the Old Testament, the first two chapters enter, by way of a beginning, into the problems of revelation and reparation that characterize the whole Bible. The eight chapters that follow do not strictly speaking deal in a uniform way with eight successive stages of God's work. Rather they give eight views on the Bible taken with filters that pick out certain colors in a multicolored whole. Just as a color reproduction is made by superimposing several one-color impressions from selective negatives, each of which is a photograph of the whole image, so, it seems to me, a balanced biblical theology can be obtained only if the reader's mind puts together several selective views taken from the entire biblical panorama. In each of these views, one part of the image will appear in special relief, since it is richer in the color chosen by this particular filter. And so I find that I have classified these views in the chronological order of the elements that they particularly emphasize. For example, in the third chapter what stands out most clearly is the coming of Moses on to the scene, while it is the Decalogue that gives character to the fourth. The fifth is concerned with the golden calf. The sixth brings out the personality of David and the seventh that of Hosea. The message of Jeremiah occupies the eighth. At the center of the ninth, the Holy Grail shines forth. In the tenth, we listen to the voice of the Paraclete.

We all know that faithful color reproduction is a difficult matter. The difficulty here is even greater, because the spectrum of the Word of God is not that of ordinary white light. It is far from easy to identify the elements that make up that perfect silence of colors which is the true light. We cannot simply focus a lens and capture on an impartially selective film one element in the spectrum of the Bible's essential radiance. One dominant color will tend to swamp the rest. A missing color will betray its absence by the consequent overemphasis of one of the others.

The text of this work has already been published in almost identical forms as ten articles in *La Vie Spirituelle*, from November 1961 to April 1963. The first eight were a much-edited version of the first six lectures in the *Cours de Science Religieuse* given in 1960–1961 in the Aula of the University of Fribourg. In this edition, a few glosses and further biblical references have been added as notes.

Fribourg, Switzerland
March 10, 1963

ABBREVIATIONS

AI R. de Vaux. *Ancient Israel*, London, 1961.

AP W. F. Albright. *The Archaeology of Palestine*. Harmondsworth, 1960.

BJ Fr. Barthélemy used the French edition of the Jerusalem Bible: *La Sainte Bible*, translated into French under the direction of L'École Biblique de Jérusalem, Paris, 1955. The page references to the Jerusalem Bible have been adjusted so that they now reference the appropriate page in the English translation, rather than the French edition. Because of this, in most cases the references are *JB*, referring to the English edition. In a few particular cases, however, *BJ* is used to indicate the author's reference specifically to the French edition.

JB *The Jerusalem Bible*. Garden City, New York: Doubleday, 1966.

GTS M. du Buit, *Géographie de la Terre Sainte*. Paris, 1958.

Passages from Scripture are largely taken from the Revised Standard Version, Second Catholic Edition, but depart from it occasionally in order to conform to the French translation used by the author.

INTRODUCTION

Rereading the ancient word

The Old Testament is not a collection of archives in the ordinary sense of the word. If it were, it would be reasonable to suppose that access to the Old Testament ought to be reserved to a particular category of men, to the few whose special vocation it is to establish continuity with the past and who are found in all countries: the archivists. The archives of the Old Testament contain a word of God. And when long ago God began to speak, the word he uttered was already very much closer to that uttered by Christ than we are inclined to think. God does not change, and what God wills to say to man is basically always the same thing. The secret message communicated by this word from God remains substantially the same.[1] Nevertheless, the people who were still in their infancy and who heard this word for the first time could not be expected to gather from it the same elements, the same fullness of understanding that a more adult people have later been able to realize. God could have said even then something that Jesus would one day say to his apostles during his discourse after the Last Supper (Jn 16:12): "I have yet many things to say to you, but you cannot bear them now." That is to say, the Word of God already intended to stir up in man echoes that would only resound much later.

[1] See *JB*, note on the first verse of St. John's Gospel, as well as the marginal references in that Bible to this verse.

This word contained riches that men were not capable of grasping at the time. But the people of God were destined to ripen little by little in the twofold experience of an immense gift communicated by God and a wretchedness whose remedy became ever more obscure. At each stage of its gradual ripening, this people, reflecting on God's words of old, were able to understand them better and to grasp shades of meaning that were formerly unfathomed. In this connection, one might quote another saying of our Lord at the Last Supper (Jn 14:26): "But the Counselor, the Holy Spirit . . . will teach you all things, and bring to your remembrance all that I have said to you." And it is precisely because the word, from Abraham to Jesus, is always so much richer than contemporaries realize, that one of the fundamental works of the Spirit is to recall to man what God has said of old, to remind him, when he has grown in depth and inspiration, of what he has heard in childhood and could not then understand. The Holy Spirit, then, who inspired the Scriptures and planted in them his secret treasures that no man living could fathom at the time of their writing, had this further role which necessarily followed from the first, of being the guide on the rereading of the ancient word. That is why this word did not resound in the ears of Abraham and his successors without leaving traces of its passage. First of all it was preserved by means of a living oral tradition.[2] Later, once the art of writing took root in Israel, the word was committed to writing. This revered Scripture remained deeply engraved in the minds of the people—not like a dead letter or forgotten archives, but as the object of

[2] For the importance of oral traditions at the beginning of Holy Scripture, see *JB*, introduction to the Pentateuch, p. 7. See also "education" in the index of *AI*.

continual meditation,[3] which ensured that understanding would grow in the direction of its original orientation.

Let us now take a third quotation from our Lord's words at the Last Supper: "When the Spirit of truth comes, he will guide you into all the truth" (Jn 16:13). The Spirit makes himself the people's guide in their rereading of that word which he had once inspired, because it is his mission to enable us to penetrate *all* truth. And even after the death of Jesus—since the disciples of the Word of God Made Flesh were not able to bear what he had to say to them—his people must continue this rereading of the word so as to come to the whole truth. But this is possible only under the leadership of the same Spirit who inspired the ancient word, possible, that is, only by belonging to that people to whom the Spirit was promised by the custodian of the promises. Such is the perspective, I think, in which the Bible truly makes complete sense for us. Now we can understand why and how Jesus could say that the Christian familiar with the ancient Scriptures is "like a householder who brings out of his treasure what is new and what is old" (Mt 13:52). Materially speaking he can bring out only what is old, but if he knows how to take stock of his treasure under the guidance of the Spirit who formerly gave life to that word, then spiritually he can bring out what is new also.

The Old Testament as light for the new man

But of what interest to us Christians can it be to know how the people of Israel gradually anticipated a gift that

[3] See the prologue by the translator of Ecclesiasticus (Sirach) in *JB*, p. 1036. See also what is said about the influences on Jeremiah and about those influenced by him in the introduction to Jeremiah, *JB*, pp. 1126–27. See also the enumeration of the sources of 1 and 2 Chron in *JB*, pp. 492–93.

overwhelms us today? Surely this is chiefly a matter of historical interest. Surely the kind of Scripture we must meditate on if we are to penetrate the whole truth is to be found in the New Testament rather than the Old. Since the Old Testament can be defined as the law of death for the old man, the New Testament can be defined as the law of entry into the life of the new man.[4] Yet the Old Testament does have more than a theoretical interest for us. Although for us the stage of being dead to the old man has been substantially surmounted, this is not altogether so. Baptism[5] has implanted in us the seed of the new man, but the old man still remains very much alive in us. All our lives we have to die and be born. And when death comes, it is important that this new man implanted in us as a seed should be still living, living for eternity. Failing this, man is born dead—conceived, but born dead. Baptism is the conception, and we ourselves, being free, are responsible for seeing that the seed remains viable throughout life, that is to say, that our essential being passes progressively from the old man to the new; and this is not achieved by itself alone.

It is almost dangerous to be a being in whom one knows the new man has been planted, because we are liable to believe that he will grow of his own accord. We may think we are cured, when in fact the old man is working away all the time and our essential vitality is still in his hands. What are his tactics? He does not attack the new man openly; the old man is too subtle for that. He knows very well that, should he show himself as an atheist in the heart of one baptized, the latter would promptly take steps to

[4] For notions of the old man and the new man, see *JB*, notes on Eph 2:15 and Col 3:10.

[5] See *JB*, notes on Rom 6:4 and Col 3:5.

exterminate him. And so the old man, atheist though he is, puts on the guise of religion. In his own way, he monopolizes and caricatures the destiny of the new man. He sucks his bones to the marrow and fastens on him as a parasite far more than he seeks to overthrow him. The old man does not present himself as an atheist but as an idolater, which is something much more delicate and cunning. In other words, realizing his inability to drive God away, he seeks instead to take him in hand and fashion him to his own image. The old man never yields himself into the hands of the living God, for that would be his death.[6] He prefers instead to make for himself a comfortable God, one easy to live with, while the new man, who is seldom very shrewd when he is young, is capable of living for a long time without suspecting that somebody else is gradually fashioning his God for him; so that instead of being placed in the hands of the living God, he finds in his own hands a dream God. Thus he tries to placate and ease his conscience by remaining faithful to a God, not perhaps a God of his own invention, but one far removed from the living God. And therein lies the drama: the old man turns monk with a taste for a gospel that has become insipid. There is nothing he will not do to make sure he is not recognized, so that he can go on living as a parasite in the bosom of those good intentions which pave the way to hell, in the bosom of all that passes for what is noblest in man's heart. For there is nothing he cannot make use of or twist to his ends.

[6] It is the old man who says, "It is a fearful thing to fall into the hands of the living God" (Heb 10:31), while the new man cries out, "My heart and flesh sing for joy to the living God" (Ps 84:2).

This explains why the old man must be put to death, why we must begin by hunting him out and expose to the light of day the work of the idolatrous old man, who tries to hide himself by making us believe we are entirely beings of the New Testament, that we are wholly capable of digesting the gospel in our wide-open hearts and of living by it. But let us turn once more to the Old Testament. There, we may clearly see the craftiness, the ruses that the old man made use of when he fled from God and was not yet disguised as a sheep of the Good Shepherd. For the Old Testament is above all the great exposure of idolatry, the great exposure of caricatures of the living God. There is a risk that we Christians, by a sort of quietism, may let ourselves be lulled to sleep in the hands of what we imagine is "the good God", instead of trying to let ourselves be formed by him who is the living God. The Old Testament brings vividly before our eyes our idolatry, our running away, and helps us to realize our wretchedness, our poverty, enabling us thus to rediscover ourselves among those poor for whom the Kingdom was made.[7]

[7] See *JB*, note on Mt 5:3.

I

A Wrong View of God: Job

Beginning in darkness

If we want to succeed in seeing things clearly, we must necessarily begin in the dark. This may appear paradoxical, but in the Old Testament it is no use seizing on the first glimmer of light in which we think we discern an obvious reflection of the New Testament. We must first approach what would seem to be the very opposite of this, because the light found in the Old Testament is only the dim light of dawn, and if our eyes are dazzled by full sunshine, we cannot perceive the twilight. The only thing to do is to begin in darkness.[1] When you go into a really dark cellar, you must first get used to the complete blackness, and only then will the obscurity take on glimmers of half-light. Students of radioscopy—the examination of objects by means of X-rays—are well aware that examination cannot be made until the eyes have been in the dark long enough to be accustomed to it. We actually have two systems of sight: one for daylight vision and the other for night vision, and to bring the second into play requires a certain lapse of time to allow the former to become dormant.

[1] In certain of Rembrandt's canvasses and etchings, lack of light near the edges enables the light in the center to stand out with emphasis.

In the same way, we have two systems of biblical perception—one for the New Testament and one for the Old. We must lay the New Testament system firmly on one side and have the courage to enter into the night of those people who were lying in darkness and on whom the light dawned[2] if, with them, we are to see that light arise. We must first accustom ourselves to the shadows, otherwise we shall always run the risk of comparing the dawn of the Old Testament with the full light of the Gospel, and so we should find that nothing there is clear to us, that no important message reaches the heart of mankind. No doubt this seems a gloomy outlook for that part of us which is accustomed to reading the Gospel. For this very reason we must put ourselves in the place of those who heard it for the first time. If we fail to put ourselves in their place, we shall never understand.

That is why the Book of Job is of fundamental importance. It is in this book that Israel wonders what is the situation of the pagan man in relation to God. By the pagan man we mean the man who knows nothing of revelation, to whom God has not yet spoken.

The Book of Job, a paleontology of revelation

The Book of Job tells us of a man who lived in a distant country, the land of Uz, and it shows him grappling with God. For man does not require some revelation to be already permanently conversant with God, to be constantly shocked, even scandalized, by the way in which God guides his universe, to feel the revolt of his conscience because of his actions, and to be discouraged by them. Man is constantly

[2] Is 9:1; Mt 4:16; Lk 1:78–79; Jn 8:12; Rom 13:12.

grappling with God, but with a God whose behavior is mysterious and who does not answer when he is questioned. Such is the God of Job. He is a God who does not explain himself. And Israel sets Job, a wise pagan, face to face with him. The people of Israel had to reach maturity before they could ask themselves: What is the relationship between God and a man who knows nothing of revelation? And this came about only fairly late. One must be already born before embarking on the study of paleontology. That is why mankind had to reach a clear understanding of itself before it could consider the question of its own origin. The Book of Job is a kind of paleontology of revelation.[3] Delving into the past beyond that first word spoken by God to Abraham could be undertaken only when man, possessed of revelation, could ask himself what he was about, and what this treasured inheritance was. How and when did he go about this self-questioning?

A Jew both scandalized and rebellious

I think man's self-questioning was at the time of the Exile, for the exile of the kingdom of Judah was a tragedy for those Israelites who were living around Jerusalem and trying seriously to mend their ways during the days of King Josiah, about 620 B.C.[4] They had done their best to be converted, but that had not stopped Nebuchadnezzar from

[3] The Book of Job is not *only* that, but this is the point of view that interests us here. Cf. the helpful introduction to this book in *JB*; in this introduction I would question only the suggested date for the editing of the book, preferring to place it during the Exile rather than after it. We should note that the theology of the book presupposes the ideas of Ezekiel but not those of the fourth song of the suffering servant (Is 53:10–12).

[4] See 2 Kings 22 and 23; also 2 Chron 34 and 35.

coming, laying siege to the city, finally taking it and deporting all the finest of the people.[5] What can it all mean? *Does God thus hunt down those that have returned to him?* And if such is the case, what is the hidden meaning of this suffering that falls so heavily on men, many of whom have striven so hard after interior conversion? And above all there is that question that goes even deeper: Is one really righteous? Is the effort to be converted enough to make one righteous before God? *Is it possible for a man to be righteous before God?* Such is the question asked by these men, many of whom find themselves exiled even after devoting themselves to most sincere religious reform. Such is the question asked by those who remain to contemplate the ruins.

They dare not ask the question in so blatant a manner. So one of them describes, not a people, but an individual, a foreigner—a pagan who, believing himself just and innocent, finds himself harshly treated by God. Through the mouth of this pagan, then, the author gives expression to his own scandalized mind, to the workings of his conscience over God's severe treatment of his people. He brings before Job a few friends who try to reason with him and make him understand why God treats him in this way. To suffer such calamities, he must be guilty of some hidden faults. And in any case it is not for man to ask God to explain his reasons, but simply to believe in his justice. But Job is by no means comforted and soothed by this, any more than the author of the Book of Job is soothed by hearing the devout and traditional wisdom of the Jews declare that Israel cannot have been sufficiently converted,

[5] On this drama, see the beginning of the introduction to the Book of Jeremiah in *JB*, p. 1126. The events are related in 2 Kings 24 and 25.

that God must have his reasons for allowing Israel to be deported.

All this scarcely convinces the author of the Book of Job. This is why Job's complaint rises higher, louder and more intense than the reasonings of these orthodox theologians who are his friends. And God has willed that this great cry of scandal before the ways of Providence should survive until our days.[6] God has willed that this man, for whom the theological reasonings of his day appear unacceptable and wholly insufficient, should cry aloud to us. There must be a reason for this.

The unbearable presence

Let us try and listen to Job. But first of all let us be quite clear that for him the existence of God is not the problem; the problem he is up against is *the existence of man*. We should be inclined to think that the existence of man is obvious but that the existence of God is by no means so clear. For Job it is just the opposite:

First text (14:1–6):

> "Man that is born of a woman is of few days, and full of trouble.
> He comes forth like a flower, and withers;
> he flees like a shadow, and continues not.
> And do you open your eyes upon such a one
> and bring him into judgment with you?

[6] God has also willed that the only words gathered by the two oldest evangelists from the lips of the dying Jesus were, "My God, my God, why have you forsaken me?" (Mt 27:46; Mk 15:34), so that believers in a state of confusion should never feel that they were intruding, but always find a place to lay their head in the paradise of Scripture.

Who can bring a clean thing out of an unclean?
There is not one.[7]
Since his days are determined,
and the number of his months is with you,
and you have appointed his bounds that he cannot pass,
look away from him, and desist,
that he may enjoy, like a hireling, his day."

1. *First drama* of man: he comes forth like a flower, he is cut down.[8] Man wants to bear fruit, and he aspires to a rich fecundity, but just at the moment when the flower buds forth, when his desires show themselves, he sees death approaching. Just when he catches a glimpse of what he thinks is desirable, he sees that his strength has already begun to fail.

2. *Second drama*: God brings this frail and fallen creature before his judgment seat and demands justice of him. Why cannot he be left to endure his confusion as best he can? Why must a reckoning still be asked of him? If man could only be left quiet for a moment, be granted at least the

[7] Instead of "Who can bring a clean thing out of an unclean? There is not one", which is a translation of the Hebrew, the Septuagint version of the Greek "translates": "Who will be clean of every defilement? There is not one, even if his life on the earth lasts only a single day." It is in this form that Philo of Alexandria and later all the Greek Fathers, as well as all the Latin Fathers up to St. Bernard and including Abelard, cite this verse. St. Jerome does the same in his theological works. But, in his Vulgate, which he wished to be faithful to the "Hebrew truth", inspired by Targum Jonathan and the Babylonian Talmud he "translated": "Who can render clean that which was conceived of an unclean seed, if not You who are unique?" This is therefore how the whole Latin scholastic tradition has read this verse. One sees by means of this example the liberty with which the Greek and Latin Bibles sometimes gloss the Hebrew. This poses a number of questions that I shall attempt to formulate in another work.

[8] Unlike the second, this idea is not peculiar to Job. See *JB*, marginal parallels to Job 14:1, 2.

right to pass the evening of his days in peace, without remorse that pierces him and drags him down interiorly! If only he could forget, could rest a while, and in that dread moment calmly sink to sleep—but God does not allow it.

Second text (14:16–17, 19c–20):

"For then you would number my steps,
  you would not keep watch over my sin;
my transgression would be sealed up in a bag,
  and you would cover over my iniquity.

  [S]o you destroy the hope of man.
You prevail for ever against him, and he passes;
  you change his countenance and send him away."

God does not even allow man to die with the illusion that he has done something worth while. God wills that man should die without hope, die with the conviction that he has ruined his life. If only God would take away from man this hopeless nostalgia, this gnawing conscience that destroys his peace!

Third text (10:20b–22):

"Let me alone, that I may find a little comfort
before I go from where I shall not return,
  to the land of gloom and deep darkness,
the land of gloom and chaos,
  where light is as darkness."

God need not worry. Why come and scrutinize this being who will disappear in an instant? This man who is about to be blotted out is no redoubtable enemy.

The fourth text (7:16b–21) resumes the spirit of the preceding three. All four texts, gathered from the first part of the book, re-echo one another. They truly give us the *leitmotif* of the Book of Job.

"Let me alone, for my days are a breath.
What is man, that you make so much of him,
and that you set your mind upon him,
visit him every morning,
and test him every moment?
How long will you not look away from me,
nor let me alone till I swallow my spittle?
If I sin, what do I do to you, you watcher of men?
Why have you made me your mark?
Why have I become a burden to you?
Let my sins pass.
Be not troubled with all my faults.
For now I shall lie in the earth;
you will seek me, but I shall be no more."

It seems that Job here expresses the drama of the silent and damning presence of God's piercing gaze. He says: "How long will you not look away from me, / nor let me alone till I swallow my spittle?" To swallow one's spittle suggests a moment's respite, a moment's calm. Job is so affected and exasperated by God's steadfast gaze upon him that he cannot swallow. His distress is exactly like that of a person who cannot feel at ease at home because his neighbor's window is only two yards away and there are no curtains. It is natural to want to be private at home. But under this gaze of God, one is never at home. There is never a moment of relief when one can say, "Nobody is looking at me now." One must always be acting a part and assume the correct bearing in front of him who is always there. Man feels crushed by the insistent and scrutinizing gaze of God, who will not leave him to himself, quiet, alone, relaxed and confident. Man for ever has this strange gaze turned upon him, a gaze not only strange, but one that demands a reckoning of him, that scrutinizes his whole being. In modern existentialism, the idea of looking has been put in the front rank. For Sartre,[9] religious experience is concerned with the fact of being looked at, of knowing oneself as looked at, and of being "in the eyes of another". It would be surprising if Sartre had learned this from Job. But what is certain is that it corresponds exactly with the analysis of Job. In natural religion (and we must start with that) where there is no exchange of dialogue, God is the silent Almighty before whom man feels himself crushed and stripped naked; he feels unprovided for in the presence of a dangerous power. Man knows that he is naked, that is to say, looked at, undermined, threatened by this gaze.

Innocent in God's eyes?

Let us now read the dream or rather the nightmare of Eliphaz. This nightmare, in spite of being that of one of Job's friends, corresponds exactly to the experiences of Job himself (4:12–20). Eliphaz the Temanite tells Job for his consolation the nightmare he has had the night before. He says:

> "Now a word was brought to me stealthily,
>   my ear received the whisper of it.
> Amid thoughts from visions of the night,
>   when deep sleep falls on men,
> dread came upon me, and trembling,
>   which made all my bones shake.
> A spirit glided past my face;
>   the hair of my flesh stood up.

[9] See Jean-Paul Sartre, *L'être et le néant* (Paris: Gallimard, 1943), p. 350 (English translation, *Being and Non-Being: Nothingness: An Essay in Phenomenological Ontology* (New York: Citadel Press, 1966).

It stood still,
  but I could not discern its appearance.
A form was before my eyes;
  there was silence, then I heard a voice:
'Can mortal man be righteous before God?
  Can a man be pure before his Maker?
Even in his servants he puts no trust,
  and his angels he charges with error;
how much more those who dwell in houses of clay,
  whose foundation is in the dust,
  who are crushed before the moth.
  . . . without any regarding it.' "

How momentary is man's existence; he springs from his native clay for an instant like a worm that nestles in the dust and that, the next instant, will be trodden underfoot without anyone noticing it. The death of a man leaves few traces, at least very few that are permanent. Is this the being that God will find righteous? When all the angels are in his sight and subject to his judgment, if God can find fault in the utterly pure spirits that stand before him, what will happen to man? Yes or no, can man be innocent? He may think that he is innocent, but what does that mean? To his drowsy conscience man seems to be more or less in order, at least as much as those around him. Strictly speaking, what connection is there between man's way of judging and that of God's, whose deepest secret desire is the blooming of his creature? Compared with that absolute that God is ready to plant in man's heart, if only man realized his need, can a "clear conscience" suffice for positive acquittal? This is the great question in Eliphaz's nightmare: Can a man really be innocent in God's sight? Is there the slightest connection between the impression of being "no worse than the rest" and the fact of being innocent in the eyes of the Lord himself?

The twofold scandal of Job before God

Fundamentally, Job experiences a twofold scandal before God.

1. How is it that the almighty creator allows man to die? How can he allow desires to spring up in the heart of man and be felt, only when man has already lost the ability to put them into effect? How can the almighty author of all that is allow such a thing, when he is able to maintain his creation and cause it progressively to develop from age to age? How is it that man, in whose heart God has planted the desire for that perfect development that his creator wishes for him, should be the only being in creation who is prevented from achieving it? This is what scandalizes Job. How can the Almighty leave man to slip away to death[10] like water leaking through the cracks in a cistern?

2. Why does God, who does not intervene to save him, intervene in a different way in the form of gnawing remorse that depresses man within, so that even his last moments are not moments of peace and forgetting but of agony and obsession with his ruined life? Why does God leave this hopeless desire in the heart of a man who is approaching death? Why does God preserve in man this destroying influence of an ineffectual conscience, capable only of condemning him, crushing him, defacing him so that he loses all hope?

Job's greatest hope is that God will forget all about man. If God will not save, at least let him not torment him further; let him neither hasten nor trouble his inevitable death.

[10] This inevitable slipping away toward death is evoked in an affected and disillusioned style by Ecclesiastes (12:1–8).

Job's blasphemy

Nevertheless, Job knows quite well that God will never abandon us. He admits as much to Bildad the Shuhite when he advises him not to question God's actions (9:2–12, 19–31). This passage is sometimes called Job's blasphemy, and indeed it deserves the name. But God can understand blasphemy like this, for the grounds for it are rarely as grave as these.

"Truly I know that it is so:
  But how can a man be just before God?
If one wishes to contend with him,
  one could not answer him once in a thousand times.
He is wise in heart, and mighty in strength
  —who has hardened himself against him, and succeeded?—
he who removes mountains, and they know it not,
  when he overturns them in his anger;
who shakes the earth out of its place,
  and its pillars tremble;
who commands the sun, and it does not rise;
  who seals up the stars;
who alone stretched out the heavens,
  and trampled the waves of the sea;
who made the Bear and Orion,
  the Pleiades and the chambers of the south;
who does great things beyond understanding,
  and marvelous things without number.
Behold, he passes by me, and I see him not;
  he moves on, but I do not perceive him.
Behold, he snatches away; who can hinder him?
  Who will say to him, 'What are you doing?'...

If it is a contest of strength, behold him!
  If it is a matter of justice, who can summon him?
Though I am innocent, my own mouth would condemn me;
  though I am blameless, he would prove me perverse.

Am I blameless? I regard not myself.
  I loathe my life. What use is it?
One can just as well say,
  he destroys both the blameless and the wicked.
When disaster brings sudden death,
  he mocks at the calamity of the innocent.
The earth is given into the hand of the wicked;
  he covers the faces of its judges—
  if it is not he, who then is it?
My days are swifter than a runner;
  they flee away, they see no good.
They go by like skiffs of reed,
  like an eagle swooping on the prey.
If I say, 'I will forget my complaint,
  I will put off my sad countenance, and be of good cheer,'
I become afraid of all my suffering,
  for I know you will not hold me innocent.
I shall be condemned;
  why then do I labor in vain?
If I wash myself with snow,
  and cleanse my hands with lye,
yet you will plunge me into a pit,
  and my own clothes will abhor me.' "[11]

[11] This cry of a man who hungers and thirsts for justice is more acceptable to God than the "proverbs of ashes" (13:12) of "worthless physicians" (13:4) who try to justify Providence by a facile apologetic made up of old maxims. After forcing Job to admit that there is no common measure between creative Wisdom and the problems that worry man, "God said to Eliphaz the Temanite: 'My wrath is kindled against you and against your two friends; for you have not spoken of me what is right, as my servant Job has. Now therefore take seven bulls and seven rams, and go to my servant Job, and offer up for yourselves a burnt offering; and my servant Job shall pray for you, for I will accept his prayer not to deal with you according to your folly; for you have not spoken of me what is right, as my servant Job has.' So Eliphaz the Temanite and Bildad the Shuhite and Zophar the Naamathite went and did what God had told them; and God accepted Job's prayer" (42:7–9).

The author of Job has revealed all that he has at heart. Is he going to stop there? No, he will go much further still, only this is the deepest point of his darkness.

"My groaning is my advocate!"

We come now to another most bitter text, but one that ends with a certain hope that is wholly paradoxical and still very obscure. If Job knows that he will die without having received an answer to his complaint, he nevertheless thinks that his appeal for justice, his shame, and his moaning before God will survive him. He believes that the complaints of the innocent will live on once those who uttered them have died in agony. Job is one of those who think that it is absolutely impossible for the echoes of an innocent sufferer's crying to be silenced in any way down the ages. Even if men have never listened to them, if all memories are forgotten, if all sense of remorse is quickly healed, yet these cries will survive because there must be an advocate and a judge for them. Such is the basis of Job's hope. But he has no idea as to when or how it will be realized.

In the text that follows, the central element is the phrase "My groaning is my advocate". He has nobody to help him, nobody to take what he says seriously, but will not his very groaning as an innocent sufferer be his advocate before a tribunal of which he knows nothing, and which he has no means of approaching today? His groaning must present his case, his tears must plead his cause. So he says (16:12–14, 17–22):

"I was at ease, and he broke me asunder;
  he seized me by the neck and dashed me to pieces;
he sets me up as a target,
  his archers surround me.

He slashes open my kidneys, and does not spare;
he pours out my gall on the ground.
He breaks me with breach upon breach;
he runs upon me like a warrior. . . .

[A]lthough there is no violence in my hands,
and my prayer is pure.
O earth, cover not my blood,
and let my cry find no resting place.
Even now, behold, my witness is in heaven,
and he that vouches for me is on high.
My groaning is my advocate;
my eye pours out tears to God,
that he would maintain the right of a man with God,
like that of a man with his neighbor.
For when a few years have come
I shall go the way from where I shall not return."

"God, whom I shall see, will be on my side . . ."

He knows very well that for him it is finished; all he will leave behind him is his cry, his protestation. May that at least abide and never be stifled!

And now, in this attitude of mind, let us read the passage that the author of the Book of Job certainly thought of as the keystone of his work (19:23–27). It begins with a most solemn introduction and is made up of three main ideas, but these three ideas bear within them all of Job's paradoxical hope, without however going back on anything he has said about his scandal or his doubts, his refusal before the ways of Providence. His hope is expressed in these words:

"Oh, that my words were written!
Oh, that they were inscribed in a book!
Oh, that with an iron pen and lead
they were graven in the rock for ever!

For I know that my Redeemer lives,
and at last he will stand upon the earth;
and after my skin has been thus destroyed,
then from my flesh I shall see God;
whom I shall see on my side,
and my eyes shall behold, and not another.
My heart faints within me!"

He knows then that his groaning, which is his advocate, will abide. And one day the Almighty will be touched and will change his expression toward him who was unjustly put to death. Even though he died in despair, outside his flesh he will see God. He will see him like one who is on his side and not against him, someone who is no stranger to him, although all his life Job had suffered from this stranger of a God. Such is Job's hope.[12]

One may hold that Job did not believe in the resurrection as a certainty acquired once and for all. Nevertheless, he felt that, given what God is, and what man or at least his present destiny is, this was the only solution that sets everything right again. A new image of God must show itself after the death of him who today is on the road that allows no return.

It is with the same conviction that he says (24:1):

"Has not Shaddai,[13] then, times in reserve?
Will his faithful not see his days?"

"Times in reserve" means that human life is short and does not leave time to see God's day, the day of reconciliation, of intimacy, of full blossoming in the hands of the

[12] The phrase "from my flesh I shall see God" is not absolutely sure. It might mean "outside from my flesh I shall see God", since the Hebrew *min* can mean "from" or "outside". For the history of the doctrine of the resurrection of the dead in Israel, see *JB*, p. 705, note on 2 Mac 7:9.

[13] This is the name of God for the patriarchs.

Almighty, who will appear as a Father. This is not yet seen. God must therefore have times in reserve for some other occasion.

When the false image of God will be driven out

For our last text, let us take those verses in which Job dreams of the day when the false image of God will be driven out, that of the divine judge, exacting and resentful, who with a single glance destroys man. Once this false image is expelled, another image will appear, on the day that God chooses and by the means he chooses (14:7–15).

> "For there is hope for a tree,
>   if it be cut down, that it will sprout again,
>   and that its shoots will not cease.
> Though its root grow old in the earth,
>   and its stump die in the ground,
> yet at the scent of water it will bud
>   and put forth branches like a young plant.
> But man dies, and is laid low;
>   man breathes his last, and where is he?
> As waters fail from a lake,
>   and a river wastes away and dries up,
> so man lies down and rises not again;
>   till the heavens are no more he will not awake,
> or be roused out of his sleep.
> Oh, that you would hide me in Sheol,
>   that you would conceal me until your wrath be past,
>   that you would appoint me a set time, and remember me!
> If a man die, shall he live again?
>   All the days of my service I would wait,
>   till my release should come.
> You would call, and I would answer you;
>   you would long for the work of your hands."

Job has the impression, then, that there has been a misunderstanding: God no longer cares about man, the work of his hands. But why does God no longer care about man? Why does man think of God in the guise of an almighty executioner who tortures and destroys him? Something must have happened about which Job knows nothing. One must enquire about what has taken place, what has caused man to be unable any longer to look at God with confidence, unable to look upon him any more as a Father: it is the transgression, in the Garden of Eden.

2

Reasons for This Wrong View

I. THE GARDEN OF EDEN

Paradise lost

Let us first examine in his natural state the old man who must die in us so that the new man may be born. It is indeed interesting to consider bodies in their natural conditions before studying their more complex forms. Now the author of the Book of Job has shown us the difficulties that are felt by pagan man in existing under the scrutiny of God:

1. Man feels his life to be a frail thing, gradually withering away, destined to return to the dust, without any human hope (at that period) of surviving for ever.

2. Already, this side of the grave, man suffers from the fact that any real intimacy with God is impossible. On the contrary, such contact with God, established through racking remorse, at once destroys man's hope, even the hope of at least being righteous, because he is ignorant of the very terms in which God considers the righteousness of man.

After disfiguring man, God cast him out. That is how Job dramatized his experience. We cannot fail to be reminded of Adam and Eve being driven out of the Garden of Eden by the angel with the flaming sword. In a word: paradise lost. On one side there is the loss of a life that was perpetually renewed, constantly blossoming with greater profusion and now broken by sudden death, and, on the other side, the loss of intimate union with God, like that of a child with his father. In this twofold loss of paradise, human life is the dramatic center. It is through what happened in the earthly paradise that we shall discover why that paradise was lost and find the explanation of the concrete situation that oppressed Job.

Broken cisterns

But before approaching the account of what happened in the Garden of Eden, we find a pointer in a brief text of Jeremiah (2:13), where God says through the prophet: "... they have forsaken me, the fountain of living waters,[1] and hewed out cisterns for themselves, broken cisterns, that can hold no water." This is the fundamental theme. Why is man now in the disconsolate situation of Job? Because he has forsaken the fountain of living water. What is meant by "forsaking the fountain of living water"? Nothing else than the wish to live for oneself alone, to cease to be dependent on any exterior source. From the fountain of living water man may draw a life perpetually renewed. The broken cisterns, unable to hold the water that continually leaks away from them, is the life seized upon by man in an attempt at autonomy. But this is no longer living water, no longer the life renewed to the heart's content; it is dead water, a life destined for death. It must even be said that the man who cuts himself off from the fountain of living water is already dead, since he no longer possesses the hope of perpetual renewal of life. For the Hebrews, death was not so much

[1] For living waters, see references given in *JB*, beginning in the middle of the first note to Jn 4, p. 153 (New Testament pagination).

the last moment of physical life as the loss of hope; so they called water dead when it had become permanently stagnant in little pools and gradually leaked away to die in the sand, without hope of renewal.

It is not the fountain of living water that has turned away or abandoned man. Jeremiah tells us: "*They* have forsaken me, *me*, the fountain of living water." It is me, God, they have forsaken. So if man is now without life in him, without intimacy with God, it is because man has forsaken God. But this only brings us back to the question: Why has man foresaken the fountain of living water? Why has he forsaken God? And this is the very point to approach the account of the earthly paradise and the Fall; that is where we shall find our answer.

The account of paradise and the Fall

In a childlike and imaginative manner, this account (Gen 3: 1–11) is packed with meaning:

> Now the serpent was more subtle than any other wild creature that the LORD God had made. He said to the woman, "Did God say, 'You shall not eat of any tree in the garden'?" . . . "We may eat of the fruit of the trees of the garden; but God said, 'You shall not eat of the fruit of the tree which is in the midst of the garden, neither shall you touch it, lest you die.' " . . . "You will not die. For God knows that when you eat of it your eyes will be opened, and you will be like gods, knowing good and evil." So then the woman saw that the tree was good for food, and that it was a delight to the eyes, and that the tree was to be desired to make one wise. She took of its fruit and ate; and she also gave some to her husband, and he ate. Then the eyes of both were opened, and they knew that they were

> naked; and they sewed fig leaves together and made themselves aprons. And they heard the sound of the LORD God walking in the garden in the cool of the day, and the man and his wife hid themselves from the presence of the LORD God among the trees of the garden. But the LORD God called to the man, and said to him, "Where are you?" And he said, "I heard the sound of you in the garden, and I was afraid, because I was naked; and I hid myself." He said, "Who told you that you were naked? Have you eaten of the tree of which I commanded you not to eat?"

One thing is immediately apparent: there is nothing unintelligible here. It is all perfectly clear as far as the story goes. One may ask: What is this tree? What is the serpent? How can man be condemned to death. How can his consciousness of nakedness arise from eating? These are the questions that spring from the story, but the thread of the account is simple enough. Nevertheless, one glimpses a mysterious depth behind it all. As an anecdote, it could pass for a fairy story. But at a deeper level it binds together those fundamental realities which form the course of man's destiny. If we would ask questions of the text, certain preliminaries must be made clear, certain states of mind must be understood.

First of all, certain points need to be clarified: in the passage quoted above (Gen 2:9) we are told of two trees, the tree of life, of which man might eat and which was not forbidden, and the tree of the knowledge of good and evil, which was forbidden to man.

The tree of life

This tree of life, of which man was normally allowed to eat, corresponds to the fountain of living water already found in Jeremiah; that is to say, it was the constantly renewed nourishment for the life God had given. In other words, the tree of life is for man's inner life, for his perfect fulfillment, what ordinary food is for man's physical life. It is like a kind of umbilical cord by which man is joined to his creator and by which he endlessly draws all that he needs for growth, renewal and self-assertion as man.

The tree of the knowledge of good and evil

The tree of the knowledge of good and evil is rather more mysterious.[2] It cannot be experience of good and evil, since by the fact of his liberty, man already possessed the possibility of doing good and of doing evil. On the other hand, he could not be forbidden to exercise this freedom. All actions are either good actions or bad actions. All the time, whatever positive choice he made, whatever act of fidelity to God he made, was an experience of good. One cannot say that the knowledge of good, in the experimental sense, was forbidden to man. What, then, was forbidden?

I believe the tree of the knowledge of good and evil denotes the possibility of man determining for himself what is good and what is evil, in other words, of becoming the

[2] Abelard, my co-parishioner from the Muscadet region, saw in this tree the vine, whose juice taken in moderation stirs up the spirit (knowledge of good), but taken in excess, obscures it by stirring up the libido (knowledge of evil). According to Abelard sinful humanity had afterward always been disgusted with this tree, the cause of its disgrace, until Noah, after the Flood, started to cultivate it, not knowing that it was the tree of sin. The same cause produced the same effect and Noah repeated the humiliating experience of nudity. It appears that today's vinters of Pallet have forgotten the intuition of their famous compatriot. Modern exegetes want to see in this tree a symbol of some supposed sexual disorder. This is a simplistic Freudianism, and I prefer the more abstract interpretation proposed by Fr. de Vaux in the note on Gen 2:17 in *JB*.

principle of his own moral conscience. Man certainly suffers from the inability to unite two scales of appreciation. On the one side he has desires that make many things appear to him as sweet or bitter, delightful or unpleasant. But this scale does not correspond exactly with the other scale that is, so to speak, that of good or evil, high or low. The two scales do not coincide. Man would always like to make the scale of his desires into his scale of values and is always distressed to feel that what is good seems bitter to him and what is evil seems delightful. Here is a kind of paradox, for there is the everlasting temptation in man to say to himself, "Well, I decree that henceforth what is delightful to me I will call good, and what is distasteful to me I will call evil." There we have Adam's temptation, and the restraining command God gave Adam was precisely to overcome man's inclination to decree what was good or bad for him according to his desires and tastes.[3] Imagine a four- or five-year-old child deciding one day that everything pleasing to him was good and everything distasteful bad, and continuing on this way of independence. He would never get beyond a certain stage of growth, never shed so many superfluities. The child is conscious of his own values in a purely instinctive manner. He can neither guess nor feel what the adult who loves him has learned from experience to recognize as his authentic good and evil.[4] And man, only just born from the hands of God, was in an analogous position.

[3] This is what the Bible calls "stubbornly following their own evil heart", an expression typical of Jeremiah, found in Deut 29:19; Jer 3:17; 7:24; 9:13; 11:8; 13:10; 16:12; 23:17. The *BJ* translates it in various ways [as does the *JB*]. Another analogous biblical expression is "they went after false idols, and became false" (2 Kings 17:15; Jer 2:5).

[4] See the insistence in the Book of Proverbs on the necessity of discipline in education (marginal references in *JB* on Prov 15:32).

There is nothing dramatic in doing evil, provided man preserves a wide-awake conscience by which he can judge himself. The sinner whose conscience remains lucid, even though it acts as a jarring discord that causes him inner suffering but which he cannot stifle, has not eaten the forbidden fruit. On the other hand, St. Paul, in his Epistle to the Romans (1:32), speaks of those who not only do evil, but consent to those who do it. This gradation from "not only" to "but" seems surprising when we first read it. One is inclined to say that to consent to those who do evil is not as bad as actually doing it. Yet it is in fact worse, because the man who does evil may do it in spite of himself. But the moment he consents to evil for himself and for others, he has stifled his conscience, he has eaten the forbidden fruit. And is not this the sin against the Spirit? Not only to fail to obey the Holy Spirit, but to endeavour to silence him.[5]

That is the way that God had forbidden for man. God is aware that man will slip up at times. Even though he is in God's hands, this free being will be drawn this way and that. But let him not eat of the forbidden tree to decide for himself what is good and what is bad, and so become oblivious of that divine call which determines for him, regardless of his own desires, what is his real good, his real evil.

The tempter's tactics

How was man tempted? Here we must embark upon the analysis of those stirrings of the soul in which the tragedy of Eden was expressed. First we must notice that it was not the man but the woman who was tempted. We shall see what were the consequences of this.

[5] See marginal references in *JB* on Amos 2:12.

So the serpent enters on the scene. First of all: the tempter. It is useless to ask whether the tempter was an angel and why he was the tempter. The Bible offers us no identity papers in this case. It simply says that there was a tempter and describes him as subtle, and that must suffice for the story. The tempter intervenes and begins by distorting God's command, not by curtailing it but by exaggerating it: "Did God say 'You shall not eat of any tree of the garden'?"[6] These words make Eve uneasy: "Have I misunderstood in thinking that we might eat of all the trees except the one in the middle of the garden?" But she resists this suggestion and corrects it for the honor of God, since she does not wish to make him appear as a rigorous despot. "No, he did not say that. He said we may eat of the fruit of the trees of the garden but 'You shall not eat of the fruit of the tree which is in the midst of the garden, neither shall you touch it, lest you die.' "[7]

Awed by God's command, poor Eve added "neither shall you touch it", which God had not said. He had only said, "You shall not eat of it." But she had said to herself, To be sure of not eating of it, the best thing is not even to touch

[6] Literally: "you shall *not* eat of *all* the trees in the garden." But "not . . . all" is a Hebraism meaning "none at all". This Hebraism is often found in the Bible. Here are a few examples that leave no place for ambiguity: Gen 9:11 (*never . . . all* flesh); Ex 10:15 (*not* a green thing remained); Ex 20:10 (*not . . . any*); Prov 12:21 (*no* ill); 2 Chron 32:15 (*no* god of *any* nation), etc.

[7] Literally: "if not, you will die". Instead of "if not", St. Jerome's Vulgate gives "*ne forte*", which shrewdly expresses an eventuality that one refuses to consider possible. Here it is God who refuses to admit that his orders might be disobeyed. But all the commentators of the Middle Ages, from Hugh of St. Victor to Nicholas of Lyre, misunderstood this shrewdness, seeing in Eve's "*forte*" as qualifying the eventual death penalty a suggestion of doubt as regards that eventuality. Such a psychological analysis contradicts the data of the original text. As we shall see, doubt is indeed the beginning of Eve's sin, but not doubt about this point.

it. Nevertheless, this precaution had the secondary effect of creating a whole imaginative atmosphere round God's command, so that it held an exaggerated place in her worried conscience. In this way the serpent gained his first object, that of making the woman obsessed by the command.

Then he touched on the motive for the command. Eve had repeated God's word: "You shall not eat of it, lest you die." The serpent immediately modified this on his side or, rather, distorted it: "You will not die. For God knows that when you eat of it your eyes will be opened, and you will be like gods, knowing good and evil." Eve was profoundly impressed; [in modern terms, she probably would have thought] "What does this mean? I thought that God was protecting me from eating of that tree because it would be deadly for me. I thought that God—like a father taking care of a child who does not understand that he must not go and touch the stove as soon as he sees it—said to me, 'Do not touch that tree or it will kill you.' And now this serpent gives me to understand that perhaps God had quite another idea in his mind; perhaps God is, as this serpent suggests, a despot jealous of his authority who wishes that on no account anyone else should acquire that clarity of vision, that ability of decreeing what is good and evil, which is his privilege alone. He wishes to remain alone on his throne,[8]

[8] After the original sin, God said something that seems to confirm Eve's interpretation (3:22): "Behold, the man has become like one of us, knowing good and evil; and now let him not put forth his hand and take also of the tree of life, and eat, and live for ever!" Does not this suggest that God *does* "count equality with God a thing to be grasped" (Phil 2:6)? Certain commentators, wishing correctly to avoid such an interpretation, see in God's remark ("Behold . . .") ironical sarcasm as regards fallen Eve's hopes. But why should God seem to be afraid that man—in this new state which could only be utterly illusory—should *live for ever*? The banishment from paradise should, it seems to me, be interpreted in the same way as the confusion of tongues at Babel (11:6–7). God is anxious to prevent man from succeeding in an

and consents to make creatures only on condition that they remain subordinate to him. But for one of them to discover the way and the gateway to becoming a god in his turn, that is something that God does not wish. God knows this and fears it, and he cuts off all access to divinity, just as Bluebeard closed the door of the room containing his seven wives."

From tree to lips

Eve was worried, possibly thinking, Is it possible that this foul-mouthed serpent is right? Or was I not right in thinking that God really wills what is best for me and protects me from the danger of death that I bear within me? Doubt has seized upon her mind. Is she responsible for it? It is the serpent who insinuates this doubt in her soul; it is he who is the tempter. But let us see what follows. "So then the woman saw [why this 'so then'? Because it was the result of the temptation] that the tree was good for food, and that it was a delight to the eyes, and . . . was to be desired to make one wise." Her imagination speculates and embellishes the tree, the object of God's ambiguous command, with a peculiarly attractive aspect.[9] Supposing this tree really was the tree that could make people into gods! How attractive it had become since the serpent's explanation had been sown in Eve's mind as a possibility! And then there comes that giddiness of imagination which no longer knows on what security it depends, whether it is a matter of

---

unauthentic destiny that would mask the true destiny that he had abandoned. For the same reason he would destroy the kingdom and the temple by means of Nebuchadnezzar's armies. The only authentic situation for the sinner is his uprooting by the Exile, to remind him that his lost fatherland is elsewhere.

[9] It is in connection with "foreign wives" that the Bible develops the theme of temptation as seduction: Prov 2:16–18; 5:2–5; 7:21–23; Eccles 7:26; Judg 16:4–21.

freeing oneself from a despotic and jealous God, or, on the contrary, of following the instructions of a provident father who cares for his scatterbrain child. At such a moment, the imagination has no roots. So giddiness causes it to fall, as giddiness usually causes one to do. If one is not giddy, one does not fall. Giddiness makes the legs like cotton wool. Yes, the legs of Eve's will had become like cotton wool. She took a fruit. She bit it.

She had hardly bitten it when she remembered that she had a husband, so she quickly passed some to him, so as not to be alone in this hazardous venture. She said to herself, What is going to happen? Immediately she shuddered, as she felt herself doing this—better that he should be in the affair with me. Let us die together or become gods together; whatever happens let it be for both of us. Her husband would never have thought of eating of the tree. His imagination was limited; he did not even realize that a serpent was in the process of turning his wife's head, despite the fact that he was standing beside her. And so, at a single prompting, both ate the fruit. Observe the subtlety of the account, ". . . and he ate. Then the eyes of both were opened." Here was the new kind of knowledge that the serpent had foretold: "You will be like gods, knowing good and evil." It is by knowledge that one enters the state of divinity: "Then the eyes of both were opened, and they knew [now comes this little fall] that they were naked." Yes, there was indeed a new form of knowledge, but a very different knowledge than they had hoped.

Responsible?

Before looking at the consequences of the Fall, let us try to clarify who was ultimately responsible for it. In the moment of temptation how can Eve be held responsible for the doubt that entered her imagination, or for the fact that once obsessed by doubt and wavering in her will she was, as it were, intoxicated by the attraction of the fruit and ate it? Where does responsibility come into it? It seems to me to be neither at the moment when Eve began to doubt nor when she committed the act, but when she left herself open to the fascination of the doubt, when she entertained the doubt. It was precisely then that she became responsible, at the moment when she began to dwell pleasurably on the eventuality, on that doubt which touched on the motive of the divine command, when she let her mind play with what the serpent suggested. It was not the fact of having heard or of having acted; it was the fact of having lent her ear willingly,[10] of having reflected and dwelt on the possibility, of having as it were forgotten in that moment all her daily experience of God's dealing with their lives, of God's dealing with creation, and of having preferred instead the most unlikely eventuality, which was at the same time the most terrifying: that she might be the sport of God.

I think it was just there that the fault lay, just as for certain sensual sins, for example, the major responsibility is not in the initial imagination, or in the stirring of desire, or strictly speaking in the gesture that at given moments can spring spontaneously from an overwhelming desire and nerves stretched to their limit, but somewhere between the two, in the moment when the thing imagined is welcomed,

[10] Does not placing the fault, as I have done in the fact of *giving ear* to the tempter, only push the question further back? Proverbs indeed says (17:4): "An evildoer *listens* to wicked lips; and a liar *gives heed* to a mischievous tongue" (emphasis added). Did Eve herself realize where her sin began that showed itself by the attention she paid to the serpent? No doubt the serpent knew better than she did.

repulsed and, finally, accepted. There we have that fragile second when there is indeed still real liberty of choice and then, an instant later, when there is liberty no longer. Although nothing has been done, one has toyed with and welcomed the idea that it might possibly be done. And in this toying, the decisive element takes the form of a sort of crazy attraction to what is worst.

Nakedness and dress

What was the main result of the sin? Nakedness, or, rather, the realization of being naked: "they knew that they were naked." Their reaction was to dress themselves: "and they sewed fig leaves together and made themselves loin-cloths." To understand what the Bible means by nakedness, we must first realize that in Israel the word is far from having the significance that it has in our modern way of speaking. We should be tempted to think: nakedness-attraction. But an Israelite of those days would have found this a most peculiar sequence of thought. Their first reaction was: nakedness-humiliation,[11] or even more: nakedness-destitution; that is to say, finding oneself stripped and disabled in the presence of somebody of whom one is afraid.[12] In Israel, all nakedness produces a sort of fear of rape, physically, but much more spiritually.

Man is a being who tries to adorn much more than to dress himself. He tries to appear as someone of importance, to cut a good figure, to have the air of an angel; woman

[11] See Gen 9:21–24; 2 Sam 10:4–5; Ezek 16:37; Rev 3:18.

[12] Moses covered his face before God (Ex 3:6), and the seraphim used their wings to conceal their faces and their genitals (Is 6:2). God said to Moses: "while my glory passes by I will put you in a cleft of the rock, and I will cover you with my hand until I have passed by" (Ex 33:22).

does this also.[13] But strictly speaking, all this is an effort to give the impression of *being*. Man is a being who tries to have the air of being, at least to be somebody in the eyes of others, even if he does not wholly succeed in convincing himself that he is somebody. He finds it soothing at least to consider that he may *seem* attractive or estimable to other people. It helps him to think that he might even really *be* so, and that it would be exaggeratedly pessimistic to think otherwise. That is what we call self-adornment, to give oneself airs in the eyes of others and then in one's own eyes. Now man seeks first of all to adorn himself. Why? Precisely because in reality he knows his *being* is evil, his being is incomplete, his being is without peace, his being is in anguish. And so he tries to appear other than he is. And to be naked is to see these appearances totter, to see this "attempt to seem to be somebody" fall to pieces, to find oneself in the eyes of all such as, unfortunately, in the depths of one's conscience, one knows only too well that one is. One does not like to be reminded of this fact. If one has sinned without anybody seeing, there is only half a sin. If one sins and others see it, it becomes dramatic. For there is the risk of being really a sinner, in such a moment, in the eyes of everybody. If one is only a sinner in one's own eyes, one can go on playing the game and try to deceive oneself.

And so, to be naked is just that: to see spread out before everyone's eyes that humiliation which we bear in the depths of our being.[14] To be no longer able to play the game in the eyes of others, we find ourselves disabled in the presence of danger. Why danger? Because in Israel, "the others"

[13] On adornment, see Is 3:16–24; 2 Kings 9:30; Jer 4:30; Ezek 23:40.

[14] By contrast, one speaks of being "covered with shame" (Jer 3:25; Mic 7:10; Ps 35:26; 109:29).

are either those speechless with admiration at such "a sight for sore eyes" or else those who, like untamed serpents, look for a chance to bite.

Snakes to charm

In certain psalms, the life of social man is likened to the life of a snake charmer. "Scoffers"[15] must be kept at a respectful distance, and we must take care that people do not begin to whisper about us nor whistle when they see us go by. That would be a sign of our nakedness. It is no use being as correctly dressed as usual; our efforts to pass as a person of importance have been seen through, the magic of the snake charmer has failed; they all begin to hiss[16] and try to bite us with that scandalous talk that causes us to lose face. There is only one way to silence slanderers and to neutralize all that malevolent spite which is seeking our undoing: it is by saving face and at any price keeping up the impression we have been trying to make. The tragedy here is not that one has lost health, fortune or happiness, but primarily that one has become the target of other people's scoffing looks and mockery. How like the snake charmer! Either he dominates and has the mastery of his group or else he suddenly realizes that he has become the prey of those ready to pounce on him.

The look that withstands all charms

Nakedness indicates first of all this collapse of the personality that we had tried to create by decking ourselves out.

[15] See Ps 12:4; 25:2; 38:16.
[16] See Job 27:23; Lam 2:15–16; Zeph 2:15.

But it is found not only in the sphere of our relations with our fellow men, but chiefly in the sphere of our relations with God. Job has described its effects: the feeling of being spied upon, stared at, judged by the Almighty, by him whose glance, as we know in the depths of our being, is all-penetrating. Such is the destitution man has undergone from the moment sin was committed. Under the gaze of God, he immediately felt that the root of life had been cut. Why? Having started by doubting his father's goodness, he has gone on to seal this doubt by an action that ratifies it like a stamp at the bottom of a document. When man made the gesture of eating the forbidden fruit, its real significance was this: I recognize, at bottom, that God is he who wishes to keep me in a state of abasement, and from this I must free myself at any price so as to become a god myself.

Eating the fruit signified this interpretation of God's motives. By this gesture was broken for ever the atmosphere of confidence, of filial submission into the hands of a Father whose love for us should be our only treasure. But with that broken, man knows that he has cut off the source of life. For indeed one cannot receive from God a life that is ceaselessly renewed unless one remains constant and open to him with all one's being. But man, by wishing to become a god, at once destroyed that relationship of complete and confident openness which alone could assure him life.

II. DISTORTED IDEAS OF GOD

Hallucinations of a shrivelled heart

Man has passed straight away from a Father-God in whose arms he had played like a child, to a Judge-God from whose face he flees.[17] Does this mean that God has changed toward man? I think not, at least not principally. The change has come about principally in the mind of man himself. After his sin, man said to himself: What is God going to think about this? And to figure out what God might think about it, his imagination is guided by his own heart, a heart already shrivelled by sin, by the act of rebellion. In his shrivelled heart, he says, "How should I myself react if somebody had rebelled against me in this way?" And from now on man's "I" signifies something different from what it was before since, by asserting himself against all manner of dependence, he has taken up a wholly new position. And this is the man, barely established in his autonomous independence, who says: "What would I do if somebody rebelled against me, as I have done against God?" Obviously such a man would nurture in his ungenerous heart sentiments of rancor and spite against the one who had rebelled against him. All relations would be severed, and humiliating reparation would be demanded before there could be any question of gradually opening the door again.

Let us recall in this connection the parable of the prodigal son (Lk 15:11–32), which begins with an account of original sin, although this aspect of it is seldom considered. This son who is far from home has also seen the springs of life dry up. He had set out for distant lands with his little inheritance, and this inheritance had been frittered away like living water that has become dead and leaked away through broken cisterns. All too soon he has nothing left. Seeing the approach of death, the end of all, he begins to

[17] This was the attitude of Cain when he had filled up the rebellion against the Father by murdering his brother (Gen 4:14, 16). The flight of the rebel is described by Eliphaz (Job 15:20–25) and is a commonplace in the Bible (Deut 28:65–67; Is 57:20–21; Amos 9:1–4).

think of the father he has forsaken. How does he picture him? He says to himself, "Ah, I was better off at home with my father than I am now. How many of my father's servants are far better fed than I am now. . . . What shall I do? I will return to him and I shall have to humble myself first to appease him. I will say to him: 'Father, I have sinned against heaven and against you; I am no longer worthy to be called your son. Take me back, I beg you, as one of your servants.' " What is the real significance of this? He supposes he will find an angry father who will say to him, "There is no question of taking you back like that, my boy; I want proofs that you know your own mind better. You may begin by spending some time in my service. I will judge from the results of this whether or not I can recognize you as my son again." It was with such dispositions as these that the prodigal returned, ready to swallow the bitter pill of having to humble himself before his father. And what does he find? His father waiting for him at the front door, and not just by chance, for all along he has lovingly awaited him.

But the son does not understand what is in his father's heart. This is shown by his promptly entering upon the little speech he has prepared: "Father, I have sinned against heaven and against you." But the father falls on his neck, embracing and kissing him, and calls out, "Go at once and fetch a ring and the best robe; let the fatted calf be killed." The prodigal can make nothing of all this. Why not? Because in rebelling against his father, he has distorted in his mind the image of the father. And this was precisely the beginning of his revolt: he began by doubting his father as a *father* and as a *loving father*. He had thought of his father as an exacting tyrant who did not wish his children to leave him and discover adult independence for themselves. It was by harboring this idea that his father was in fact no more than a wicked stepfather, someone who wished at any price to keep his sons about him to do his bidding, and for whom the son's happiness did not count. It was by hardening his heart by this resentment that he summoned up the strength to quit his father, to free himself. His departure had become a necessary thing, a normal consequence of the circumstances.

He had begun by falsifying the image of his father in his own mind, having allowed himself to doubt his father's love.[18] And this falsifying of his father's image would continue in what followed, and in the bitterness of his failure would become hardened into a caricature. This was what made his return to favor appear as a humiliation hard to accept, a new enslavement to which he must resign himself. He did not say to himself, It is my father's love that I need; he said, I no longer have anything to eat, they are better fed at home with my father. Perhaps, after all, that servitude I tried to escape would be better than dying of hunger. I'd better resign myself to accepting it. And so he comes back, not because he has discovered his father anew, but because he sees no other way of keeping himself alive. He returns to his father only as a last resource.

Assuredly these gestures of submission, of humiliation, of admitting his failure, are hard to make, but it seems to him that they are the only terms possible if reconciliation is to be achieved. For to his rebellious eyes, which have caricatured the image of his father, all he can expect is a demand

[18] It was to Hosea that this father whose love had been scorned tells of his grief (Hos 11:1–4): "When Israel was a child, I loved him, and out of Egypt I called my son. The more I called them, the more they went from me.... Yet it was I who taught Ephraim to walk, I took them up in my arms; but they did not know that I healed them. I led them with cords of compassion, with the bands of love, and I became to them as one who raises an infant to his cheeks, and I bent down to them and fed them."

for reparation from the father's self-respect and outraged authority. He cannot conceive that his father's love has in fact been wounded, is suffering, is broken, and that he longs for the return of his son—that his father has simply no idea of bargaining with him but only wants to be able to call back to his inmost heart this son who has gone so far astray, and whose very return would be enough to fill him with joy. The father knows that even if it is only necessity that has brought his son back again, yet love can eventually be born again, through a real relationship with his father, and not with that caricature that his son had made of him.

The fear of God is born

It was the same misunderstanding that separated man from God in the first sin. In his normal condition, man was not afraid of God; he did not feel naked before him. But once he had disfigured the image of the Father in his mind, imagining him to be a suspicious despot, jealous for his authority, he began to fear him, because this was the chief image of God that lay at the root of his sin. And perhaps the drama of the first sin lies not so much in the fact of man's trying to become God in God's place—man knew perfectly well that he could never achieve this, that stumbling against the impossible he would be hurled back—but that at the root of this idea there is misunderstanding of what the Father is, followed by the determination to delude himself as to the truth, to imagine the Father as a jealous tyrant and so justify himself in his desperate rebellion. It is this caricature of God's image which is the hardest thing to root out of man. Man will quickly realize that he is not a god; he will quickly realize that this lost paradise was the only possible place in which to find happiness. But what keeps him from turning again to his God is that he cannot rid himself of the belief that this return must involve a humiliating deal in which remorse and personal disavowal of the past would be required of him in order to appease the offended authority of God. Man has become incapable of imagining this return as the rediscovery of a misjudged heart, which in fact is what it is. And so from God's point of view, man's return will consist chiefly in his becoming tractable once more.

Unbearable gentleness

Man has become wild; he flies in terror toward death, in terror because he can no longer bear the gaze of his Father, whose love he has in fact disowned and flouted. I would say, moreover, that it is because the Father's eyes are too gentle for man to bear, with a gentleness that torments him, that man, as though to palliate his sin, attempts to force himself into the conviction that in fact the Father had laid an unbearable yoke upon him that he must shake off at any price. Yes, at the sound of God's first words, "Adam, where are you?" the sinner at once recognized that the true face of God was that of a loving father and not of a tyrant jealous for his authority. But this only frightens him the more, because once he has broken the bonds that held him he can no longer bear love, which becomes the greater torment when he realizes that he has misjudged it.

There are families in which things like this happen. It all starts when one of the partners is guilty of some unfaithfulness. The other knew nothing about it. But for the one who has sinned, the disgust caused by the memory of his fault grows the stronger when he feels himself enveloped by the trust of his unsuspecting partner. This trust becomes unbearable, worse even than suspicion. And because he realizes exactly what he has destroyed, and nevertheless has always before him that contact with a faithful heart always open to him, for that very reason he tries to caricature the other and says to himself, "I just had to run away; I was right in doing so." Is this why he tries to silence within himself everything that might revive that trust and tear his heart still more, now that he has made another choice that worries him, and which he forces himself to accept for fear of something worse? How often do we erect a caricature of people's minds, because once we have given way to doubt and suspicion, we no longer have the strength to recognize at last that we have passed love by? We may try to persuade ourselves that we were right to doubt, that there could no longer be any question of love, that it was necessary to quit. This is what man has done before God.

Humanity to be tamed anew . . .

So God would have to tame man again, laboriously, as one tries to tame a frightened bird. It is no use picking him up at once; he must first get used to you. A little bread is put outside the closed window. The bird will come when the window is closed, but not when it is open. You repeat this for several days. Then, one day, the window is left ajar; the bird comes all the same, because he is accustomed to doing so. Eventually you go so far as to put the bread on the edge of the table; little by little the bird will come, even though your least movement disturbs and frightens him. This is just how God acted with man. But the bird summons up courage to approach you, only because it is winter. In summer you would never succeed in taming it, but in winter, when it cannot find enough to eat, it comes to the windows of these frightening humans.

God will be able to tame his people only in winter. Jacob's descendants in Egypt are a people in winter, a people ready to die, who see death staring them in the face. God will be able to tame a people in conditions like these. It is not immediately that he will be able to take them by the hand on Sinai. He must begin by saving them from death in a wholly unexpected manner—hence the exodus from Egypt and the passage through the Red Sea. He will not expect this people to start calling him God, a name that evokes terrifying almighty power, immediately. He asks them to call him by the name he gives himself, Yahweh,[19] which for Israel means "Savior", since this name is linked up with their experience of the escaping from Egypt[20] and passage through the Red Sea.

. . . to be formed again in the image of God . . .

And Israel will grasp the hand of this Savior as their guide, since it is he who has saved them from death. Afterward, they will allow this saving hand to fashion them anew. It is very necessary that God should fashion man once more in his own divine image. For man was made in the image of God. But this same man has fled from God's hands and has fashioned in himself a caricature of God's image. God cannot therefore make himself recognized by man unless he first fashions in him the true image of God, unless he begins

[19] Actually, the vocalization "Yahwoh" would be preferable to "Yahweh", which is not so well attested. See W. Vischer, "Eher Jahwo als Jahwe", in *Theologische Zeitschrift* (Basel), XVI, 1960, pp. 259–67. To this enquiry with such decisive results may be added other data that confirm the conclusions.

[20] In the heart of Israel, to the thrice-holy name (Is 6:3) must be associated the solemn commentary on it that God himself gave at Sinai as introduction to the Decalogue (Ex 20:2 = Deut 5:6): "I am Yahweh your God, who brought you out of the land of Egypt, out of the house of bondage."

by refashioning man in his own image. If the word "fatherhood" begins once more to mean for man what it means for God, if the word "love" begins once more to mean for man what it means for God, in other words, if God refashions his image in man, then man will one day be able to recognize God once more. But in order to fashion man in his own image once more, God must first take in hand this fugitive, terror-stricken man who flees his presence, bearing with him the remains of the stolen water of life until it is all spent in a hopeless death. God must first take hold of this man who flees from him toward death; otherwise he cannot refashion him. But he cannot take hold of him again until that day when, at the very gates of death and destruction, man is prepared to accept the hand that will deliver him from the land of servitude, lifting him out of the great waters[21] of the Red Sea.

. . . so that it can discover him again

Once he is saved, man will follow his Savior. He will offer himself to be kneaded anew by him who has seized hold of him and whom he still does not realize as the God he was fleeing. While God refashions him, man will begin to recognize in himself the image that God is forming there, rediscovering the God he had misjudged.

We shall now witness God taking in hand a wretched people. It happened in the land of Goshen, only thirty-two hundred years ago.

[21] If water is life for the nomad and his flocks in the desert, the sudden rising of water from the wadi that is swollen by rain might swallow up camps set up a few hours before in its dried-up bed. From this arises the ambiguity of the theme of water in the Bible. For waters that engulf, see the note in *JB* on Ps 18:5.

3

A God Who Chooses

Why was Israel chosen? This looks like a very dangerous question. What, in fact, do we know of God's designs? God may have chosen Israel, but he has never told us explicitly why he did so. So it may not seem prudent to attempt questions that God himself, through revelation, has not set us to answer. Nevertheless, it is a key question for the man who, seeing the present destiny of the people of Israel and understanding how deeply rooted is all Christian destiny in that of Israel, wonders why God willed that his gospel, his good news, should spring from Israel. I think we cannot ask this question with modern terminology, because it was not present-day Israel that was chosen. The Israel of today is a people that has already lived three thousand years of history in the hands of God, so it is no longer the same as when it was chosen. It is a people that already has a whole history of faithfulness and struggle in the matter of its own vocation. On the other hand, the Israel that God chose was a people that did not even know the name of him who at that moment was taking it in hand.

God's choice of people

If we want to understand the motives for choosing Israel we must realize first of all that God could perfectly well have spoken to every man born into the world by the light of his conscience instead of choosing one particular group out of the mass of humanity. He could have progressively brought to maturity by interior guidance the whole of mankind at once. But this is not what he chose to do.

Similarly, God might have made another choice—a choice that seems most logical, at least to human logic—and used some chosen being, some genius appearing at the head of one of the great civilizations, and thus assured a vast cultural expansion of his word. But, again, this is not what he chose to do.

The solution God chose was between the two, or appears to us to be so. He chose out a particular human group that was only a small part of mankind in general, but one in which individuals swarmed. At the time of his choice, the persons in this group of human beings were by no means exceptionally brilliant and the group was famous only for its confusion and the threat of extermination that weighed upon it. Nevertheless, it was to this group of human beings, situated as they were, that God began to speak. Taking their destiny in hand, he made of this group a people.

I. THE PATRIARCHS

The great themes of salvation

But before the birth of Israel at the time of the exodus from Egypt, this people had had a prehistory: their conception in the promise made to Abraham. Indeed, all through the time of the patriarchs, we see, like the overture of some opera, the great themes already showing themselves, treated as though for themselves alone, whereas eventually they were to have their part within the age-long divine conduct of affairs.

First of all came the initial uprooting. God makes of Abraham a wanderer and sets him on his wandering way. Why? Because that is the condition in which God must take hold of man again, since it was like this that man had fled away from him. When Adam left the earthly paradise, he became a wanderer. It was only to be expected, then, that when God decided to lay hold of Abraham he turned him into a wanderer. Meanwhile, man had tried to establish himself. The tower of Babel had been an attempt at a systematized gathering of the clans (Gen 11:4), but man did not succeed in recovering his unity and stability by this means. And so, little by little as best they could, strangers knocking at the doors of strangers, men built up cities for themselves, and the family from which Abraham sprang was accustomed to migrating from one city to another.

It was, then, to a man of this family among so many others that a message was given (Gen 12:1): "Go from your country and your kindred and your father's house to the land that I will show you." The speaker is unknown. As yet Abraham has no knowledge of him. What was the manner of his speech? Was it some interior suggestion that gradually impressed itself upon him? Was it all of a sudden, like a sort of hallucination that turned out to be true? We cannot tell. But what we surely know is that Abraham was convinced that he had heard these words spoken by a supremely authoritative voice. This unknown Being who speaks to him will very soon impose himself on all his conduct. But in the first words he speaks, the unknown One promises Abraham "the land that I will show you".[1]

[1] This wandering of the patriarchs toward an unknown destination has been recalled in an unforgettable manner by the author of the Epistle to the Hebrews (11:8–16): "By faith Abraham obeyed when he was called to *go out*

Like a vanishing mirage

So Abraham sets out for the land of which he knows nothing, and one day, as he is pitching his camp (Gen 12:7), God says to him: "This is the land, this one here, but it is not to you that I will give it. I will give it to your descendants" [paraphrased]. Abraham can do no more than pass through it like a nomad; it is only his descendants who will possess it. Abraham himself will have no more than a foretaste of it. But these descendants, where are they to come from? His wife is barren. His first thought is to adopt his favorite servant. But God speaks out firmly: No, your "own son shall be your heir" (15:4). So then he takes his wife's handmaid, as is customary at the time, so that she should bring forth a son for him in the name of his wife. Hagar presents him with Ishmael, but again God insists: "No, but Sarah your wife shall bear you a son" (17:19). But how? Abraham is old, Sarah is barren. It is then that, on the occasion of the visit of the three mysterious persons who come asking for his hospitality,[2] a promise is made to him: "I will surely

to a place which he was to receive as an inheritance; and he *went out,* not knowing where he was to go. By faith he *sojourned* in the land of promise as in a foreign land, living in tents with Isaac and Jacob, heirs with him of the same promise. For he looked forward to the city which has foundations, whose builder and maker is God.... These all died in faith, not having received what was promised, but having seen it and greeted it from afar, and having acknowledged that they were *strangers and exiles on the earth.* For people who speak thus make it clear that they are seeking a homeland. If they had been thinking of that land from which they had gone out, they would have had opportunity to return. But as it is, they desire a better country, that is, a heavenly one. Therefore God is not ashamed to be called their God, for he has prepared for them a city" (emphasis added).

[2] The creator of the earth accepts the pressing hospitality offered him by the wandering Abraham. The next day, he will punish with fire the city of Sodom for not having obeyed the laws of hospitality (19:8–9) and spare Lot,

return to you in the spring, and Sarah your wife shall have a son" [Gen 18:10]. Sarah laughs and says to herself: "After I have grown old, and my husband is old, shall I have pleasure?" (18:12), and the visitor reproaches her for laughing. In due course she indeed bears a son, Isaac, the child of the promise that God himself has made.[3] So God first uproots Abraham and brings him into an unknown land that he himself will never possess but which God promises to his descendants as their possession, descendants who will be born, not of man's fecundity but of God himself.

So Abraham watches Isaac grow up as his descendant who will later possess the land in his name. Then suddenly one day he hears a voice saying (22:2): "Go to the mountain that I will point out to you [remember: 'the land *that I will show you*', and now 'the mountain *that I will point out to you*']—and there you shall offer up Isaac, your first-born son, whom you love", the sole heir, Abraham's whole future. What shocks Abraham so overwhelmingly here is not so much to hear God, in his fatherly love, commanding him to sacrifice his son. In the region of the land of Canaan, the sacrifice of firstborn sons to God was a well-known custom.[4] Men felt they had no right to be fathers until they had acknowledged the primacy of the divine fatherhood by sacrificing their firstborn. It is a case of anxiously disfiguring God's face, such as we have seen began among men at the coming of sin. Abraham, then, is not so surprised by this demand of God, even though he is ignorant of its true significance. On the other hand, what seems

---

who has shown himself hospitable (19:1–3). A similar crime against the law of hospitality would later suffer a terrible punishment (see note in *JB* on Judg 19:23).

[3] See Rom 9:7–9; Gal 4:28.

[4] See *AI*, pp. 443f.

extraordinary to him is that the very one who had miraculously given him this offspring, contrary to all expectation, now wishes to take him back again. What does it all mean? Is Isaac not God's gift after all? In the logical sequence of his work, is God going to take back and destroy his gifts? Is that promised offspring always going to disappear like a faint mirage?

A gift to possess as gift

God wills to lead Abraham to the very limits of faith. Abraham obeys blindly, and we must remember that this is not the only time in history when God seems to destroy what he himself has built. It is to prevent us from insidiously appropriating things to ourselves that God goes so far as to take them away from us, only to give them back to us in the end so that henceforth we may possess them as coming from his hand alone. We realize the gratuitousness of a gift only when it is taken away from us, or at least after it has very nearly escaped us entirely. How many people who have never been bedridden really understand what it is to walk? How many really appreciate the gift of sight who have never nearly lost it? How many of those who have never been confined in hospital or in prison for long periods realize what it is to breathe in the pure fresh air with wondering delight? We possess God's gifts, knowing them truly the gifts of God, only when like Abraham we receive them a second time from his hands, having been ready to surrender them to him without seeing why, in blind faith[5] stripped

[5] The author of the Epistle to the Hebrews comments on the sacrifice of Isaac (11:17–19): "By faith Abraham, when he was tested, offered up Isaac, and he who had received the promises was ready to offer up his only-begotten son, of whom it was said, 'Through Isaac shall your descendants be named.'

of all human understanding about the mystery of faithfulness that blind faith contains.

This was the case with Abraham. He was Isaac's father, and he had indeed received this son from God himself, but he might have ended by slipping into the habit of thinking he was his father in the ordinary human way. God claimed the boy for himself and gave him back to Abraham only when he had stretched out his sword to slay him. That was the moment when Abraham learned that he was the boy's father in God's name, not in his own, so that he must not appropriate to himself even his own son. And there we already have one of the keys to biblical history.

To this we might add the story of Jacob, that crafty man whom God converted by the consequences of his misdeed.[6] And again, there is the case of Joseph, the predestined one, persecuted because he was predestined—betrayed, delivered up by those who were jealous of him, and later by means of his sufferings becoming their savior.[7] These are some of the great themes that God wants us to hear before the children of Israel begin to exist as a people. Later on, God alludes to these incidents when, through the mouth of Moses, he says to his people (Deut 7:7–8): "It was not because you were more in number than any other people that Yahweh set his love upon you and chose you, for you

---

He considered that God was able to raise men even from the dead; hence he did receive him back and this was a symbol."

[6] By a dishonest trick, Jacob deprived Esau of his father's blessing (Gen 27:1–40). Later, by a clever trick, he increased his flock (Gen 30:31–42); then, by a virtuous trick, he effected his reconciliation with his brother (Gen 33:1–16). But he had to suffer the mean tricks of his uncle Laban (Gen 29:25–27), the Machiavellism of his own sons (Gen 34:13–30), before a final ruse of these latter broke his heart (Gen 37:18–35).

[7] See in *JB*, p. 59, note a, introducing the story of Joseph at Gen 37:2.

were the fewest of all peoples; but it is because Yahweh loves you, and is keeping the oath which he swore to your fathers, that Yahweh has brought you out." As with Abraham the wanderer, this came about not because Israel was a particularly imposing people, but *out of love* (there is absolute gratuitousness here, an intended paradox in this love), and also for the *keeping of the oath* sworn to your forefathers, precisely because the oath made to Abraham was made under the sign of complete gratuitousness.

Everything comes from God who gives all to him whom he has first deprived of all, to him whom he has found in a state of utter dereliction, wholly abandoned, completely uprooted. Such is the man whom God enriches, and with what does he enrich him? With a promise.[8] What more tenuous, humanly speaking, and yet what richer than a promise—a seed rather than a fruit! Man can appreciate its fruitfulness only by beginning to experience what it means to be in God's hands. And even at death man has only a hope.

Loving the hand that brings to birth

These experiences of the divine ordering of things are only the wellspring of hope, but we have clearly seen that for Israel life is precisely this: a hope that is no illusory expectation. First, God snatches away all human hopes, and in their place he gives a hope that is unique. If human hopes are multiple, it is because they are recognized as fragile, and so man tries to keep at his side a certain number of decoys that will last at least for a time and bear him up in certain

[8] It is surprising to note that biblical Hebrew has no word for "promise", in spite of this phenomenon having so prominent a place in God's dealings with the patriarchs. This only goes to show that biblical theology must be built on notions and not merely on words.

circumstances. But God alone can give real hope, for that is life. God's only pledge to man, therefore, is the experience of being led by his hand. And from the hand of God, man has experienced only uprooting, more in the nature of a surgical operation than of maternal nurturing. But he knows already by experience that this hand that is working in him loves him better than he loves himself, better than those who say they love him actually succeed in doing. And man prefers this hand that destroys and this mouth that promises but does not promise for the immediate future, that does not promise something to fill man with joy today, but will dig deep into him so that there may be born in him the man whom God intends eventually to shower with gifts. This is the hand man loves better than any other known to him.

And this is the way God leads Abraham during that little stretch of road that makes up his earthly life; this is the way God will lead countless generations afterward, each one bringing into the world the generation that follows, because God is guiding not a single individual but a people. Man has surrendered himself and God has given to all these isolated individuals a new fruitfulness, so that the posterity[9] that will possess the land should be brought into the world. We must remember that Adam was the man who was banished from the earth. So God takes a remnant of this banished humanity and, beginning with this, forms a new posterity that will possess the land. In this way, the exact response to Adam's sin is effected. First of all God begins to acclimatize these men, to tame them so that they will love the hand that works upon them—men who, when God

[9] The idea of "seed", that is promised posterity, holds in the theology of the patriarchs the same place as the idea of "remnant" in the theology of the prophets. For the first, see marginal references in *JB* on Gen 12:7. For the second, see the note in *JB* on Is 4:3.

laid his hand upon them, were no more than a group of good-for-nothings, creatures of dust condemned to extermination. It is important to recognize that God begins to effect the promise made to Abraham at precisely the moment when, like a second sacrifice of Isaac, the vastly increased posterity of Abraham once again has the knife at its throat. It is then that God grasps them. How did it all happen?

II. THE HEBREWS

The Hyksos invasion

We must first take a glance at the conditions in which these men were living. At that time, Egypt maintained on its frontiers a vast crowd of slaves: the Hebrews. Why were they slaves? Egypt, we must realize, is a country formed in such a way that it runs no risk of invasion from either east or west, for it is like a long ribbon of land protected on each side by impassable deserts. On the other hand, it was open to invasion from the south, from Ethiopia. Many a time dynasties came from the south to invade Egypt and replaced the local dynasty. There was also danger of invasion from the north, either at the delta where "the people of the sea" landed at about the time of the Hebrew's departure from Egypt, or else by the isthmus of Suez. An invasion of this kind had already taken place in the eighteenth century B.C. Foreigners from the north had come down across Palestine, which Egypt always considered as its line of defense. Who were these invaders? They had at their head the famous *hyksos*, shepherd kings of whose origin nothing is really known. They brought with them a certain number of semite nomads from Syria and Palestine. The invaders took possession of the delta, that is to say, the kingdom of Lower Egypt. Traditionally Egypt was made up of two kingdoms united under the double crown of the Pharaohs, the red crown and the white crown that made up the *pschent.* The northern kingdom, then, had been mastered by the *hyksos*, forcing the local dynasty to retreat into the south.

During the occupation of the delta by the *hyksos*, many Palestinian semites followed them there without difficulty, since the delta offered them the advantage of an assured agricultural life. Whenever the rains, on which Palestine was entirely dependent,[10] failed and famine ensued, it was customary to go down toward the delta where the flooding of the Nile was a regular feature. So it was that a good number of poor folk established themselves there and settled on the eastern frontier of the delta in the land of Goshen. One must place the coming down of Joseph's family (Gen 47:4) in this context. So there they were, firmly established, these one-time Palestinian seminomads, now become fellahs. At any rate their sustenance was assured, and when very undeveloped people find themselves better fed than of old, the first result is that they proliferate. This frequently leads to extreme wretchedness, which was the very thing they had been trying to overcome. Jacob's posterity had become prolific in this

[10] In *GTS*, I, there are precious indications about seasons and rain in Palestine (pp. 27–31), vegetation and agriculture (pp. 41–5), demography and conditions of population (pp. 49–57). The fact that the fertility of Palestine depends wholly on rain has very important religious consequences. See Lev 26:19–20; Deut 11:10–17; 1 Sam 12:16–18; 1 Kings 17:1–7; 18:1–5, 41–45; Is 5:6; Jer 3:3; 5:24–25; 10:13; 14:2–6, 22; Hos 2:23–24; Amos 4:7–8. Rabbi Samuel bar Nachman sees four advantages in a country being watered by rain rather than irrigated by rivers: (1) the powerful cannot monopolize the water; (2) the atmosphere and the vegetation are washed of their dust; (3) the high ground receives as much as the bottom of the valleys; (4) men must raise their eyes toward heaven to pray.

way in Egypt (Ex 1:7) between the end of the eighteenth and the beginning of the thirteenth century B.C.

Meanwhile, the Pharaohs who had been driven back into the south succeeded in driving out the *hyksos* and taking possession of the delta again. The foreign warriors with their chariots were able to cross the desert and make off. But the poor immigrants who, thanks to these Pharaohs of their race, had been able to settle in the delta now took on the appearance of a dangerous fifth column left behind by the invaders of yesterday. They were therefore looked upon with the greatest suspicion by the Egyptian nationalists who had just regained possession of the land (Ex 1:9–10).

What was to be done with them? A double policy, exactly like Hitler's policy toward displaced persons, was decided upon.

1. Because there were urgent defense works to be accomplished, and because these people were subjects who had been justly seized as dangerous for national defense, make them work for national defense by forced labor (Ex 1:11–14).

2. According to the needs of the work to be done, let us try to exterminate them rather than help them toward self-development (1:16–22).

In this way the Pharaohs alternated their two policies: sometimes exterminating these dangerous people, sometimes making the utmost use of them to fortify the frontier that was admittedly vulnerable at the time of the *hyksos*.

And so overnight the Hebrews became a people with nobody to take their part, attracting nothing but suspicion, kept firmly under control, exploited to the utmost; and it was hoped they would be utterly destroyed once they were of no more use. Israel was destined to find itself in exactly the same condition thirty-two hundred years later.

But I think that this was the very first time in the history of mankind that a people had been treated in this way as mere human trash, destined for extermination. Before a situation like this can arise, there has to be great bureaucratic empires, in which men know how to make systematic use of a human mass, in terms of profit pure and simple. Now Egypt is the oldest example of this type. It is true it fostered a humanism of exceptional quality, but this was centered in the Pharaoh, who was the man with unlimited power. All the rest of the people were to varying degrees considered merely as servants of Pharaoh. As for those who were not of the nation (I am thinking specially of the Hebrews), they were no more than material to be made use of, like the ropes and pullies used to build the pyramids. It needed an empire like this that knew how to blend the most refined humanism at its head, the most effective bureaucracy at the intermediary level, and at its base the human rabble, completely exploited and ground down, for a section of humanity to find itself in such a state of distress that none but an almighty savior could preserve them in being. But because Israel's misery was too extreme even to let them cry aloud to the Lord, their very cries stuck in their throats, until they forgot the meaning of freedom. And one cannot speak of real misery until it has reached the stage where man forgets the possibility of liberation.

III. MOSES

He chose to be one with them

In the face of this refuse of mankind stands Moses. He had been brought up at Pharaoh's court (Ex 2:10). It has often been suggested in this connection that he must have had a first-class education and have learned the secrets of the Egyptians, and so on.[11] But what is more important is that Moses was brought up as a free man, while the rest of his people were slaves. The decisive point is this free man's reaction when he reached adolescence.[12] It was then that his sole concern was to get to know his own people (2:11), for he knew that he was not an Egyptian by birth. Many an unwanted child brought up by some charitable institution is obsessed by the need to know who were his real parents and is prepared for all sorts of disillusionment and disappointment rather than remain in ignorance of who they were. Moses was such a child. He visited the brick kilns and was there told by the foremen, "Those are the Hebrews there." And Moses saw *them*, and where *they* were. In that moment Moses' choice was made. His education had given him a high ideal as to what man is, and he knew why man had been made. But he did not wish to live out that ideal by himself; he felt the need to be one with his brothers. Now these brothers of his were in a bondage that he, with his experiences of a free man, could neither undergo nor allow. He was torn by this twofold attachment of his heart, between the need to be with his brethren and the impossibility of living with them in their servitude. It was this twofold attachment that turned him into a savior.

[11] See Acts 7:22.

[12] Stephen (Acts 7:23) supposes this to have taken place when Moses was forty years old. Some rabbis agree with Stephen; others think Moses was only twenty at the time, which is more likely. The number forty is an attempt to divide Moses' life into three equal parts: forty years in Egypt, forty years in Midian (Acts 7:30) and forty years as leader of Israel (Deut 1:3), which makes a total of 120 years (Deut 31:1), reached by a calculation that is more ingenious than probable.

Moses would never have intervened if he had been born like all the rest of the Hebrews, if he had lived and grown up in their midst. Neither would he have intervened if he had remained at Pharaoh's court and cut himself off from those from whom he sprang. But to be one with his brothers and not to be able to live in the conditions in which he saw them living moved him to try and draw them out of their distress, not by some preconceived plan but by spontaneous reaction. When he saw an Egyptian overseer strike a Hebrew, he intervened, and the Egyptian found his last resting place in a few feet of sand (2:12).

But next day, we are told, he saw two Hebrews quarrelling. Before they could be liberated, it was necessary that they should not be divided among themselves, should not trample on one another and add yet more to their bondage. However, among those who are enslaved and in dire wretchedness, it is often easy to find individuals ready to take on the role of intermediary, act as leader and keep their fellow bondsmen quiet for a few meager advantages. Moses could not tolerate these kind of *Kapos*[13] who had spread among the people. Immediately he reproved them (2:13), but the protagonists objected to his reprimand and said to him, "Who made you a prince and a judge over us?" (2:14). They had no wish for anybody to interfere with them, especially in their quarrels and their personal interests, even if it was to save them. So Moses, realizing this division among the people, realizing that the first blow dealt for their liberation when he killed the Egyptian would be sure to reach the ears of the overseers

[13] *Kapos* was the name given during the last war to certain prisoners in concentration camps who set themselves up as leaders of their fellows and cultivated the good graces of the prison warders by little services that won them some trifling recognition.—TRANS.

by denunciation,[14] realized also that nothing could be done. It is impossible to deliver from bondage a people that has lost the very taste of freedom, as well as its sense of unity. No earthly power would ever be able to drag it from its despair. It is beyond cure, just as gangrene is too much for the body affected by it.

Beyond the beatitudes

Such was the state of the people who were to be saved. Their poverty was not of the kind to make them cry to God for aid; they were so utterly wretched that they no longer wished to cry out, even preferring their misery in which at least they could sleep to a liberation in which nobody believed. Egypt had succeeded in killing in them not only liberty itself, but the very taste for liberty and all faith in justice. Such beings as these are beyond the beatitudes: they are not the poor[15] who cry out for food, they are not those who hunger and thirst for justice,[16] and it is in this extremity that God takes hold of them. God chose Israel because the divine plan for the Hebrews is already the same as it would be for the dockers of Corinth fifteen centuries later (1 Cor 1:27–29): "God chose what is foolish in the world to shame the wise, God chose what is weak in the world to shame the strong, God chose what is low and despised in the world, even things that are not, to bring to nothing things that are, so that no flesh might boast in the

[14] As Stephen explains (Acts 7:24–25), "And seeing one of them being wronged, he defended the oppressed man and avenged him by striking the Egyptian. He supposed that his brethren understood that God was giving them deliverance by his hand, but they did not understand."

[15] See Lk 6:20; Mt 5:3.

[16] See Mt 5:6.

presence of God." In other words, so that no man should try by himself to fill up by a false glory, which is a snare and a delusion, that void which God has reserved for himself to fill with his own glory. This is what God chose long ago at the gateway of Egypt. This is what he has always chosen.

Yet one still meets people who think that the Christian domination of the world would have been more easily assured if Jesus had been born the son of Caesar. But that is not what God chose. God chose to begin in an unknown place, in hearts that did not even know how to suffer any more and that seemed beyond all resistance and all human effort to save the world; for what God dreads more than anything is a heart that lets itself be satisfied with something other than him. Rather an empty heart that no longer knows how to call out or even to want than a self-sufficient heart[17] that will suddenly discover the vanity of what it had regarded as all-important. God prefers to make use of beings who are helpless and abandoned, rather than this Pharaoh of the fourteenth century B.C., Akhenaton, who nonetheless had come to the conclusion that the world must be guided on its way by a single almighty one. In his faithfulness and wholehearted loyalty, the Pharaoh reached this conclusion and was not afraid to put his throne in jeopardy, expelling all the priests, each of whom pleaded for his local deity, saying, "No, I do not believe in a federation of gods, because the Almighty, Aton, alone rules the world." Yet it was not he whom God chose; it was a people who did not know, and who in their misery had lost sight of the fact, that their ancestors had had a God.

[17] See Lk 6:24–25.

"On the spot"

We must now go back to Moses, who had fled into the desert after his disappointing rebuff. Sitting by a well, he met a shepherdess. She brought him to her father, who accepted him as a son-in-law. In due course a son was born to him (Ex 2:21–22). So it seemed that Moses had found a future for himself by becoming the son-in-law of a sturdy Midianite sheik who lived in the neighborhood of Mount Sinai. But it was not for nothing that God had led him there. One day Moses, who retained enough of his former inquisitiveness to be interested in things that did not concern him, saw in the desert a bush that was burning but was not consumed (3:2). His curiosity getting the better of him, he went up to it to see what it was. At once he was stopped by a voice that said to him, "Do not come near; put off your shoes from your feet, for the place on which you are standing is holy ground" (3:5). Moses covered his face and then heard a further message: "I have seen the affliction of my people who are in Egypt, and have heard their cry because of their taskmasters" (3:7).

Why should he be the one to hear this? It was because he was the man most "on the spot" in both meanings of the term—he was there present, and he was ready. And when God speaks, it is the man who listens to him who is most "on the spot". Indeed Moses also, and perhaps only he, really knew the sufferings and the distress of his people. He also had heard their cry but with this difference: he had given up all idea of delivering them, since his first overtures had brought nothing but bitter disappointment. When he understood that the God of their fathers had also been touched by the sufferings of this people, Moses was afraid. He feared that this word of God might mean that he had been chosen to go and deliver the people, and he did not wish to undertake such a task at any price. His past experiences had shown that it was beyond all human strength to bring out of Egypt a people who had no will to be delivered, who did not understand the extent of their misery.

Called against his will

Besides, God did not say, "I have heard their appeal, their supplications". They did not know how to appeal, to supplicate, to pray; they had no idea of how to wrest their liberty from God. They only knew how to cry out to relieve their sufferings; and this was the cry God heard. But he understood and interpreted this cry as an appeal, because he knows better than Moses why man was made. And so he issued his command (Ex 3:10): "Come, I will send you to Pharaoh that you may bring forth my people, the sons of Israel, out of Egypt." Moses felt crushed by the task: "Who *am I* to do this thing?" God replied, "*I will be* with you; and this shall be the sign for you, that I have sent you: when you have brought forth the people out of Egypt, you shall serve God upon this mountain" (3:12, emphasis added). Yes, when they have come out of Egypt, but what about now?

Moses realizes he has been called, but he has no wish to follow up the call (4:10–12). He replies, "Oh, my Lord, I am not eloquent,[18] either heretofore or since you have spoken

[18] Jeremiah made a similar objection on the occasion of his calling (Jer 1:6–9), in contrast with the prompt readiness of Isaiah (Is 6:8). For Ezekiel, a tragic prophetic mission (Ezek 2:10) appeared to him as "sweet as honey" (3:3). The author of the Book of Revelation felt his mission as a prophet sweet in his mouth, but bitter in his stomach (Rev 10:10), uniting the impressions of Ezekiel and Jeremiah (Jer 20:9).

to your servant [a slight reproach here? your word is not able to free my tongue]; but I am slow of speech and of tongue." Yahweh replies, "Who has made man's mouth? Who makes him mute, or deaf, or seeing, or blind? Is it not I, Yahweh? Now therefore go, and I will be with your mouth and teach you what you shall speak." If God sends him, God who himself created the word will produce it on his lips.

Moses has no further arguments but is as obstinate as a donkey that refuses to budge. He sticks to his motiveless "No" (4:13): "Oh, my Lord, send, I pray, some other person." Then Yahweh was angry with Moses and said to him (14–15): "Is there not Aaron, your brother, the Levite? I know that he can speak well; and behold, he is coming out to meet you, and when he sees you he will be glad in his heart. And you shall speak to him and put the words in his mouth;[19] and I will be with your mouth and with his mouth, and will teach you what you shall do." Moses can resist no more, and now these two, Moses and Aaron, must walk with God's staff to keep them on the right path and must go and find audience with Pharaoh.

Between hammer and anvil

No need to say that the result of this mission will be very slight. We know what reaction to expect from the king of Egypt (Ex 5:6–9):

> The same day Pharaoh commanded the taskmasters of the people and their foremen, "You shall no longer give the

[19] Here we have the institution of cooperation between prophet and priest in the service of God's word. This will not be without difficulty, since the priest is inclined to be jealous of the prophet because of the intimacy that binds him to his God (Num 12).

> people straw to make bricks, as heretofore; let them go and gather straw for themselves. But the number of bricks which they made heretofore you shall lay upon them, you shall by no means lessen it; for they are idle; therefore they cry, 'Let us go and offer sacrifice to our God.' Let heavier work be laid upon the men that they may labor at it and pay no regard to lying words."

Pharaoh's thought is this: "If these people are capable of thinking of making an expedition into the desert, it is a sure sign that they have not got enough to do. They must therefore be made to lose all taste for excursions by being crushed with work." Faced with such a reaction, the people themselves are scarcely likely to respond enthusiastically to Moses' mission and its first results.

Moses and Aaron are aware of Pharaoh's anger; and they are anxious when they hear that, just after their visit, the *Kapos* charged with organizing the forced labor of their fellow Hebrews had held a meeting. When they hear, "Well, my friends, there is going to be no more straw, but there must be just as many bricks", they are heartily disgusted by the lack of efficiency in their delegate Moses' visit to Pharaoh. As they come out from the meeting, Moses and Aaron gather the people together to try and explain how it had happened. But it was the "scribes of Israel" who took up the offensive (5:21–23): "Yahweh look upon you and judge, because you have made us offensive in the sight of Pharaoh and his servants, and have put a sword in their hand to kill us." Then Moses turned again to Yahweh and said, "O Lord, why have you done evil to this people? Why did you ever send me? For since I came to Pharaoh to speak in your name, he has done evil to this people, and you have not delivered your people at all." Moses is between the hammer and the anvil, between God who has sent him and the people who cannot bear the excess of misery that this mission starts by bringing upon them. Still believing, however, that it is indeed for the liberation of this people that he has been sent, he implores God to take the matter in hand himself, for Moses can no longer bear to see the merciless crushing of this people whom theoretically he ought to save.

Before the people's unbelief, Moses clings to God, for he knows that if he has intervened, it is not because he has dreamed he should, not because he had any wish to do so, but because somebody has sent him. All the murmuring and doubts of the people only force him to attach himself more closely as a suppliant to this God[20] who has catapulted him into a mission that he has accepted against his will.

But now we must ask why it was that God chose Moses precisely at that moment and after the boyhood experiences he had had.

Man cannot deliver man

To answer this question, let us regroup the elements that motivate and condition Moses' vocation. God began by preserving him in his infancy, so that he should know what freedom means. Without this, he would never have understood the people's servitude. And God chose someone who not only had been liberated, but who had been loyal enough to acknowledge himself one with the people from which he sprang. Far from abandoning them, he came back to them to try and get them out of their predicament by rescuing them from slavery. Yet it was not when Moses first tried to save them that God chose him. So that Moses should be ripe for his mission, it was necessary that he should intervene, should fail,

[20] See Ex 15:24–25; 17:1–4, 11–12; Num 11:1–2; 14:1–19; 20:2–6; 21:4–7.

and should give up the idea. This is very important. God intervened for those who have already had experience of human enthusiasm and human attempts at intervention and have seen where such things have led. Only then do they come to realize that they are not great enough, that the problem of man's liberation is not a human problem.

If men on their own intervene, in the belief that they can deliver themselves, they either break themselves or make compromises with concessions that change the liberation of their dreams into another form of slavery. Moses would have nothing to do with compromise; he had no wish to bring about a deformed liberation. He preferred to abandon the idea altogether and go into exile, his hope broken. And God chose to intervene just when Moses had no longer the least human wish to enter on the scene, when having made trial of his strength, or rather of his weakness,[21] he knew that it was not his arm or his word that would save Israel. The conditions of the contract were perfectly clear then: when God chose him, Moses knew beyond a doubt that it would be only in God's hands that he would again find the hope to do anything.

This is surely a lesson for general application. More often than not, our human instinct persuades us to undertake the very thing for which we were made, but our aim is crooked; we miscalculate our strength and come to the conclusion that the thing cannot be done. At such a moment, the danger is that like Moses we marry[22] and get busy with our flocks. But the moment God himself speaks, just when we

[21] See 2 Cor 12:9; 4:7–10; 6:4–10; 1 Cor 4:9–13; Is 50:4–7; 1 Kings 19:14; Jer 15:10–11, 15–21; 18:18–20.

[22] Moses was already married at the time of his calling, whereas Jeremiah (Jer 16:2) and Paul (1 Cor 7:7–8) remained celibate in faithfulness to their mission.

no longer have the heart to intervene and act, it is essential that we should do only two things: *listen* first of all and not close our ears on the pretext that we no longer wish to intervene, and *believe*, that is to say, stake all on the word of God. Only thus will we have the courage to take again, without any personal inclination, the way we took before with so much enthusiasm, and on which we failed—because now we are walking with God. Before, in our youthful enthusiasm, it was not with God but with our personal illusions that we walked. It is nevertheless a good thing to be logical about our early illusions. For if we are not logical in these, we have not loyally experienced them right to the end, as we should. But after that, once the illusions are exposed, it is good to keep our ear open for faith.

A faith that opens up the sea

And so Moses, crushed by the weight of a demoralized people and by the resistance of Pharaoh, who will not hear of liberating them, succeeds nonetheless by the power of God in leading his people out of Egypt at last, till they come to the Red Sea. The people, seeing themselves caught between the sea and the Egyptians pursuing them, say to Moses (Ex 14:11–13):

> "Is it because there are no graves in Egypt that you have taken us away to die in the wilderness? What have you done to us, in bringing us out of Egypt? Is not this what we said to you in Egypt, 'Let us alone and let us serve the Egyptians'? For it would have been better for us to serve the Egyptians than to die in the wilderness."

Seeing that the situation was, humanly speaking, desperate, Moses replied:

"Fear not, stand firm, and see the salvation of Yahweh, which he will work for you today; for the Egyptians whom you see today, you shall never see again."

Then Moses stretched out his hand over the waters, and the waters separated so that the people passed through them. There is the faith of Moses. That grain of mustard seed that is capable of moving mountains (Mt 17:20), capable of opening up the sea, had taken root in Moses' heart. And I believe that the people's very incredulity caused Moses' faith to grow. Seeing the saving will of God's heart unappreciated, Moses took it wholly to his heart, and from then on felt himself entirely one with his mission. So he now asserted himself and ordered the Israelites to step into the sea; the sea divided and the people passed through it. The Egyptians chased after them and the sea closed up again. How are we to imagine this miracle? Impossible to say, but what is certain is that only this miracle can explain how Israel became the people of Yahweh, how they accepted as bridegroom a God with whom it was difficult to live, because Yahweh is not a God you would choose; he is a God who chooses you. Man would never choose to submit himself to such a hand, that slays in order to bring to life, if this hand had not been first stretched out to him as the hand of a savior, as the hand of the last resort reaching out when there is nothing but death ahead, the hand that drives back the waves of death[23] and makes a despairing rabble into a people. For those who set foot on the other side of the sea were no longer the same. One could never understand why Israel alone, out of the

[23] The memory of the miraculous passage through the Red Sea was deeply engraved in the hearts of the Israelites: Neh 9:11; Ps 66:6; 77:16–20; 78:13; 89:9–10; 106:9–11; 114:3; Wis 10:18–19; Is 51:10; 63:12–13; 1 Cor 10:1–2, etc.

whole world, agreed to be led by the living God, if he had not adopted them when they were mortally wounded.

Let us praise him who does wondrously

On the other side of the sea, the Sea of Reeds as the Bible calls it, the Israelites sang the song of their betrothal, with the energy of a thunderbolt, occasioned by God's having so suddenly saved them. It is the Canticle of the Sea (Ex 15:1–11):

> . . . "I will sing to Yahweh, for he has triumphed gloriously;
> the horse and his rider he has thrown into the sea.

Miriam, Moses' sister, danced with her timbrel, while the women of Israel took up this refrain as a chorus, between the following couplets that Moses improvised then and there:

> Yahweh is my strength and my song,
> and he has become my salvation;
> this is my God, and I will praise him,
> my father's God, and I will exalt him.
> Yahweh is a man of war;[24]
> Yahweh is his name.
>
> "Pharaoh's chariots and his host he cast into the sea;
> and his picked officers are sunk in the Red Sea.
> The floods cover them;
> they went down into the depths like a stone.
> Your right hand, O Yahweh, glorious in power,
> your right hand, O Yahweh, shatters the enemy.

[24] The Greek of the Septuagint has translated this epithet by inverting its meaning—"breaker of wars" (found in Jud 9:7; and 16:2), an expression that has a messianic nuance (see Is 9:4; Zech 9:10; Hos 2:20). This reveals the originality of the work of the Greek translators who gave the Bible an adaptation suited to the Hellenistic world.

In the greatness of your majesty you overthrow your adversaries;
  you send forth your fury, it consumes them like stubble.
At the blast of your nostrils[25] the waters piled up,
  the floods stood up in a heap;
  the deeps congealed in the heart of the sea.
The enemy said, 'I will pursue, I will overtake,
  I will divide the spoil, my desire shall have its fill of them.
  I will draw my sword, my hand shall destroy them.'
You blew with your wind, the sea covered them;
  they sank as lead in the mighty waters.

Who is like you, O Yahweh, among the gods?
  Who is like you, majestic in holiness,
  terrible in glorious deeds, doing wonders?"

The whole drama of Israel will be to succeed in perpetuating this moment of bethrothal[26] in which they truly became the people delivered by the Almighty; to live as a people actually liberated by the Almighty, when through the burden of years Israel will have to bear the alliance with the Lord as an actual condemnation to liberty.

[25] In Hebrew, the same word *aph* signifies both nostril and anger.

[26] This nostalgia for the time of Israel's betrothal with her Lord first appears in Hos 2:16–17 and later forms an introduction to the oracles of Jeremiah (2:2).

4

A People Condemned to Liberty

From the time of the Persian Empire down to our own day, Israel has found itself in difficulty, dispersed among other nations, living as a small closed community, always unable to live at ease in an open-hearted manner with the peoples among whom it has found itself. Why should this be so? It all springs from what happened at the Red Sea. What I mean is that after this event God required, as a strict condition of life from the people he had liberated, that they should never acknowledge a human master, never recognize any power other than his. From this it becomes immediately clear why Israel, dispersed among various empires, could never offer sacrifice to the powers in which those empires believed. We know that at the beginning of the Christian era, both Jews and Christians were called "atheists" [1] in the Roman world. Since their faith forbade them to sacrifice to local gods and so acknowledge the divinity of the gods worshipped by other people, the last looked upon them as "repudiators of the gods", [2] that is, as atheists.

[1] This is the reason given by Dio Cassius for the condemnation of the Christians Clement and Domitilla by Domitian. Apollonius Molo brought the same accusation against Jews in general: "atheists and man-haters".

[2] According to Dio Cassius, "the Jews are distinguished from the rest of humanity chiefly because they refuse to honor any other gods." According to Pliny the Elder, Judea is a nation "celebrated for its disdain of the gods".

For Israel could recognize no power other than that which had liberated them from Egypt. "There is no divinity other than God." This was the confession of faith that Mohammed later demanded of the idolatrous nomads he brought to Islam, that is to say, the true religion as opposed to idolatrous superstitions.

The Creator's authority of freedom

The Israelites realized that there is no divinity exercising dominion over them other than the God who made heaven and earth.[3] That is the sole authority recognized as being over Israel and in Israel. At the very base of the Old Testament there is this axiom which is too quickly forgotten, especially in our days: if man fails to recognize his creator's unique authority over him,[4] he will very quickly lose his liberty. He will invent myths and pseudo-divinities for himself, prostrate himself before other powers and no longer be his real self. There is only one power that can impose himself on the whole of creation without violating any part of it: the power by which creation itself exists in the fulness of its liberty. As soon as man no longer recognizes this power

[3] "He who made heaven and earth" is the classic title of the God of Israel, the characteristic that distinguishes him from false gods: 2 Kings 19:15; 2 Chron 2:11; Neh 9:6; Ps 115:15; 121:2; 124:8; 134:3; 146:6; Esther 4:17c; Is 37:16; Jer 32:17; Acts 14:15; Rev 14:7, etc.

[4] God is the "moulder" (*yōṣer*) of the universe (Jer 10:16; 51:19; 33:2; Gen 2:19; Ps 74:17; 104:24; 95:5; Is 45:7, 18; Amos 4:13), of events (2 Kings 19:25; Is 22:11; 37:26; 46:11; Jer 18:11) and more especially of man (Gen 2:7–8; Ps 33:15; 94:9; Is 27:11; 29:16; 43:1, 7, 21; 44:2, 21, 24; 45:9, 11; 49:5, 8; 64:7; Jer 1:5; 18:6; Zech 12:1). In all these passages, the Hebrew uses the same verb *yāṣar* (to mould), although *BJ* gives several variants. In the following passages, which are proper to the Greek Bible, *plassein* expresses exactly the same notion: Gen 2:15; 2 Mac 7:23; Job 10:8–9; 34:15; 40:19; Ps 90:2; 119:73; 139:15; Prov 8:25; 24:12; Wis 15:11; Hab 1:12; Rom 9:20; 1 Tim 2:13.

or fails to discover it, other powers, existent or nonexistent, enter into play. For man feels the need of giving himself a master so as not to be tormented by the emptiness and vagueness of a condition that opens everything up before him but does not point out his way, leaving him in indecision and ignorance. Wherever man is no longer under the domination of his creator, or, rather, wherever man does not know his master, he invents for himself powers that are different from the Almighty,[5] and can therefore neither enslave nor liberate him. There is only one way by which man can discover his liberty and live by it, and that is to remain in the hands of him who brought him into being and who only enslaves him to something else out of his good pleasure as creator. It is a good pleasure that has nothing gratuitous, whimsical or sadistic about it, since it is creative[6] and hence sets man in the context of the real reason for his existence and not of those elements which would subject him to some other power than God, his creator.

Giddy because free

All that comes from the mouth[7] of the Almighty will be stories of the inmost accomplishments of his creature, and so of his liberation, because liberty is not just the shaking off of bonds that browbeat and disfigure man's real development. Such a liberation is no more than a foretaste of

[5] "Almighty" comes from the Latin Bible, where the word *omnipotens* translates the Greek *pantokratōr*, which itself translates the mysterious divine epithet *ṣ^{e}bâ'ot* (literally, "of armies").

[6] The notion of "good pleasure" is typical of the Hebrew Bible (*ḥēpheṣ* or *rāṣōn)*. The Greek and Latin Bibles have generally substituted for this the notion of "will", which has no exact equivalent in Hebrew.

[7] See Deut 8:3; Mt 4:4.

that liberty which also implies the possibility of realizing far more deeply the reason for one's existence, of discovering one's real meaning, of reaching one's goal. Deliverance from usurping powers[8] is only the door that gives access to liberty, whereas real progress in liberty is to fulfill one's being. Only he who made man enables him to fulfill himself truly. It is in his hands that man passes from the germinal state of a dreamed-of destiny to birth, fulfillment and fruition. It is in these same hands that he proceeds on his way, and if he does not try to escape from them, man will achieve his liberty. If he abandons them, he finds himself in a state of privation and distress. For man must never imagine that what he needs is to be his own master. The only man to let himself be deceived by such a dream is the slave of false masters, even though the influence of the false master has been as discreet as that of the tempter himself. What man really wants is to be in the hands of a master who has real rights over his being, who does not usurp this almighty sovereignty. If a man finds he has no master once he has driven out the false masters he very soon discovers that he is like a demagnetized compass and that any harvest he garners is worthless. Not knowing the true fruit that it should be his to bear,[9] man once again looks for other masters who, even if they fail to bring him real and total fruitfulness for his perfection, help him nonetheless to drive out a

[8] God appears as the one who breaks the yokes of bondage in Lev 26:13; Is 9:3; 10:27; 14:25; Jer 30:8; Ezek 34:27.

[9] Separated from the true God, humanity suffers the pains of childbearing without being able to bring forth the fruit to which it must give birth (Is 26: 17–18). On the other hand, a humanity united to God brings forth the people to come before having any pain (Is 66:7–8). Another simile: the unfaithful people are like a barren fig tree (Lk 13:6–9), while the faithful are trees that bear their fruit twelve times a year (Ezek 47:12). Or again: unfaithful Israel is a vine that has gone wild and only produces sour grapes (Is 5:2, 5; Jer 2:21).

certain anxiety and fear of emptiness that assail him. At least these other masters will enable him to realize something, even if illusory and inauspicious, which will save him from being an isolated atom and will incorporate him into some organism that works and from which there comes a certain dignity that he likes to think of as influential. And that "something" which is preferable to solitude may be the grinding system of the totalitarian state. Even if it crushes him, it frees man from that obscure giddiness of his useless nothingness.

Israel's freedom—obedience or anxiety

But in the case of Israel, the dilemma is very strict: there is only the choice between her true master and the agony of darkness. Any substitute for God's authority is severely forbidden. For a man overwhelmed by hunger and distress is capable of discovering his true master. On the other hand, a man in the state of estrangement—that is, one who has surrendered power into unauthorized hands over his liberty and who betrays by false satisfaction his need of developing properly in the hands of the Almighty—such a man is not free for God, is not open to grace, is not obedient to the leading of him who alone can bring him to true development. God requires of Israel either solitude and thirst[10] or else happy development in his hands; there is no third possibility. Every idol is forbidden. And this necessity of abiding, if not in the perfection of liberty, at least in that freedom of solitude and privation which allows man's true master to keep a real hold on him, this need of liberty was experienced by Israel as the hardest of God's demands; it is

[10] Thirst is the beginning of conversion: Is 55:1; Amos 8:11–13; Jn 7:37; Rev 21:6.

at the root of the Ten Commandments. The Ten Commandments, like the whole law, which is their commentary, have no other aim in view than to preserve Israel from a twofold slavery into which both ancient and modern civilizations have fallen and continue to fall. On one side there is an *exterior* slavery that would supplant the people's exclusive dependence on the Almighty. On the other side there is the whole master-slave relationship, which would put each individual in danger of being no longer immediately dependent on the Almighty, since one or the other of his brothers would blot out that dependence by usurped authority.

I. THE PEOPLE'S IMMEDIATE DEPENDENCE ON GOD

We must now single out three situations that offer distinct problems: (a) when the people are enjoying peace and prosperity; (b) when hard times overwhelm them; (c) in everyday life. Let us see in each of these cases how the domination of the almighty master is assured.

A. WHEN ALL GOES WELL

When the harvests spring up from the earth as though by themselves and when the rains come at their appointed times, when no enemies are making sudden raids, in moments such as these, Israel accustoms itself to thinking of nature as a trustworthy nurse. People begin to think that by their own cunning and strength[11] they have succeeded in getting

[11] See Deut 8:17; Judg 7:2; Amos 6:13.

from their land all that it has to give. That is why in times of peace and prosperity there is danger that people may become forgetful.[12] At times like these, when the Savior does not have to enter on the scene to snatch his people from the abyss, there is a tendency to forget that every dawn is a daily salvation, a new gift.[13] There is the tendency to think that it is perfectly normal for the stalk to come from the seed, for the baby to come from the womb, for the adult to grow out of the baby, and that such is the drama of everyday life. So shortsighted does man tend to become. In the so-called normal situation, a few little tricks, a few little ruses are enough to make sure that tomorrow is no worse than today. So long as such craftiness holds good, the shortsighted man continues to pull the levers that he sees close at hand and gets into the habit of thinking that by these conditions which he sets working, he assures the prosperity and continuity of this creation in which he finds himself, whereas actually he only lays down certain conditions that are not causes in the strict meaning of the word. In the shortsightedness of a prosperous life, man fails to look at its real author. It is inevitable; forgetfulness does its work. Since man succeeds in providing for most of his needs without having to go further than a few yards, why bother to look further? One can say, then, that a state of peace and prosperity tends to produce in man a certain materialism (by no means limited to our day), a certain shortsightedness that makes him live entirely on the creaturely plane, between the walls of things created, walls that end by becoming impenetrable to man's eyes.

[12] See Deut 31:20; 32:15; Jer 5:7; Hos 13:6; Prov 30:9.

[13] See Deut 8:12–14; Hos 2:10; Ps 104:27; 136:25; 145:15–16; Mt 6:26; Acts 14:17.

Things masking the inaccessible

A second danger can be added to this: that of not reaching complete forgetfulness of God. Indeed it might almost be better for the remembrance of God to be totally obliterated, because when prosperity came to an end, the memory of him to whom man must turn for help might arise afresh. But normally man's prosperity does not lead him immediately to atheism. Unconsciously he passes from religion to superstition, provided he does not wish deliberately to disown his past and brutally cast out that Savior in whom he truly believed during the time of his distress. He is content to disfigure little by little the face of that Almighty Savior until it is no more than the face of a docile "good Lord" who makes no demands on one, like the *baalim* or *astartes* of ancient times. One must be very careful. There is an inevitable slipping away from the true God, on whom man realizes his dependence in his more enlightened moments, toward a simple memory of God, who assumes a face and a heart that are only too human, and little by little is no more than a means of satisfying his need of dependence that man can no longer gratify at its true source. Formerly a voice made itself heard, and this voice came from a particular place. Now that silence reigns, one no longer knows exactly what that voice sounded like. One tries to recall it, but unconsciously our memory falsifies the sound of it, until we no longer know if it comes from our own wavering heart, or if it is a genuine memory of the voice we knew of old.

In the matter of faith there is always the risk of slipping away from the living God, who has intervened on our behalf in a manner at once so devastating and so consoling, toward a God to whom our fidelity wants to cling; but since no word of his can now be heard, we end by wondering if after all we ourselves invented that voice in our lives. In Israel, the final result of this sliding was false gods, those wretched masks obscuring the unbearable face of God. No doubt, sacrifice was offered to them, things that cost much to give were consecrated to them, but they can never make up for him who spoke of old and who guides his creation. The *baalim* and the *astartes* thus become accommodating gods, making no great demands in times of Israel's peace. But it is precisely against this degradation that man must react by refusing to trust in those false images that he makes for himself in the place of the true image of God, who is now silent. It is better to remain in expectancy and silence, perhaps even in great distress, knowing who is the master to whom one belongs. This is how man should behave in times of peace and prosperity.

B. IN DAYS OF DISTRESS

With the coming of danger, the *baalim* and the *astartes* are quickly thrown away as utterly incompetent as saviors.[14] The custom had grown up of attributing to them those harvests which would have come about even if they had not been there. But when everything goes awry, one is too sceptical of their very existence to pray to them. On the contrary, the existence of another is brought to mind, one to whom man was bound of old by another kind of intimacy. It is to him alone that prayer is made in days of distress. But what answer will come in reply to this appeal? Will it be salvation? Not necessarily, because God did not

[14] See Deut 32:37–38; Is 2:20; Jer 2:27–28.

choose Israel simply to enrich it and fill it with joy. God chose Israel to be the witness of his holiness, and according to whether this people is forgetful of God or is docile and pliant in his hands, it will be the wasted or the shining witness of that holiness. This holiness works two ways: either it gives life and fulfillment to the man who abides joyfully in the hands of the Most Holy or it burns and consumes interiorly almost to destruction[15] the people who have tried to escape from the hands of their liberator. It does not completely burn to destruction; it burns until there remains no more than a fragment, a weak remnant, but a remnant that, from this renegade race, will succeed once more in bringing forth a faithful people. Thus the holiness of God borne by Israel will often consume almost the entire people, leaving no more than a fragment that it can vivify and from which it can bring forth a new people. And God's hold on Israel is not only equivocal in this double sense; very often it involves a quasi-destruction in order that a new birth may take place, which is in keeping with the evolution of a humanity that is on the way to re-creation: Israel.

C. IN DAILY LIFE

If one wants to make sure that the devouring holiness of the God who has been disowned does not consume almost the entire people, his hold on the people must be assured in ordinary daily life. This is achieved by keeping the people in a state of fear of God, fear that does not mean "being afraid", but "relying on", "reverencing", "being mindful

[15] See Is 66:15–16; Ezek 21:3–4; Amos 7:4–5; Zech 13:9; Deut 32:22; Zeph 1:18; 3:8.

of". The people must think of God's power as paramount. God's judgment and scrutiny must be preferred to all other judgments and scrutinies,[16] especially those of neighbors. This is a fundamental matter for Israel, and when one of the greatest rabbis of the first century, Johanan ben Zakkai, was dying, he said to his disciples who were asking him for a spiritual testament: "God grant you that his fear may be as vivid a reality within you as the fear of men." The disciples were shocked by this comparison "as vivid ... as". But he answered them, "When a man commits a sin, he says to himself: 'I hope no man saw me.' But what is needful is that God's judgment should be for each individual at least as vivid a reality as that of those about him." Every hope must be rooted in God's power, rather than in such empty desires.[17]

"You are my tenants"

This dependence must be as all-embracing as possible where Yahweh is concerned, and to make it realistic, very precise and exacting laws were formulated. An example of this was the law saying that men are only tenants of the land that falls to their lot, not its real owners. In Israel, there is no absolute right of landed property. To ensure this, for the whole of one year in seven the land must be left fallow[18] so that it can return to its natural state. It is given back into the hands of its only creator, so that the hold of its so-called human "owners" should be realized

[16] See 1 Kings 8:39; 1 Chron 28:9; Ps 7:11; 33:15; 90:8; 139:1–4; Prov 15:3, 11; Jer 11:20; 17:9–10; Heb 4:13; Rev 2:23.

[17] See Ps 146:3–5: Is 2:22; 31:1–3; Jer 17:5–8.

[18] See *AI*, pp. 173 ff.

as something provisional and transient. The Bible establishes an explicit relationship between this custom and the Sabbath that once in every seven days abolishes man's right to share by labor in the creative work of God,[19] so that he may remember that it is this work of his creator that gives value to whatever man may add to it. In the Book of Leviticus (25:4–6) we read: "in ... the seventh year there shall be a sabbath of a solemn rest for the land, a sabbath to Yahweh; you shall not sow your field or prune your vineyard. What grows of itself in your harvest you shall not reap, and the grapes of your undressed vine you shall not gather; it shall be a year of solemn rest for the land. The sabbath of the land shall provide food for you"; in other words, you shall eat what grows wild that year, and this alone will nourish you. In verse 21 of the same chapter it says, "I will command my blessing upon you in the sixth year, so that it will bring forth fruit for three years." This blessing of God will guarantee produce for the end of the sixth year itself, for the seventh when there will be neither sowing nor reaping, for the eighth when there will be no harvest because no sowing was done in the previous year, and for the beginning of the ninth year until its harvest is gathered. If man thus shows that he is filled with the fear of God, one year will be worth three. All this indicates a way of thinking: man's tenure of land is only transient because, as God says in Leviticus 25:23, "you are strangers and sojourners with me". Man ... must therefore always remember that he is not the real owner, but a tenant who must renew his lease every six years, and for the seventh year he must leave the whole property in the hands of its real owner.

[19] For the Sabbath, see *AI*, pp. 475 ff.

Firstborn and first fruits

Similarly, when a man thinks he is a father, he must remember that it is not he who is the real father but God. He will remind himself of this by sacrificing the firstborn of all animals to God. Every firstborn animal must be sacrificed (Deut 15:19–20).[20] This animal may be eaten at home, but it must not be made to work, and it must not be of service to man or domesticated by him. It must remain in its wild state and be killed to show that man does not make use of it. This law holds above all for the firstborn of man; while they are not immolated to God, they are redeemed, that is, replaced by an animal that is immolated to God instead. The same idea requires that the right of exploiting the earth be limited by sacrificing the first crops of all fruit trees. The Hebrew Bible calls this "the foreskin of fruit trees" (Lev 19:23–25), meaning the beginnings of its fruitfulness. It is forbidden to gather the fruit of any tree during the first three years of its fruit-bearing. After that, the first good harvest that one would be happy to enjoy must be offered to God alone. Only in the following year may the fruit be taken for the use of man. Even so, each year at a special feast, the first fruits of every harvest[21] must be offered to God; the first of everything, even if symbolically, must be for God, and only then may man make use of it. From the fact that man must sacrifice to God what might have been the first reward of his labors, it is seen that all man's rights must be exercised as rights delegated to him by the Almighty. All these observances keep vividly before Israel's mind the fact that there is no human power that has not been conferred by God.

[20] For the sacrifice of the firstborn, see *JB*, p. 93, note a, on Ex 13:11.
[21] See *JB*, p. 249, note a, on Deut 26:1.

II. EACH ISRAELITE DEPENDS DIRECTLY ON HIS GOD

There was always a danger that there might grow up in Israel a master-slave relationship that would be for all those in subjection like a screen obscuring the authority of the one true master. How was this to be avoided? We have already insisted enough on the fact that immediate dependence on God is the only sure pledge of liberty, so that the essential importance of this fresh aspect of a unique demand may be properly grasped. As long as one fails to make this demand the basis of the law of Sinai, one cannot understand it. Here, then, are a few details that will show us the law in perhaps an unfamiliar light, that is to say, as the guarantee of brotherhood between Israelites by the strict prohibition of the institutional and permanent condition of servitude within the people. The underlying principle is "nobody shall exploit his brother". By "exploitation", I understand: to treat a brother as an object from which one expects a return. The reason for this is that all Israel is made up of persons who have been freed. To turn them into a people of slaves would be to disfigure them.

Neither forced labor nor loans at interest

This is how the Book of Leviticus seeks to prevent abject poverty from becoming slavery (25:35–36):

> "And if your brother becomes poor, and cannot maintain himself with you, you shall maintain him; as a stranger and a sojourner he shall live with you. Take no interest from him or increase ..."

In other words, he shall enter into the house of some well-to-do Israelite who is to adopt him, but as a free man. There must be nothing suggestive of mortgage in return for service, for such conditions would be prejudicial to liberty.

Exploitation can be practiced in two ways: by granting tenure in return for work, which amounts to forced labor, or by demanding interest on a monetary loan, which is usury.[22] Both of these are forbidden to the brotherhood of Israel. It may be said that this was largely compensated for by permission to make loans at interest to persons other than Israelites. This is true, but loans at interest were not allowed within the family of Israel (Deut 23:20–21). And this formal prohibition is very important, because Israelite morality is a kind of "moral bubble", if one may use the term, a moral type that is still only formally valid for a limited group of men, the group of liberated brethren; that is all it is. Alongside this are relationships of mercy, and of humanity, but not of fraternity in the strict sense of the word. And this morality which establishes in the world a kind of closed brotherhood, which is the people of Israel, is to be found at the root of the most general morality that can exist, although it is, to use Henri Bergson's expression, still provisionally closed. Social morality in Israel is extremely far-reaching, but it refers to "the neighbor", a neighbor who is still limited to members of the covenant made at Sinai: the Hebrew brotherhood. It is Jesus, in the parable of the good Samaritan (Lk 10:29–37), who will teach us what to do to become the neighbor of a man by caring for him in his misery. It is then that we discover that our neighbor can be any man, that every man has the right to expect us to show we are at one with him, that we draw near to him

[22] For usury, see *AI*, pp. 170 ff.

to show ourselves in the guise of the "neighbor" that he is in theory and even in fact. However, we must not fail to notice that a widening of the idea of neighbor can be foreseen in certain verses of the Pentateuch (Lev 19:34), whose spirit went far beyond other laws of the time.

Slaves of God alone

Here is the continuation of the text of Leviticus that, as we saw, prohibited forced labor and usury among Israelites themselves (25:36–38):

> "... but fear your God; that your brother may live beside you. You shall not lend him your money at interest, nor give him your food for profit. I am Yahweh your God, who brought you forth out of the land of Egypt to give you the land of Canaan, and to be your God."

God is saying: It was I who rescued you from slavery, I who gave you all, and you must therefore not speculate among yourselves about what I have given you. You have no real right of ownership, it is I who gave all this to you as a pauper. Therefore you have not the right to negotiate over your brother, who today is poor, in things that were my gratuitous gift to you. Such a law has grave obligations, but we have here the foundation of the social morality of the Old Testament:

> "And if your brother becomes poor beside you, and sells himself to you [he began by selling all that he had, and now has no more to sell. But so as not to lose entirely the land he has mortgaged, he is now ready to sell himself, which is only logical], you shall not make him serve as a slave: he shall be with you as a hired servant and a sojourner.... For they are my servants, whom I brought

> forth out of the land of Egypt; they shall not be sold as slaves. You shall not rule over him with harshness, but shall fear your God" (Lev 25:39–43).

At the end of the same chapter, the principle is laid down even more clearly:

> "For to me the sons of Israel are servants, they are my servants whom I brought forth out of the land of Egypt: I am Yahweh your God" (Lev 25:55).

Do not make yourselves slaves of slaves!

This principle involves certain consequences: those who have sold themselves into slavery because it was impossible for them to pay their debts shall be freed at the end of six years of service.[23] Nevertheless, the Bible foresees cases in which they will refuse this freedom.[24] In spite of the provision the master must give them to facilitate their rehabilitation in life, there will be some who fear that they may not be able to manage on their own, preferring to remain as servants in a well-organized household. In this case, the master must take him to the door of his house and thrust an awl through the lobe of his ear into the doorpost (Deut 15:12–17). Johan ben Zakkai makes the following commentary on this rite: God means by this: "This ear deserves to be pierced for not understanding me when I said at Sinai that the children of Israel are my servants, for it was I who bought them in Egypt. Let them

[23] For the law concerning Israelite slaves, see *AI*, pp. 80 ff.

[24] However, the obligation to release Israelite slaves every seven years was not faithfully observed, as is shown in Jer 34:12–14. The same must be said of many of the regulations mentioned in this chapter. But that does not stop their being the logical and coherent framework for Israel's idea of justice, and this is the point of view that concerns us here.

therefore not make themselves slaves of slaves!" For this reason also it is forbidden to deliver up a fugitive slave to his master. The man with whom he has taken refuge must keep him with him as a free agent (Deut 23:16–17). On the other hand, whoever takes one of his brethren to sell or exploit him shall be put to death (Deut 24:7).

The prohibition against making loans at interest has for its object the avoidance of accumulated debts, a slippery slope that tends toward the loss of liberty. Pledges for loans, however, are permitted. The pledge could be a mere symbol, in which case a sandal was offered.[25] That is why Samuel, when the people no longer would have him for their leader, replied, "Have I received pledges or sandals from any one of you?" (1 Sam 12:3), while Amos condemned those that "buy the poor for silver and the needy for a pair of sandals..." (Amos 8:6). But the simple recognition of a debt symbolized by a sandal was not always enough for the lender. When he demanded a more substantial pledge,[26] he was not allowed to enter the house of the borrower to seize it. It was for the latter to bring the pledge outside, since the Bible forbade the sinister ways of bailiffs (Deut 24:10–11). There were certain objects of basic need, such as the millstone, which could not be taken as pledges. What would be the use of borrowing corn if one had to give one's millstone as a pledge for it? As the Bible says, it would be "taking a life in pledge" (Deut 24:6). If a poor man is obliged to pledge his cloak, his creditor must return it to him at nightfall, lest chilled by the night cold he should cry to the avenger of the oppressed who would hear his voice (Ex 22:25–26; Deut 24:12–13).

[25] See *AI*, pp. 170 ff.
[26] See *AI*, pp. 171 ff.

Abolish your debts

With the permanent aim of preventing the accumulation of debts obliging a man to sell himself into slavery, the Bible provides for the annulment of debts by the return of all pledges and acknowledgments of debts every seven years (Deut 15:1–3). But this prospect risks making lenders less generous when they see the seventh year approaching, which will take away their whole right to whatever somebody may want to borrow. For this reason the Bible requires men to lend to their brethren out of compassion, trusting in Yahweh's blessing alone (Deut 15:9–10).

To make sure that an individual can be helped in difficulty, it is necessary for the family to remain well provided for.[27] It is undesirable that in some city two or three big families should monopolize all the wealth, while many other families are overwhelmed and impoverished. To prevent this from happening, every forty-nine years there must be a reconstruction of basic family patrimonies. This was known as the jubilee.[28] The price for the sale of land was reckoned in practice by the more or less close proximity of the jubilee year, because it would really be a certain number of harvests that were sold (Lev 25:8–16). Even before the jubilee year arrived, the nearest relative of somebody who had been obliged to alienate house or lands—or even the vendor himself if he could—had the right and the duty of repurchasing the goods sold (Lev 25:25–28).

All this legislation shows how deeply the biblical legislators were concerned with rooting out slavery in Israel. From this came their anxiety to open every possible door

[27] For the sociological importance of the family in Israel, see *AI*, pp. 19 ff.

[28] See *AI*, pp. 175 ff.

to allow deliverance from slavery, and their efforts to build up barriers on the road that leads to it.

The rights of the poor man

The Bible takes great care also to ease the lot of impoverished brethren. The wage[29] of a workman must be paid daily (Lev 19:13), "for he is poor, and sets his heart upon it; otherwise he would cry against you to Yahweh, and you would be in sin" (Deut 24:15). As we have said, the primary object of the weekly rest is that for one day in seven man should surrender the success of his own hands into the hands of God, the source of all success. But it is instituted also so that man's ox and donkey, his slave and his servant may also have their rest. "You shall remember that you were a servant in the land of Egypt" (Deut 5:14–15). This obligation of a weekly day of rest for slaves is wholly exceptional in antiquity, yet the Bible grants it even to oxen and donkeys (Ex 23:12), and similarly prescribes "You shall not muzzle an ox when it treads out the grain" (Deut 25:4).

Still with the object of easing their lot, the poor must be allowed leisure to gather whatever grows on the fallow land during the sabbatical year (Ex 23:11). Even during the years of normal harvesting, it is forbidden to reap right up to the edge of a field or to come back and glean what is left. What remains is for the poor man (Lev 19:9; 23:22). A forgotten sheaf is also for him (Deut 24:19). When one harvests an olive grove and some unripe olives are left, they must not be gathered. They are for the poor (Deut 24:20). The same applies to all clusters of grapes left by the harvesters and all early windfalls in the orchards (Deut 24:21;

[29] For wage earners, see *AI*, p. 76.

Lev 19:10). When a man goes through a field of wheat or a ripe vine, he has the right to eat as much as he likes, rubbing the ears of corn and the clusters in his hands, but he must not take away any in a basket (Deut 23:25–26). Finally, every three years the tithe of the harvest must be placed on the doorstep so that the poor may be satisfied (Deut 14:28–29; 26:12).

A single Master who makes us brothers

We see, then, how the Old Testament, by detailed laws and profound compassion, opposed the progressive proletariatization of the people and always sought an abiding compensation for those caught on the slippery path of poverty. These precepts and laws, although scattered about in the books of the Bible, constitute a well-built jurisprudence whose aim is to prevent any Israelite from having one of his brethren for master, so that all may only have for master the unique Master who made them all brethren.[30]

And so this section of mankind which is Israel will find itself taken firmly in hand by the divine artist who seeks to restore in Israel his image that has been disfigured. It will still be necessary for Israel to renounce utterly any attempts to imagine (in the strict sense) him who is in process of remodeling it. Meanwhile Israel can do no more than caricature him. From this comes the law in Israel prohibiting all idols.

[30] Early Christianity did not fight against slavery on the plane of social restoration, but it took away its sting by announcing to both slaves and masters that they now have only one Master, the Lord (1 Cor 7:20–24; Col 3:22—4:1; Eph 6:5–9).

5

The Idols and the Image

I. THE IDOLS

It was God's will to remodel in his own image that section of mankind that he had taken in hand in Egypt. To make possible this patient restoration of his image in man, he began by taking two protective steps. By forbidding his people to recognize any authority except his own, he insisted that the people to be remodelled should remain exclusively in the hands of him who was remodeling them. This is the first of the Ten Commandments, and we have already studied its implications. The second commandment,[1] which forbade the making of images of God (idols), is the second protective step. Its aim is to make sure that the relationship of artist to model should not be reversed. It is for God to model man in his own image, not for man to model God in his. We must now see what exactly is meant by idolatry.

To mask God or to express him?

In making an "idol", man tries to give himself an imaginary substitute for that unbearable presence from which Adam the sinner fled away. As he cannot endure letting himself be worked upon by an unknown being with bewildering

[1] Ex 20:4–6 = Deut 5:8–10.

power, as he cannot submit to being pliable in the hands of the one his anxious and hallucinated heart immediately imagines as a sadistic Almighty, man tries to veil this face, which is a devouring fire,[2] by means of a mask on which he feels he can look. It is not his intention to turn this mask into a caricature. To make the mask, he uses what he feels is most sublime and gives his God perfections that he does not himself possess but for which he feels a certain nostalgia induced by the remains of God's image that he still bears within him.

After all, did not God create man in his image as creator,[3] and did he not by this very fact give to the most perfect of the creatures, which he made on the sixth day, a power over those already created (Gen 1:25–28),[4] the power to perfect by his intellect their creation in giving them names (Gen 2:19), that is to say, assigning to them their definitive *raison d'être* in a cosmos made to be administered by man? Is it not reasonable, then, that man, in the desire to contemplate his God, should try to decipher the image of the creator that he has within him and devote all the means in his ability to express in matter (of which God had made him master) his own Master's characteristics that he has glimpsed? Is there a more sublime activity for the administrator of the cosmos than to model the whole cosmos entrusted to him according to the image of him who entrusted it, according to that image whose Master made him the exclusive guardian? The religious man dreams thus to make of the world one immense idol, as authentic as possible, reminding all his senses of the one in whose image he was made man.

[2] Ex 24:17; Deut 4:24; 9:3; Heb 12:29.

[3] See Gen 1:26–27; 5:1; 9:6; Sir 17:3; Wis 2:23.

[4] See Sir 17:4; Wis 9:2–3.

Danger of the distorting mirror

Why then does God reject this idea? Because although such a design would have been quite all right for Adam before the Fall, for the man completely docile to the divine artist, it is no longer licit for one who has fled away from the hand of his God, and it would become possible only when God's true image has again taken possession of man. Even if man as sinner has no intention of caricaturing his God, his finest insights cannot give him an adequate idea of the image of God that his rebellion has distorted within him. To want to mark the world with this distorted image, with a glimpse of God seen in a distorting mirror, is to give consistency to man's hallucinations, confirming him in the state of a frightened slave. That is not the way to discover the real face of the creator. And so, in forbidding man all images,[5] God wishes to draw man away from the hallucinating fascination of his distorted image, so as to keep him in his hands with eyes closed for a moment, long enough for his image to take once more its real form within him. During this time, if his consuming glory blinds man every time he tries to raise his eyes to him,[6] this is to make him understand that it is not a matter of laying hold of God, but of submissively letting himself be held by him.

Subject or object?

There is also a more secret motive for God's prohibiting man the sinner to make idols. What basically is idolatry for the man who does not recognize God for what he is, but an attempt

[5] See Deut 4:15–18; Is 40:18; Acts 17:29; Rom 1:23. For the impossibility of discovering in the physical or spiritual creation any being that can be said to be like God, see Ex 15:11; Ps 86:7; 89:7; Is 40:25; Jer 10:6.

[6] See Ex 33:18, 20; 19:21; Lev 16:2; Num 4:20; Judg 13:22; Is 6:5.

to reverse the order of subject to object that defines the relationship of God to man? In this relationship, God is by definition the subject and man the object. By idolatry, however, man seeks to become the subject and make God the object. This is an inversion. In other words, God is the absolute source of all action, while man is the result of one of his actions and, no doubt, the crown of creative activity in matter that God has begun to reduce to order. Man is at the summit; but even as a being sharing in liberty, and as the virtual center of creation, he is still not more than a product of God's activity. God alone, therefore, is absolute subject, and in relation to him man can only be the object of God's creative activity, even when he is a free subject.

Now it is just this relationship of object to absolute subject that the sinful man finds insufferable. Whether it is Adam saying to God, "I was afraid, because I was naked; and I hid myself" (Gen 3:10), or Job crying out, "How long will you not look away from me . . . you watcher of men?" (Job 7:19–20a), man wants God to disappear, and no longer to fix him with that unbearable look which he knows he cannot face up to. This sovereignly powerful and free presence of God, constantly interfering with what man thinks is his liberty, never stops reminding him of the source, once life-giving but now disowned, of that same liberty. In contact with him who is the absolute center of life, man recognizes his own life as wounded and finished. And so he implores God kindly to disappear, mercifully to let himself forget the one who has denied him.

Creating his creator anew

However, man knows that he cannot always flee, that he will never succeed in finally eluding this presence which the remains of clear-sightedness eternally force him to recognize in his worst moments. And so another idea springs to his mind: to replace the unbearable presence with another presence, tamed and made to his own measure, which will become the symbol of the other—to make for himself an *object* that will be the image of that absolute *subject*. Man will thus replace the insufferable presence of the absolutely free and almighty being by another presence, the fruit of his own labor and the child of his dreams, easily tamed because born of man's own subjectivity. In other words, the old man, in his idolatrous attempt, seeks to make an object of the absolute subject, to make a valid image of it, and afterward to give the image such an important place in his religious observance that it ends by concealing the one it was supposed to represent.

Instead of letting himself be painfully modelled by God's hands, which he knows would involve laceration and the breaking of all that he has done wrong, man prefers to make God in his own image. This image will be far superior to himself, the image of a dream that he would be quite incapable of realizing fully, and yet an image that remains fundamentally his own, never coinciding with the one that God wishes to remodel in him. Idolatry, then, is a passionate effort at objectification, the substitution of a created image for the being whose created image man is said to be.

This is an inversion of sacrilegious proportions. The clay seeks to replace the potter. This simile may seem strange, and indeed it would lack sense if man were not a very special "clay", into which God has not printed a mere passive image of himself but an active image. And man's great temptation will be to try and re-create his own creator in his own manner. Finding his condition as creature intolerable, but realizing nevertheless that his intimate relationship with the creator cannot be destroyed, man attempts to turn his creator into the most sublime of manmade creatures. This is what gives a dramatic turn to the making of the golden calf, Israel's real original sin.

II. THE GOLDEN CALF

Israel's original sin

Whereas the original sin of man was to flee away from the hand that was molding it, Israel's original sin was to try and mold God in the image of one of his creatures. When the Bible speaks of a "calf" as the creature chosen for this, the choice strikes us as a shameful caricature. Ever since Moses' condemnation, without appeal and in the name of God, of this whole enterprise, nobody, Jew or Christian, can sufficiently express his disgust for this calf.[7] However, I would like to be able to interview some of the contemporaries of that calf and ask them what it was they saw in it. They would certainly say that the calf had nothing of the placid and somewhat languorous character that we usually associate with this animal. It was a young bull in the acme of his age,[8] pawing the ground and wanting to mate. Why should such an image have been chosen? Because ever since the middle of the third millennium at least, this is what expressed, in the Near East, the essential qualifications of divinity: strength and fecundity. And for his worshippers God was primarily the one who gives life, and the strong defender.

[7] See, already, in the Bible: Ps 106:19–20; Jer 2:11.

[8] The image of a dynamic young bull is found in Ps 29:6 and Jer 31:18.

In the exclamations of the people at the sight of Aaron's golden calf, "This is your God, O Israel, who brought you up out of the land of Egypt" (Ex 32:4), we must not see the least feeling of disgust,[9] but merely an extremely naïve enthusiasm. This cry must have delighted Aaron, not only out of the self-love of an artist, but in his troubled conscience as lieutenant of his brother Moses. After all, why had he given way to the demands of those who asked him for a God who would be able to lead the people (32:1)? In acting in this manner, Aaron had no intention of usurping the mission of his brother Moses, nor of turning the people away from their new Master.

Vowed to whom?

Moses had led the people as far as the foot of Mount Sinai, following the pillar of smoke. But now, for more than a month, the people's guide had been called by his God to enter into the storm cloud that had come on the top of the mountain with crashes of thunder, and he seemed to have no intention of leaving it (Ex 24:17–18). The people, keeping their distance from the mountain that could not be touched on pain of death (19:24), began to fear that they had been led far into the desert simply to be witnesses of the incomprehensible holocaust of the person who brought them out of Egypt (32:1). And so, approaching the brother of Moses, the Israelites asked him to take in hand the people's destiny by "making a God" who would be able to lead this crowd, which had been so quickly

[9] It was when the exiled Jews in Babylon could compare at close range their religion with that of other people that their contempt for idols found its most sarcastic expression. See marginal references in *BJ*, Is 40:19–20.

abandoned by its liberator, to a place where they could live.

Aaron had no idea of leading the people into apostasy, but mindful of the people's confusion his one idea was to give them an object of adoration more accessible to human imagination than the storm cloud in which the insupportable presence was hidden. Far from turning Israel away from Yahweh, he meant by the creation of a symbol to give grounds for faith in the inaccessible God and so to avoid the apostasy of a bewildered and distracted people who no longer knew to whom they should bind themselves.

God recognized

So Aaron attempted to satisfy the people's wishes while, at the same time, guiding them in a way that would respect basic fidelity to Yahweh. "Take off the rings of gold which are in the ears of your wives, your sons, and your daughters, and bring them to me" (32:2). In this way Aaron sought at the same time to diminish the Israelite's taste for luxury and to attach them more intimately to Yahweh by the consecration of their most treasured possessions. "So all the people took off the rings of gold which were in their ears, and brought them to Aaron. And he received the gold at their hand, and fashioned it with a graving tool, and made a molten calf" (32:3–4). When Aaron broke the mold, what his joy must have been to see the excited people immediately recognize in the statue of gold him who had rescued them from Egypt!

This result was all the more remarkable since the Hebrews at that time were scarcely artists. When they came to invade Palestine, the local civilization suffered a severe setback.[10] To be convinced of this, it is enough to go through the galleries of the Palestinian Archeological Museum in Jerusalem and to note there the sudden artistic decadence that seems to have taken place when the Neo-Bronze Age gave way to the First Iron Age, just at the time of the Hebrew invasion. One has the impression there of the unleashing of a wave of barbarians. In ancient times among slaves whose lot was manual labor, it was rare to find workmen who had profited by professional training.[11] Yet God was not ashamed to make use of a people devoid of culture to bear witness to his will in the midst of far more refined peoples round about them. Looking through archeological remains, we are once again struck by the extraordinary way of acting of him who "raises the poor from the dust, / and lifts the needy from the ash heap, to make them sit with princes" (Ps 113:7–8).

Science and adoration

But sure enough, for so uncouth a people, what enthusiasm when one of their number succeeds in producing from a clay mold something that manages to evoke the dream of him that made it! Nowadays we can no longer imagine, in our age of learning and breathless mastership, the effect produced by the work of those who first succeeded in making clay into something that had a human face, in carving a bone into a skiff for distant cruises of the imagination. We

[10] See *AP*, p. 119.

[11] It was dearth of clever artists that caused the name of those employed in making the tabernacle and its furnishings, not long after the escape from Egypt, to be conserved for posterity (Ex 31:1–6; 35:30—36:2). For the building of the Temple, Solomon employed a master craftsman and specialist workmen from Tyre (1 Kings 5:20, 32; 7:13–14; 9:27).

are no longer familiar with that quality of admiration which only needs two letters changed to turn it into adoration. We are, indeed, the direct heirs of an age in which art, understood as a mastery of precision, has long since reached its heights, waiting for less talented men to find once again the memory of genius in their hands.

It is not in that sphere, therefore, that the productions of our dexterity will move us to adoration. Rather is it in purely technical spheres, in productions that are strictly functional, that the present-day man finds himself lifted out of his anxiety. He expects his technical skill to project him irresistibly into a future of which his plans give so captivating a picture, whatever the difficulties that may arise later in integrating even a modestly harmonious and peaceful humanism with the new monsters that gush forth one after another from the fevered mind of this impenitent dreamer. The ever-increasing rhythm of the vortex in which man's life is lived maintains within him a kind of exaltation that saves him from being obsessed by his own want of balance, just as the unrestrained whirling of a heavy flywheel regularizes the vibrations of some great engine. In this way, present-day mankind finds in the unfolding of its technical creations a kind of compensation for the loss of the true absolute, the possession of which alone can really tranquillize man intimately. It is precisely in this sense that our modern technical achievements take on a certain character of idols, that is to say, substitutes for the absolute.

God, jealous of a statue

But in Aaron's day it was not like that at all. Admiration for the most modest work of art irresistibly called forth prostration; and Aaron acted as one who knew the cause, wishing to develop and anchor, by means of this image, the people's faith in the unique liberator. So he built an altar in front of the statue that the Israelites had just recognized as their God and proclaimed, "Tomorrow shall be a feast to Yahweh" (Ex 32:5). Aaron must have gone to sleep in peace that night, happy to have given the much-admired statue the name whose memory must be preserved at all costs. Nothing could have been further from his mind at that moment than that God should angrily cut short his dialogue with Moses with the words:

> "... [T]hey have made for themselves a molten calf ... and said, 'This is your God, O Israel, who brought you up out of the land of Egypt'... now therefore let me alone, that my wrath may burn hot against them and I may consume them..." (Ex 32:8, 10).

Aaron would have thought this sudden outburst of jealousy wholly unjustified. Why should God take the thing in the wrong way? Does he who manifests his glory through prowess[12] not understand the relationship of a sign to the thing signified? Except for a few thick-headed folk who would never get beyond the superstitions of fetishism, most of the Israelites certainly saw in Aaron's statue only the image of God, who had brought them out of the land of Egypt. But it was just this ambiguity of the image that God could not tolerate. Like all symbols, the image

[12] The authentic manifestations of Yahweh were the mighty deeds he accomplished to save Israel at the Exodus (Ex 15:6; Deut 4:34; 7:19; 11:2–7), and again at the time of the return from the Exile (Is 41:2–4, 20; 42:8–9; 46:9–11; 48:3–7; Ezek 28:25–26; 34:27, 30; 36:11, 23, 36–38; 37:6, 12–14, 28). In an analogous sense, the miracles of Jesus were the sign of his messiahship (Jn 2:11; 5:36; 9:3–4; 10:25, 32, 37–38; 14:10–11).

is both a transparent sign and an object. It can either be an introduction to the reality it signifies or it can take the place of that reality. That is why it stirred up God's jealousy.

The shattered footbridge

Yahweh will not tolerate any idol made by man's hand because he will not tolerate man's reversing the relationship of molder to the thing molded. He will never give man any image distinct from himself, for fear that the image, instead of playing the part of a transparent sign, should become a veil that masks him. Only one possibility remains: that he should raise up among men an image that would not be distinct from himself, that would not be other than himself. That would be the Incarnation.

But it is always a temptation for priests (*pontifices*, "bridge builders") to try and throw bridges between man and his God. They tend to forget that God allows only the bridges that he himself builds. And the divine architect was just then busy discussing with his foreman the type of bridge to be built between man and himself. So it is not surprising that he ruthlessly batters down the ridiculous footbridge that has sprung from the all too human imagination of Aaron. The type of bridge conceived by Aaron is called an "idol". The type of bridge conceived by God is called "Incarnation". And God could throw the bridge "Incarnation" only toward a humanity that had wholly renounced the idea of throwing the bridge "idol" toward him.

Let us now see how God proceeds to build the bridge of the Incarnation, how he prepares mankind for the coming of the only true "image", that of God made man.

III. THE KNOWLEDGE OF GOD

The opposite

God had now established his hold on that section of mankind that was to be remolded, and from the first disfiguring of his image by their original rebellion, he had forbidden them to fabricate any supposed image of himself. Now, in remolding man's heart to resemble his own, God is going to establish between his chosen ones and himself a secret understanding that will prepare them to recognize his true image on the day it appears among them. By teaching them to look on their brethren exactly as he does himself, God will create between men and himself that deep intimacy, that heart-to-heart relationship which will prepare them for meeting him face to face on the last day. Realizing this, we shall not be surprised to see the prophets of Israel give to the "knowledge of God" a meaning that is the very opposite of gnosticism.

Jeremiah explains this very clearly to Jehoiakim:

"Do you think you are a king
because you compete in cedar?
Did not your father eat and drink,
and do justice and righteousness?
Then it was well with him.

He judged the cause of the poor and needy;
then it was well.
Is not this to know me?
says Yahweh."

(Jer 22:15–16)

Or as the prophet Micah says,

> He has showed you, O man, what is good;
> and what does Yahweh require of you
> but to do justice, and to love kindness,
> and to walk humbly with your God?
>
> (Mic 6:8)

Only the man who walks in God's footsteps among men will discover God. And there is only one way of walking in God's footsteps: to practice justice, in its widest sense, with those around one. Only thus can man be really "heart-to-heart" with Yahweh, who is "he that does justice." ". . . [L]et him who glories glory in this, that he understands and *knows me*, that I am Yahweh who practice steadfast love, justice and righteousness in the earth; for in these things I delight, says Yahweh" (Jer 9:24, emphasis added).

Favorites of the Most High

God may seem terribly strange to man the sinner whom he takes in hand, and the bond that unites this man with his God seems so tenuous that in his anxiety he fears he may be quickly abandoned by his Savior, and yet:

> Behold, Yahweh's hand is not shortened, that it cannot save,
> or his ear dull, that it cannot hear;
> but your iniquities have made a separation
> between you and your God,
> and your sins have hidden his face from you
> so that he does not hear.
>
> (Is 59:1–2)

For my thoughts are not your thoughts,
  neither are your ways my ways, says Yahweh.
For as the heavens are higher than the earth,
  so are my ways higher than your ways
  and my thoughts than your thoughts.

(Is 55:8–9)

But what then are these heavenly ways, these transcendent thoughts?

For thus says the high and lofty One
  who inhabits eternity, whose name is Holy:
"I dwell in the high and holy place,
  and also with him who is of a contrite and humble spirit,
to revive the spirit of the humble,
  and to revive the heart of the contrite."

(Is 57:15)

. . . Heaven is my throne
  and the earth is my footstool;
what is the house which you would build for me,
  and what is the place of my rest?
All these things my hand has made,
  and so all these things are mine,
  says Yahweh.
But this is the man to whom I will look,
  He that is humble and contrite in spirit,
  and trembles at my word.

(Is 66:1–2)

Because God is the Most High, he disdains all human grandeur.[13] When a man succeeds in setting himself up somewhat above the crowd and is flattered with praise, God is not in the least impressed. Men of this kind will

[13] See Deut 10:17; 2 Chron 19:7; Job 34:19; Wis 6:7; Sir 35:11–12; Acts 10:34; Rom 2:11; Gal 2:6; Col 3:25; 1 Pet 1:17.

have their reward on earth,[14] and God's heart remains closed to their smug satisfaction. But if certain members of the mass of humans should be downtrodden[15] by those who seek to exalt themselves, driven far from the source[16] of life by those who seek only their own satisfaction, then God's heart is moved for his oppressed children and he will vindicate their right to life, for his heart is the heart of a Father.

He will cry out: "Here I am!"

Where then can one meet this Most High who is inaccessible to man? At the deathbed of his children who have been trodden underfoot by their brethren, in the dungeons of slaves and in the solitude of the abandoned. Whoever approaches, with the heart of a brother, these disowned sons of the Father will be surprised to find there him for whom he had looked in vain from the heights of gnosticism to the depths of asceticism. For indeed:

> "Is not this the fast that I choose:
>   to loose the bonds of wickedness,
>   to undo the thongs of the yoke,
> to let the oppressed go free,
>   and to break every yoke?
> Is it not to share your bread with the hungry,
>   and bring the homeless poor into your house;
> when you see the naked, to cover him,
>   and not to hide yourself from your own flesh?
> Then shall your light break forth like the dawn,

[14] See Lk 6:24; 16:25; Ps 17:14; 73:12, 17–20.
[15] See Amos 5:11; Ps 36:12.
[16] Ezek 34:17–21.

and your healing shall spring up speedily;
your righteousness shall go before you,
  the glory of Yahweh shall be your rear guard.
Then you shall call, and Yahweh will answer;
  you shall cry, and he will say, Here I am.

(Is 58:6–9)

And so you will discover that:

> ... [H]e who loves is born of God and *knows God*. He who does not love does not *know God*; for God is LOVE (1 Jn 4: 7–8, emphasis added).

Now we understand what Hosea means when he says:

... Yahweh has a controversy with the inhabitants of the land.
There is no faithfulness or kindness,
  and *no knowledge of God* in the land;
there is swearing, lying, killing, stealing, and committing adultery;
  they break all bounds and murder follows murder.
Therefore the land mourns,
  and all who dwell in it languish,
and also the beasts of the field,
  and the birds of the air;
  and even the fish of the sea are taken away. . .
My people are destroyed for *lack of knowledge*. . . .

(Hos 4:1–3, 6, emphasis added)

The guide's disguise

But when God, by the mouth of Hosea, was lamenting in this way, the prophets we have just quoted had not yet shown Israel the way of true knowledge. Eight centuries had still to pass away before the son of thunder[17] would discover

[17] See Mk 3:17; Lk 9:54.

that God is love. Why then did the Savior of Israel require a thousand years to reveal who he is?

Here I am reminded of young Tobias, whose blind father had entrusted him to "brother Azarias,"[18] a stranger who knew the way to Media, where the young man had to go. They walked together side by side for days and days without the stranger saying a word to the young man about his real identity. On the way, Tobias learned from him about the medicinal use of the gall, heart and liver of a mysterious fish. Following his advice, Tobias married the young Sarah, driving out the jealous demon who, out of love for her, had already killed her first seven husbands. The mysterious companion undertakes to go to Rages to recover the sum of money owed by Gabael, then, having brought the newly married Tobias back to his father, he taught the young man how to restore sight to the old man. After that, he spent the seven days of marriage celebration with the reunited family. But it was only at the moment of taking leave of them, refusing the presents that Tobias wished to give him out of gratitude for his services, that he revealed to his young friend who it was he had had as travelling companion: Raphael, one of the seven who stand before the Lord.[19]

Ehyeh ašer ehyeh

God led Israel in a similar manner, with the same disguise on the part of the guide who led Israel toward the promised land. There were the same long testing stages during which the people learned little by little to walk in step with him who was

[18] See Tob 5:4–13; 6:7, 14; 7:1, 9; 9:1.
[19] See Tob 12:15–21.

leading them by the hand. Only at the end of time is there the revelation of the mysterious guide's identity.

For example, we should note God's care to remain incognito[20] when he sent Moses to bring Israel out of Egypt. In what terms did he make himself known? "I am the God of your father, the God of Abraham, the God of Isaac, and the God of Jacob" (Ex 3:6). This merely means: he who speaks to you is he who led your forefathers. And when Moses asked him his name, he replied with the mysterious "*ehyeh ašer ehyeh*" (3:14), for which the most accurate translation would be something between "I am: I am" and "I will be who I will be". Such a formula expresses the divine being as a mystery adequately grasped by God alone, but which he will progressively reveal to his people in the course of the centuries of intimacy that are about to begin. Meanwhile, God gives himself a name, "Yahweh" (6:3), which is a pure appellative by which he may be invoked but does not evoke any notion already known. It follows from this that it is an appellative that leaves itself wholly open to the steadily progressive revelation of his being, a revelation culminating in the last phrase of the sacerdotal prayer of Jesus, "I made known to them your name, and I will make it known . . ."[21]

IV. THEOPHANY IN THREE ACTS

At first, God refrains from declaring explicitly to the people he has rescued from Egypt that he is not one god among many but is the unique Creator and master of the world. He also conceals the fact that his most correct name is

[20] See Gen 32:30; Judg 13:17–18.
[21] Jn 17:26.

"father" and that his being is "love". So when the Israelites fix their mind's eye on him who guides them, what do they see? By day, a column of smoke, by night, a pillar of fire.[22] The unfathomable being appears as darkness to our light and shines in our darkness. It will be in the course of a theophany in three acts, separated from one another by 650 years, that an image will gloriously reveal itself.

First act: the fire in the storm

On Mount Sinai, the glory of God was manifested in the sight of all the people. The word "glory", which in Greco-Latin culture suggests prestige and grandeur,[23] suggests to the Hebrews[24] a heavy burden that is imposed from above, and indeed the presence of the God of Israel shows itself as unbearable and oppressive:

> On the morning of the third day there was thunder and lightning, and a thick cloud upon the mountain, and a very loud trumpet blast, so that all the people who were in the camp trembled. Then Moses brought the people out of the camp to meet God; and they took their stand at the foot of the mountain. And Mount Sinai was wrapped in smoke, because Yahweh descended upon it in fire; and the smoke of it went up like the smoke of a kiln, and the whole mountain quaked greatly (Ex 19:16–18).

Only Moses could enter into the cloud and talk as a friend with him who dwells within the blazing fire (Ex 33:11; Num 12:6–8).

[22] See marginal references in *BJ* on Ex 13:21–22.
[23] In Greek, *doxa* is derived from the verb *dokein*, "seem", "appear".
[24] In Hebrew, *kabod*, comes from *kabed*, "weighty".

In Psalm 18:6–15 (= 2 Sam 22:7–16), we read an analogous description of God's intervention to save a suppliant:

> . . . From his temple he heard my voice,
> and my cry to him reached his ears.
>
> Then the earth reeled and rocked;
> the foundations also of the mountains trembled
> and quaked, because he was angry.
> Smoke went up from his nostrils,
> and devouring fire from his mouth;
> glowing coals flamed forth from him.
> He bowed the heavens, and came down;
> thick darkness was under his feet.
> He rode on a cherub, and flew;
> he came swiftly upon the wings of the wind.
> He made darkness his covering around him,
> his canopy thick clouds dark with water.
> Out of the brightness before him
> there broke through his clouds
> hailstones and coals of fire.
> Yahweh also thundered in the heavens,
> and the Most High uttered his voice,
> hailstones and coals of fire.
> And he sent out his arrows, and scattered them;
> he flashed forth lightnings, and routed them.
> Then the channels of the sea were seen,
> and the foundations of the world were laid bare,
> at your rebuke, O Yahweh,
> at the blast of the breath of your nostrils.

As Moses declares, when God speaks in the midst of the fire, it is impossible to recognize any visible form there (Deut 4:12, 15). There is nothing but a *blinding brightness*, thundering out of the *cloud* that veils him to spare the dazzled sight of unclean men. And it is because no created form can be distinguished in the brightness that it is forbidden for man to make use of any created form to represent God.

Second act: the figure of a man in the rainbow

The theophany at Sinai took place about 1240 B.C. Some 650 years later, Ezekiel tells us of a vision he had when he was among the exiles on the bank of the river Chebar:

> As I looked, behold, a stormy wind came out of the north, and a great cloud, with brightness round about it, and fire flashing forth continually, and in the midst of the fire, as it were gleaming bronze. And from the midst of it came the likeness of four living creatures ... Over the heads of the living creatures there was the likeness of a firmament, shining like crystal.... And above the firmament over their heads there was the likeness of a throne, in appearance like sapphire; and seated above the likeness of a throne was the likeness as it were of a human form. And upward from what had the appearance of his loins I saw as it were gleaming bronze, like the appearance of fire enclosed round about; and downward from what had the appearance of his loins I saw as it were the appearance of fire, and there was brightness round about him. Like the appearance of the bow that is in the cloud on the day of rain, so was the appearance of the brightness round about. Such was the appearance of the likeness of the glory of Yahweh (Ezek 1:4–5, 22, 26–28).

What are the new features found in this vision? Fundamentally there are two: the *figure of a man* and the *rainbow.* Whereas Moses emphasized the absence of all created form in the shining brightness, Ezekiel, six and a half centuries later, perceived in the center of his vision the *figure of a human being* shining like gleaming bronze. Why this difference? Because after the remolding of humanity into the image of God had begun again, the human form began to take on once more its authentic character of Godlikeness. No doubt the prohibition of all idols remains as strict as ever. The time of the Exile in which Ezekiel lived would even see the decisive extirpation of the use of idols in Israel, an extirpation for which the reform of Josiah was the definitive moment. And Ezekiel understood the second commandment of the Decalogue as applicable to the idols that man hides in his heart (Ezek 14:3–7). But that section of mankind in which the old man had been subjected to the painful upheaval of the Exile was, by that very fact, made capable of bearing once more the likeness of God, like a metal that is purified by the burning holiness of the crucible of glory.

Although the divine apparition is still surrounded by the thunder cloud that veiled him on Sinai, Ezekiel perceived in its midst, around the flame that radiated from the figure of a man, the multicolored shining of a *rainbow*. Now the rainbow appeared after the Flood as a sign of the covenant between God and the earth (see Gen 9:12–13). It was the sign of an angry God's reconciliation with his creation that had been perverted by man's rebellion. In Ezekiel's vision, therefore, the shining rainbow expresses the promise of universal reconciliation, which, for the entire universe, radiates the restoration of the divine image in man.

Third act: a lamb standing, as though it had been slain

By leaping ahead another 650 years, again we see the divine glory, this time appearing to the seer of Patmos. What does he see? He recognizes the throne on which "someone" sat, the rainbow that surrounded him (Rev 4:2–3), a sea of glass like crystal, and the four living creatures (6–7). But he also discerns ". . . between the throne and the four living creatures[25] . . . a Lamb standing, as though it had been slain, with seven horns and with seven eyes, which are the seven spirits of God sent out into all the earth" (Rev 5:6).

John no longer recognizes the human form of Ezekiel's vision in him who sits on the throne. But at the center of the vision, a new figure appears, endowed with the plentitude of divine vision (the seven eyes), and all the powers of God's intervention in his creation (the seven spirits). It is no longer a matter only of a formal appearance like the human figure in the glory witnessed by Ezekiel. John does not see *something like* a lamb, but actually *a lamb*, and this lamb is in a paradoxical position: standing, although apparently slain. Then there rises up a cosmic song of praise to the glory of him who sits on the throne and of the Lamb (Rev 5:13). If the Lamb has the right to this typically divine praise, it is—as the heavenly worshippers explain—because he was slain (Rev 5:12) and that this slaying enables the Lamb to liberate for God, at the price of his blood, men of every race, language, people and nation (5:9).

This slain Lamb, on which the Patmos vision converges, is evidently the silent lamb whose life was cut off from the earth and who was depicted by Second Isaiah.[26] It was this that, fifty years earlier, had intrigued a eunuch of the Ethiopian Candace as he travelled along the road in southern Palestine, until an exegete, asking him for a lift, taught him to recognize in this lamb a certain Jesus of Nazareth, executed a few years before (Acts 8:26–35). The Lamb then is Jesus, alive after being put to death, and now sharing the divine lordship as liberator, through his sacrifice, of a new and

[25] The Greek *en mesō* shows that the lamb was the central figure in the vision. See Rev 7:17.

[26] Is 53:7–8.

worldwide people. In this final theophany his glorified human destiny is not set forth as a likeness of the divinity, but as a divine incarnation suddenly rising up in the midst of the Godhead. In this incarnation, the human image caught sight of by Ezekiel as a kind of blended reality now finds its definitive features. The suffering servant of the Book of Isaiah is now found at the center of the divine mystery, immolated and triumphant.

From the theophany of Mount Sinai to that of the island of Patmos, and by way of that of the river Chebar, we witness the gradual clarifying of God's restored image. These three soundings, equidistant in time, of the divine glory, provide us with a progressive deciphering of the image that God reveals to the eyes of those who are fascinated by his glory.

V. TRANSFORMED INTO HIS IMAGE

When God led Israel out of Egypt, the only hold upon him he gave to his people was the enigmatic name of Yahweh. To Moses, who asked him for something more explicit, he replied: "I will be who I will be", in other words, "My conduct toward you will be sufficient commentary on my name." The first of these "conduct commentaries" will be the deliverance from Egypt. The Decalogue opens with a reminder of this:

> "I am Yahweh your God, who brought you out of the land of Egypt, out of the house of bondage. You shall have no other gods before me. You shall not make for yourself a graven image, or any likeness of anything that is in heaven above, or that is in the earth beneath, or that is in the water under the earth; you shall not bow down to them or serve

them; for I, Yahweh your God am a jealous God ..." (Ex 20:2–5 = Deut 5:6–9).

That is: I am jealous to keep you in my hands alone to guide you toward the deliverance of your brethren, so that you may attain a connatural knowledge of him who delivered you. Thanks to this likeness that will be formed in you, you may be able to recognize in the ultimate liberator of the whole human race the adequate and definitive image that I have been forming in that race ever since the evening of the sixth day. For only when "the light of the gospel of the glory of Christ, who is the likeness of God" (2 Cor 4:4), has shone forth, will man be able "with unveiled face, beholding the glory of the Lord" to be changed "into his likeness from one degree of glory to another; for this comes from the Lord who is the Spirit" (2 Cor 3:18).

Then those who have "borne the image of the man of dust" by the fact of their descent from the "first Adam" will be able, by the brightness of the "second Adam", to bear "the image of the man of heaven" (see 1 Cor 15:45, 49), of whose glory Ezekiel caught a fleeting glimpse. For "He is the image of the invisible God" (Col 1:15). And it is thus that humanity, having "put off the old man with his practices", will be able to "put on the new man, who is being renewed in knowledge after the image of his creator" (Col 3:9–10).

God takes a body among the human race

If God forbade Israel to make images of him, it was because the people he had chosen for himself were "predestined to be conformed to the image of his Son" (Rom 8:29). It was because he was getting ready to throw the bridge of the

Incarnation between himself and the human race that God forbade men to attempt to build the "footbridge" of idols. The true image was to be God himself taking a body within the human race, so as to glorify it in its entirety. Then the brightness of glory would no longer blind mankind but transfigure it, and its shining would be life-giving and no longer destructive. Let nobody therefore waste his time in trying to obscure by means of masks the unbearable visage of glory. Rather let men discover the Most High at the bedside of sufferers. In this way an intimacy will be formed, a heart-to-heart relationship that will make it possible to recognize, in the face-to-face relationship that is to come, the risen Lord, the human image in divine glory.

When did we see you?

The recognition of the risen liberator can be really effective only in the awakening of a vocation in man to be a liberator for his oppressed brethren. When the Lamb who has become shepherd, the liberator of the human race who today sits at the right hand of him whose image he is, comes again

> . . . "in his glory, and all the angels with him, then he will sit on his glorious throne. Before him will be gathered all the nations, and he will separate them one from another as a shepherd separates the sheep from the goats, and he will place the sheep at his right hand, but the goats at the left. Then the King will say to those at his right hand, 'Come, O blessed of my Father, inherit the kingdom prepared for you from the foundation of the world; for I was hungry and you gave me food, I was thirsty and you gave me drink, I was a stranger and you welcomed me, I was naked and you clothed me, I was sick and you visited me, I was in prison and you came to me.' Then the righteous will answer

him, 'Lord, when did we see you hungry and feed you, or thirsty and give you drink? And when did we see you a stranger and welcome you, or naked and clothe you? And when did we see you sick or in prison and visit you?' And the King will answer them, 'Truly, I say to you, as you did it to one of the least of these my brethren, you did it to me.' Then he will say to those at his left hand, 'Depart from me, you cursed, into the eternal fire prepared for the devil and his angels; for I was hungry and you gave me no food, I was thirsty and you gave me no drink, I was a stranger and you did not welcome me, naked and you did not clothe me, sick and in prison and you did not visit me.' Then they also will answer, 'Lord, when did we see you hungry or thirsty or a stranger or naked or sick or in prison, and did not minister to you?' Then he will answer them, 'Truly, I say to you, as you did it not to one of the least of these, you did it not to me'" (Mt 25:31–45).

Recognizing in order to be recognized

Meeting with the Almighty, the deliverer, then is not exclusively achieved in the liberation of the oppressed, which would bring about a kind of secret conformation with his work, and so establish a mysterious heart-to-heart relationship with him. It is not only *with* the oppressed but *in* the oppressed that he is to be found, for "though he was in the form of God ... [he] emptied himself, taking the form of a servant" (Phil 2:6–7).[27] His love suffers the loneliness[28] of the unloved, while he seeks to fill the heedlessness of our hearts. That the Almighty should be a beggar on the lips of the poor is all one with the Incarnation. God's likeness is to be sought there-

[27] See Mt 20:25–28; Mk 10:42–45; Lk 22:25–27; Jn 13:3–5, 12–17.

[28] See Lk 2:7; Mt 8:20; 26:30–33, 40, 56, 69–74; 27:75; 2 Cor 8:9.

fore at the very opposite pole to that imagined by the philosopher or the artist. And in this discovery of the liberator in the form of a slave, it is not just a matter of preparing to recognize later the unique image of God in the glorified Son. It is really a matter of a heart-to-heart recognition of the Son in his humiliated state; in his glorified state he will appear face to face as the only true image of the Father.

To *recognize* him who is the glorious image, on the day when he will manifest himself as such, will not be enough. It will also be necessary *to be recognized* by him.[29] And on that day, only those will be recognized who have recognized him in the day of his humiliation in the form of a slave. Only those will share in the glory of the Lamb who will have shared[30] in his immolation.

If it is true that the most infallibly dramatic plot is confusion as to the identity of persons, one understands the vastness of the drama written in the heart of human destiny. The prohibition of idols aimed at preventing man's outlook from being misled by will-o'-the-wisps reflecting God's glory at a time when his presence was accessible to man only under cover of darkness, preserving man's heart from undue elation because of some sublime presentiment at a time when God can be recognized only in the abyss of dereliction, nailed to the instrument of execution.

Now that we have traced in outline the way of the biblical discovery of God, it remains for us to follow some of the great friends of God in their painful gropings to know the heart of their Master: Moses, David, Hosea.

[29] See Mt 7:23; 10:33; Lk 9:26; 13:25–27; Jn 10:14; 1 Cor 8:3; 13:12; Gal 4:9; 2 Tim 2:19.

[30] See Mt 10:38; 16:24; Mk 8:34; Lk 9:23; 14:27; Mt 20:22; Mk 10:38–39; Jn 15:20; Col 1:24.

6

Two Shepherds Who Discovered God

If God will never countenance idols, it is because he himself intends to restore his own image in man's heart. So we will now follow up this work in two great shepherds of Israel, Moses and David.

To become leaders of their people, both of these did their apprenticeship as shepherds of sheep. God loves this school of contemplative silence and busy compassion in which those he destines to be leaders of his people must take their degrees. Before his experience at the burning bush, Moses had to make a strict retreat among Jethro's sheep. And out of all Jesse's sons, the one chosen to rule Israel was the youngest, the one who was doing his novitiate with the flocks (1 Sam 16:11). Professional shepherds are in fact the ones best suited to interpret the gestures of the Shepherd[1] of Israel to the people committed to their care.

We have already followed the destiny of Moses as far as the crossing of the Red Sea. Now we must consider an isolated scene that was deeply engraved on the people's memory: that of Moses' intercession for Israel after the making of the golden calf.

[1] For the rich biblical theme of shepherd, see *JB*, p. 1403, note on Ezek 34:1.

For David, the Bible gives us a sequence of most vivid scenes, gathered together by a chronicler of no mean talent. We must therefore follow him in the sinuous ways of his destiny if we want to grasp the manner in which God leads him and reveals himself on the way.

I. MOSES

Thwarting God's plans

When, by worshipping the golden calf, the people "exchanged the glory of God for the image of an ox that eats grass" (Ps 106:20), God said to Moses, "I have seen this people, and behold, it is a stiff-necked people;[2] now therefore let me alone, that my wrath may burn hot against them and I may consume them; but of you I will make a great nation" (Ex 32: 9–10).[3]

Although God said, "Let me alone", and promised to raise up a new people from him, Moses refused his consent to the plan God had just made known to him. He opposed God, thwarting his plans, and this was out of fidelity to the initial design God had called him to realize. Since he was vowed to the liberation of the sons of Jacob, Moses refused to see them replaced by his own descendants. Since he had been called to realize the promises made to Abraham, Moses would not hear of any other promises.

[2] "Stiff-necked" signifies contumacy and at the same time the refusal to admit errors: Ex 33:3–5; 34:9; Deut 9:6, 13; 10:16; 31:27; 2 Kings 17:14; 2 Chron 30:8; 36:13; Neh 9:16, 17, 29; Prov 29:1; Jer 7:26; 17:23; 19:15.

[3] This offer made by Yahweh to Moses is also recounted in Deut 9:13–14. Num 14:12 tells of another event at Kadesh-barnea.

A flagrant breach

As it happened, Moses' descendants did not enjoy a brilliant destiny. He was not succeeded by one of his sons in the task of leading God's people. The genealogies of the First Book of Chronicles give only very succinct information about his descendants (23:14–17), telling us that they were in charge of the sanctuary treasury (26:24–25). Only one of his grandsons, the young Levite Jonathan, appears in any biblical narration. This was when a wandering priest let himself be enticed by a rich man to serve his household god, and who later went off with the Danites on their travels when they, after stealing the idol, offered him a situation that was much more favorable financially. The salaried servant of an idol! That is what became of the grandson of him who, on seeing the golden calf, had smashed to pieces the tables of the Law. After that, it is not surprising that the scribes of Israel were scandalized and tried to replace the name of Moses by that of the wicked king Manasseh[4] in the idolater's genealogical tree (Judg 18:30).

But Moses refused all honor for his descendants, striving only to turn away the divine wrath from the descendants of Jacob. This complete disinterestedness is the more surprising when we remember that Moses lived at a time when men, knowing nothing of the prospect of personal happiness after death, were wont to place all their hope in the survival of their name honorably borne by numerous

[4] Since Hebrew writing has only consonants, the name Manasseh (*menaššeh*) is indistinguishable from Moses (*mōšeh*) except for the addition of a *nun*. This *nun*, which was inserted here out of respect for Moses, remained "suspended" a little above the normal line, so that it should not be forgotten that it was not in the original text. Unfortunately, most recent Hebrew Bibles pay no attention to this formal precept of the Massoretic text and insert this letter in line with all the rest.

descendants.[5] So it was out of reverence for the name of Moses that the scribes wanted to blot him out from the genealogical tree of the idolatrous priest. According to the ideas of the time therefore, the misfortune in Moses' personal destiny was flagrant. But this stems from the fact that he had completely identified his own destiny with that of God's people.

Identified with his mission

Moses was far from trembling with excitement when he heard from the mouth of God, "Of you I will make a great nation." Here was Moses, called to the supreme honor of giving his name to the chosen people. But what is Moses if not the instrument for the realization of a similar promise made five hundred years earlier to Abraham? And who is it that speaks to him if not "the God of your fathers, Abraham, Isaac and Jacob", as he had called himself at the time of their first meeting at the burning bush (Ex 3:6, 15–16)?

So Moses becomes the suppliant: "Remember Abraham, Isaac, and Israel, your servants, to whom you swore by your own self, and said to them, 'I will multiply your descendants as the stars of heaven, and all this land that I have promised I will give to your descendants, and they shall inherit it for ever'" (Ex 32:13).

What must we see in this intercession? The earnest protest of the shepherd who refuses to see the Master slay the flock that he had confided to his care? Certainly. And Moses there shows himself as utterly identified with his mission

[5] See Num 27:4; Deut 25:6–7; 2 Sam 14:7; 18:18; Job 18:17; Ps 9:6; 41:5; 109:13; Prov 10:7; Eccles 6:4; 7:1; Wis 2:4; Sir 37:26; 39:9; 41:11–12; Is 48:19; 65:15; 66:22.

whose successful issue is the only thing that counts for him, making all thought of personal success valueless. He had suffered so much for this people and from this people when, in spite of himself, he was called upon to save them. He had taken Israel's salvation so much to heart that his life would have no more meaning if Israel must be exterminated by him who had entrusted him with their liberation.

The specter of a despot

But there is more than this in Moses' intercession. He appeals from the God of today to the God of yesterday, from him who today speaks of exterminating the descendants of the fathers to him who once promised those fathers, "swearing by himself",[6] that he would multiply their descendants and bring them into the promised land. It is by using the promise as his buttress that Moses appeals to the God of promises. He cannot bring himself to believe that the anger of a jealous God is the true face of the one who defines himself as faithful to his promises. What indeed would be the use of a new promise made to his descendants if it is acquired at the cost of a former promise for which God had made himself the guarantor? It strikes at the very identity of God! For faithfulness to the promise made to Abraham is bound up with the very essence of him who has called upon himself as witness of the fulfillment of that promise. Either God must never go back on the promise made to Abraham or else Yahweh's intervention in the destiny of Moses is no more than a lie from

[6] This oath recalled here (Ex 32:13) by Moses took place just after the great test of Abraham's faith: the sacrifice of his son (Gen 22:16). The author of Hebrews comments on it (Heb 6:13–18).

the powers of darkness.[7] And the name of him who delivered the Hebrews from slavery in Egypt simply to "slay them in the mountains" (Ex 32:12) will be held in detestation[8] among the people who have witnessed his sadistic exploits. The human race will know for sure that there is an Almighty God, but their certitude will reduce them to despair. They will think it best to flee from before his face, when they consider the lot of those who had submitted to being led by his hand. And so Moses utterly refuses the prospect of becoming the doubtful favorite of this ferocious despot whose terrifying specter God's words bring to his mind's eye. His intercession for Israel is an agonized effort to exorcise this specter. "Alas, this people have sinned a great sin.... But now, if you will forgive their sin—and if not, blot me, I beg you, out of your book which you have written" (Ex 32:31–32). If I have been mistaken in thinking myself the instrument of a savior God, if I cannot appeal from your justice to your promise, if the book you write among men is other than a book of fidelity and love, then give proof of the preference that you say you have for me by blotting me out of that book whose meaning has deluded me.

If Yahweh's design is not what Moses had understood it to be at the burning bush, Job was right in envying those

[7] See in Jer 15:18 a similar test of Jeremiah's faith: he says to God, "Will you be to me like a deceitful brook, like waters that fail?"

[8] Ezekiel firmly insists on the fact that when Yahweh saves Israel from the Exile, it will be "for the sake of [his] holy name" (36:21–23; 39:25), which the Israelites had profaned during the Exile (36:20–23), by saying that God had not been able to protect them (see Deut 32:27; Ps 140:9; Is 10:12–15). This is not the point of view that Moses develops here, but he does so on an analogous occasion at Kadesh-barnea (Num 14:13–17; Deut 9:28). Joshua (Josh 7:9) did the same after the defeat at Ai.

who never existed[9] and Moses, like him, implores the Almighty to forget him and make him forget God.

The intercession of Moses and the sacrificing of Isaac

By preferring God to his gifts, by preferring the God of promises to the promises of God, Moses sealed his intimacy with Yahweh. For this intercession holds in the life of Moses the same place as the sacrifice of Isaac holds in the life of Abraham. Nevertheless the two trials seem to ripen in God's two chosen ones' revelations that are different from, and almost opposed to, one another.

God had indeed allowed Abraham to intercede for a criminal city destined for destruction (Gen 18:22–23). But his intercession was not able to save the city, because he had no formal promise from God on which to rely, as Moses had when he was able to throw down the dividing wall of God's jealousy by the irresistible lever of his faith. God reserved this discovery for Moses. From Abraham, he required the first trial of faith, faith that would bind him to the God of the promise, not to the pledge of the promise, for he was obliged to surrender this pledge into God's hands. Abraham's faith therefore sealed his intimacy with God when, at his command, he undertook to sacrifice Isaac.

God secretly requires of Moses to withstand the immolation of Israel, even though God himself has proposed it to test him. This is because, at the time of the golden calf incident, the people of Israel are no longer the simple pledge of the promise once made to Abraham. A covenant between

[9] Job was not the only biblical author to wish he had not been born (Job 3:11–16; 10:18–19). It was the case of Ecclesiastes also (6:3). Jeremiah was tempted by the same idea in moments of distress (Jer 20:14–18).

Yahweh and the people has just been sealed with blood at the foot of the mountain (Ex 24:8). No doubt God, in litigation against his people, could argue that this covenant has been concluded with a demand for Israel's obedience to the Decalogue, the charter of the covenant (24:3, 8), and that he is therefore now free of his obligations toward a people who have failed in their own by worshipping the golden calf. But, by his intercession, Moses attests that this covenant is not a contract between equals, in which God's initiative and that of the people converge. It seals a work of liberation for which the initiative has come from God alone.[10] On the night of the Passover, God had spared Israel's descendants without any merit on their part. The substitution of the lamb for the firstborn of Israel[11] is related to the substitution of the ram for the son of the promise[12] at the time of Abraham's testing. In revealing himself to the faithful Abraham with the characteristics of a God who spares gratuitously, God bound himself in thus defining himself. And this gives Moses the right to appeal from God's stipulated justice to the gratuitous yet essential mystery of God's faithfulness to his promise.[13]

A faith that protests

Hardly had the covenant that sealed the Law been concluded, when God caused Moses to discover that the ultimate guarantee of the divine protection is not to be sought in the contract that the people will constantly be breaking,

[10] Ex 3:8, 10, 15, 17; 4:15, 23; 5:1; 6:6–8, 11, etc.
[11] Ex 12:3–14, 21–28, 43–49.
[12] Gen 22:13.
[13] Yahweh defines himself as faithful in Ex 34:6; Is 65:16; Mal 3:6.

but in the identity of him who, out of mercy, had spared these wretched people even before giving them his commandments. It is to this end that he tests Moses' faith. If he speaks to him of exterminating Israel, it is to hear bursting from his lips this appeal from the strict judge to the author of the promises that will make of Moses the confidant of Israel's Savior.

This, then, is the way in which God let himself be discovered by Moses, not by telling him who he is, but by leading him, by a protestation of all his faith, to bear witness as to who he is, in spite of what he appears to be. Rooted as he was in his intimacy with the God of the promises, Moses thus exorcised by his faith the mocking mask of the angry judge that causes mankind to tremble with fear ever since the drama of the Garden of Eden.

II. DAVID

A dramatic plunge into the mystery of God was reserved for David also. God said to Moses, "Not so with my servant Moses; he is entrusted with all my house. With him I speak mouth to mouth, clearly, and not in dark speech; and he beholds the form of Yahweh" (Num 12:7–8). But he described David as "a man after [my] own heart" (1 Sam 13:14).

Saul's long obstinacy

If we are going to understand what it is all about, we must begin by comparing David with his predecessor Saul. The Bible presents David as a well-knit personality, but much more supple than Saul. In the career of Saul—that man all of one piece—there is only one real *incident*, only one example of personal initiative: the cutting up of the oxen (1 Sam 11:7) following on the action of Samuel at Ramah (9:22—10:8) and at Mizpah (10:20–24). Once he had personally come to power by this gesture, he became obstinate in that power as he understood it, and it was this obstinacy that made him act contrary to God's designs. Because of a narrow-minded idea of his own authority, he could not bear to see that authority threatened (13: 11–12) and consequently would not see that it might have been saved by God (13:13). It was his obstinacy also that made him defend the façade of his condemned authority (15:30–31) against David, whom he knew to have been chosen by God to supersede him (18:8, 15, 28–29). So Saul, the prisoner of his own mistrustful egoism, resisted just as a dead oak resists while its branches fall one by one in a storm.

THE THREE TURNING POINTS IN DAVID'S LIFE

David on the contrary is like a reed in the face of Saul the oak. That is why he survives the worst storms, that is why events score deeply into his destiny and bend him without ever breaking him. Three of these major events mark three turning points in David's career:

1. The acclamation of the women: "Saul has slain his thousands, and David his ten thousands" (1 Sam 18:7).
2. David's being sent back to Ziklag on the eve of the battle of Gilboa (1 Sam 29:10).
3. David's walking on the roof of his house and catching sight of Bathsheba (2 Sam 11:2).

Each of these events inaugurates a new period in his life: (1) Trials; (2) Victories; (3) Passion.

But before we follow David's personality through these roundabout ways, we must find out exactly who he was.

A harp for the Holy Spirit

We shall put on one side two well-known incidents in David's life: his anointing by Samuel (1 Sam 16:1–13) and his victory over Goliath (1 Sam 17), both of which illustrate the traditional biblical idea of God choosing the humblest instruments as saviors of his people. The first picture to strike us is that of a young harpist playing before Saul, for David is first of all an excellent musician. He is all harmony. He is naturally attuned to the Spirit of God. In his dealings with men, he never gives way to the presumption of him who, having no ear himself, violently obtrudes himself at the wrong time. On the contrary, he has a feeling for psychological situations and gently adjusts himself to suit them. His amazing luck does not signify—as we shall see presently—that he always advances with a fair wind without meeting with hazards on his way. But when the squall strikes him with full force, arresting his progress, he knows like the sea gull how to make use of the wind so that instead of being dashed to earth, he makes it raise him up higher still.

This young, red-haired musician with beautiful eyes radiates around him that harmony which is his chief characteristic: "And whenever the evil spirit from God was upon Saul, David took the lyre and played it with his hand; so Saul was refreshed, and was well, and the evil spirit departed from him" (1 Sam 16:23). In David was manifested that secret power, that charm which the angel of light (the good spirit of Yahweh) still exercises over the angel of darkness (the tormenting and tormented spirit of Yahweh). It is not surprising therefore that Saul became deeply attached to David and made him his armorbearer. In that capacity he distinguished himself in several battles with the Philistines, so that soon all the women in Israel were dreaming of him. If they had been content to dream, it would have had no great influence on his life, but unfortunately they gave way to their enthusiasm somewhat loudly, so it was only to be expected that their new slogan caused the suspicious Saul's hand to tighten on his lance (18:11).

FIRST PERIOD: TRIALS

The first great period of David's life was inaugurated by the women's acclamation of him as victor; this was the period of trials. Rather than recount a number of very complex events, let us take a psychological look at the David of this period. With him we find an outstanding feature, so constantly recurring as to be typical, that was already apparent with Joseph: that of a specially chosen soul being persecuted precisely *because* he seems to monopolize the blessing of God.[14] He is persecuted by the envy of the one from whom the blessing has fled.

David did not commit a single offense against Saul. He refused to take vengeance on his predecessor who repaid him evil for good. He continued to respect the divine anointing that Saul had received and did nothing to try and supplant him. Acting in this way, he won the affection of Jonathan, so that the son of the persecutor became his warmest champion (1 Sam 19:1–7; 20:1–17, 30–34). But the

[14] A similar sentiment stirred up Cain against Abel (Gen 4:3–8), Ishmael against Isaac (Gal 4:28–29), Esau against Jacob (Gen 27:41; cf. Mal 1:2–3; Rom 9:13), the sons of Jacob against Joseph (Gen 37:3–11), Joshua against Eldad and Medad (Num 11:28–29), Miriam and Aaron against Moses (Num 12:2).

jealousy of Saul's old companions in arms had no difficulty in stirring him up against their much-gifted colleague, and the madness of Saul's persecution was driven to its limit by the skillful play of his opponent. At bottom, it is the persecutor who was afraid of the persecuted, while the latter knew himself to be in God's hands.

Victories of the persecuted

In this pursuit, it is the one persecuted who always wins, but his victories are of a very special kind, as the following example so clearly shows. David had again escaped from Saul and was taking refuge at En-gedi:

> When Saul returned from following the Philistines, he was told, "Behold, David is in the wilderness of En-gedi." Then Saul took three thousand chosen men out of all Israel, and went to seek David and his men in front of the Wildgoats' Rocks. And he came to the sheepfolds by the way, where there was a cave; and Saul went in to relieve himself. Now David and his men were sitting in the innermost parts of the cave. And the men of David said to him, "Here is the day of which Yahweh said to you, 'Behold, I will give your enemy into your hand' and you shall do to him as it shall seem good to you." Then David arose and stealthily cut off the skirt of Saul's robe. And afterwards David's heart struck him, because he had cut off Saul's skirt. He said to his men, "Yahweh forbid that I should to this thing to my lord, Yahweh's anointed, to put forth my hand against him, seeing he is Yahweh's anointed." So David persuaded his men with these words, and did not permit them to attack Saul. And Saul rose up and left the cave, and went upon his way. Afterward David also arose, and went out of the cave, and called after Saul, "My lord the king!" And when Saul looked behind him, David bowed with his face to the earth, and did

obeisance. And David said to Saul, "Why do you listen to the words of men who say, 'Behold, David seeks your hurt?' Behold, this day your eyes have seen how Yahweh gave you today into my hand in the cave; and he bade me kill you, but I spared you. I said, 'I will not put forth my hand against my lord; for he is Yahweh's anointed.' See, my father, see the skirt of your robe in my hand; for by the fact that I cut off the skirt of your robe, and did not kill you, you may know and see that there is no wrong or treason in my hands. I have not sinned against you, though you hunt my life to take it. May God judge between me and you, and avenge me upon you; but my hand shall not be against you. As the proverb of the ancients says, 'Out of the wicked comes forth wickedness'; but my hand shall not be against you. After whom has the king of Israel come out? After whom do you pursue? After a dead dog! After a flea! May Yahweh therefore be judge, and give sentence between me and you, and see to it, and plead my cause, and deliver me from your hand." When David had finished speaking these words to Saul, Saul said, "Is this your voice, my son David?" And Saul lifted up his voice and wept. He said to David, "You are more righteous than I; for you have repaid me good, whereas I have repaid you evil. And you have declared this day how you have dealt well with me, in that you did not kill me when Yahweh put me into your hands. For if a man finds his enemy, will he let him go away safe? So may Yahweh reward you with good for what you have done to me this day" (1 Sam 24:1–20).

Compound interest of vengeance

David thus reaches the paradox of obliging his enemy to bless him. Nevertheless, David's attitude of non-intervention, his refusal to repay evil with evil, must not be understood as forgiveness of the harm done. On the contrary, he treasures up his vengeance at compound interest. He heaps coals of fire on his enemy's head.[15] This is a thoroughly Old Testament attitude, but David was its instigator. He feels that to refuse to take vengeance is a pledge of divine protection for the future. Indeed, although vengeance would permanently restore the balance of divine justice, the refusal to take vengeance systematically upsets the balance still further and obliges the divine justice to intervene. Moreover, this way of acting won for David invaluable sympathy in the camp of his adversary, instead of hardening hatred as bloody vengeance would have done. In this way, David isolated Saul and reduced him to despair. Finally, by respecting the inviolability of "Yahweh's anointed" even in his persecutor, he made sure in advance of the stability of his future royalty.

David would act with the same composure as regards Nabal. He mastered his anger and God himself took revenge (1 Sam 25:39).

Like a ripe fruit

There is no need to spend time on the events that followed: David took refuge among the Philistines and found himself confined to the city of Ziklag. There he played a double game, but saw no harm in deceiving the uncircumcised enemies of God's people. He gained the confidence of his suzerain Achish, letting him believe that he was busy raiding the cities of Judah. In actual fact, he was busy winning the hearts of the men of his tribe by delivering the cities of Judah from bedouin raids (1 Sam 27:8–12).

[15] See Prov 25:21–22; Rom 12:20.

But the Philistine coalition against Israel was going to put David in a very delicate situation. If he was to escape reprisals, he would have to come to the Philistine camp as a faithful vassal, tired of remaining in the rearguard, and then turn against the Philistines in the midst of a battle, as the "Hebrews" had sometimes done during earlier engagements (14:21). Fortunately, the distrust of the Philistine chiefs cleared up his case of conscience by obliging Achish his suzerain to send him back to Ziklag (v. 29). Once there, all he had to do was to take up the kingship of Israel, which, after the defeat and death of Saul and Jonathan, fell into his hands like a ripe fruit.

SECOND PERIOD: SUCCESSES

David's being sent back to Ziklag inaugurated the second period of his life: successes. It was now that David pushed to its limits his sincere fidelity to Saul's house, transforming it into a body of political friends. He won people's hearts by three acts of loyalty to the man who had held power before him.

First and second acts of loyalty

First of all, David put to death the Amalekite despoiler of the royal corpses who brought him Saul's crown and armlet, and who by claiming to have slain Saul with his own hand hoped to gain a rich reward (2 Sam 1:5–16). It was then that David composed the magnificent "Song of the Bow" in memory of Saul and Jonathan (1:19–27).

The men of Judah then anointed as their king their tribal brother who had just rendered them such great services (2:1–4), and David started his reign by sending an envoy to congratulate the men of Jabesh-gilead for having saved the body of Saul from profanation (2:5–7). Thus, at the very outset, he showed himself as heir to the memory of his persecutor.

Two regrettable murders

But Abner, sometime Saul's chief of staff, had long looked on David as a rival and now raised the standard of one of Saul's sons who had been set aside, Ishbaal. Part of Transjordan, where they had taken refuge, rallied to their side and tried to win over the central tribes to the new king's cause. Then there took place the meeting at Gibeon between Abner and the three sons of David's sister Zeruiah: Joab, Abishai and Asahel. Abner had the bad luck to kill the young Asahel, although he had tried to avoid doing so for fear of the vengeance of Joab and Abishai (2:8–23).

Some time later, Abner, having quarrelled with Ishbaal over Rizpah, formerly Saul's concubine, decided to abandon this half-wit and rally to David. He undertook to negotiate the submission of all Israel to David, hoping that this would gain a prominent place for him in the new kingdom. Abner came to David at Hebron and everything was arranged satisfactorily (3:6–21). But Joab got wind of this meeting, and on joining Abner he treacherously killed him, evidently to avenge his brother but chiefly to make away with a dangerous rival. This immediately put David in a difficult position and threatened the collapse of all his plans. Obviously everybody would think that it was he who had enticed Abner into a trap and had him assassinated. Immediately he acted with a stroke of genius in the same way in which he had already so often succeeded. He vigorously dissociated himself from Joab's act, cursing him roundly, so that Abner's blood should not stain his kingship. He then obliged Joab and Abishai to mourn for Abner at the solemn funeral he gave him and composed a lament for him. He then prolonged the funeral fast beyond the appointed time, so as to make it clear that this was no mere formality (3:22–37).

Third act of loyalty

David's attitude soon produced its fruits. Two leaders of Ishbaal's forces rose up and slew Ishbaal while he was resting and brought his head to David. David, always acting on the same principle, began by putting them to death as regicides, and then reverently buried Ishbaal's head in Abner's grave (2 Sam 4). After that, the whole of Israel, now leaderless and conquered, fell into David's hands (5:1–3).

It is impossible not to feel embarrassed by David's attitude. It savors too much of the theatrical. Is it not more like political roguery, Machiavellism, than sincere fidelity? Yet one cannot speak of roguery unless the sentiments were feigned, whereas faithfulness is such a deep and constant characteristic of David's personality that we cannot doubt his basic sincerity. It is merely that David amplified and dramatized this sincerity in a brilliant manner.

"I will make merry before the Lord"

Another of David's characteristics that is interesting and revealing comes to light at this period of his success. It is well known with what shrewd political sense David chose an independent capital: Jerusalem, which was part of neither Judah nor Israel but forms a hinge between the two territories, so that no susceptibilities were offended. For the inauguration of the capital, David transferred Israel's greatest treasure, the ark, which would make Jerusalem the center for the people's pilgrimages. Such pilgrimages had an important role to play in maintaining the unity of the tribes in times of peace. When the procession bringing the ark entered Jerusalem, David danced before the ark when it was carried up in the midst of shouting and the sound of horns (2 Sam 6:14–15). But when David returned to his house, his wife Michal, the daughter of Saul, said to him, "How the king of Israel honored himself today, uncovering himself today before the eyes of his servants' maids, as one of the vulgar fellows shamelessly uncovers himself!" But David put Michal in her place, saying, "It was before Yahweh, who chose me above your father, and above all his house, to appoint me as prince over Israel, the people of Yahweh—and I will make merry before Yahweh. I will make myself yet more contemptible than this, and I will be abased in my eyes; but by the maids of whom you have spoken, by them I shall be held in honor" (6:20–22).

Wisdom and folly

It is indeed David who speaks here, always the same, in striking contrast with Saul. When Saul stripped off his clothes at Naioth (1 Sam 19:24) in the presence of Samuel and David, he reached the rock bottom of his dethronement: the proud and jealous king thrown by God naked at the feet of his rival. David on the other hand humbled himself, but spontaneously. He did not cling to his glory as to something that was threatened. He casts it at God's feet like a child playing, sure of the fidelity, even the love of him who had chosen him. To offer glory as homage to God is to receive it back tenfold. But it was not as a premeditated bargain that David acted in this way. By an inspired intuition, he left his glory to God, just as under persecution he had already left the matter of his rescue in the hands of his divine avenger. His personality is all of a piece. The antics of this dancer radiate the supreme wisdom, quizzical and happy, of the children of God. His exaltation has nothing in common with the violent obsession of Saul (1 Sam 10:10–13; 11:6; 19:23–24).

THIRD PERIOD: FROM PASSION TO THE PASSION

When David said to Michal, "I will make myself yet more contemptible . . . I will be abased in my eyes", he little realized how that prophecy would be realized for him. It began on the roof of his house, one summer evening. And now we enter on the third phase of David's life: passion. It began with a small "p", but was quickly transformed into a capital "P". No need to record the details: the sin, David's effort to try and cover it up, then the letter to Joab and the death of Uriah by the enemy's hand (2 Sam 11). Nathan, who knew David's rightness of heart, had no difficulty in making him ashamed by means of his parable of the poor man's ewe lamb, and David accepted the death of the child of his sin as a sign of pardon (2 Sam 12). David here experienced a new kind of humiliation, not the spontaneous exultant humiliation with which he was already familiar, but that secret remorse that gnawed his heart and tortured him with agony when he realized that he himself had broken the bonds that united him to his God. But this was no more than the beginning of David's Passion. He now had other sufferings to endure when misfortune fell on his own household.

"If I find favor in his eyes . . ."

Amnon seduced Tamar, and Absalom avenged his sister by killing Amnon. David suffered deeply but forgave, for it was contrary to his nature to nurture a grudge. Absalom then succeeded by David's pardon in detaching Israel from his father, had himself proclaimed king at Hebron and marched on Jerusalem. David fled with his bodyguard and a few faithful friends.

> . . . [T]he king crossed the brook Kidron, and all the people passed on toward the wilderness . . . and behold, Zadok came also, with all the Levites, bearing the ark of the covenant of God . . . Then the king said to Zadok, "Carry the ark of God back into the city. If I find favor in the eyes of Yahweh, he will bring me back and let me see both it and his habitation; but if he says, 'I have no pleasure in you,' behold, here I am, let him do to me what seems good to him" (2 Sam 15:23–26).

The antithesis between Saul and David goes on: David does not cling to the royalty that seems to forsake him. He will not confiscate for his own profit the divine protection by taking the ark with him like a sort of magic pledge taken from God. Let Yahweh's good pleasure be done! And once again this surrender of himself into God's hands is, he feels sure, the most precious pledge on the heart of Yahweh. David is always the same, but now at a deeper level.

"To see me humiliated . . ."

His attitude is the same toward the curses of his old enemies who come to mock at the dethroned king:

> When King David came to Bahurim, there came out a man of the family of the house of Saul, whose name was Shimei, the son of Gera; and as he came he cursed continually. And he threw stones at David, and at all the servants of King David; and all the people and all the mighty men were on his right hand and on his left. And Shimei said as he cursed, "Begone, begone, you man of blood, you worthless fellow! Yahweh has avenged upon you all the blood of the house of Saul, in whose place you have reigned; and Yahweh has given the kingdom into the hand of your son Absalom. See, your ruin is on you; for you are a man of blood." Then Abishai the son of Zeruiah said to the king, "Why should this dead dog curse my lord the king? Let me go over and take off his head." But the king said, "What have I to do with you, you sons of Zeruiah? If he is cursing, it is because Yahweh has said to him, 'Curse David', who then shall say, 'Why have you done so?'" And David said to Abishai and to all his servants, "Behold, my own son seeks my life; how much more now may this Benjaminite! Let him alone, and let him curse; It is Yahweh who tells him in order to see me humiliated and can give back his curse to me in fulness today." So David and his men went on the road, while Shimei went along on the hillside opposite him and cursed as he went, and threw stones at him and flung dust (2 Sam 16:5–13).

Hunted by Yahweh?

David has a presentiment of a mysterious alchemy in this humiliation. In curses of men, he feels a secret pledge of divine blessing. And so he will no more hinder Shimei from cursing him than he did Saul from persecuting him of old. God's heart does not change, and if there is one thing that is sure to touch him, it is the situation of a man unjustly persecuted who commends himself to divine justice. David had already lived in this certainty when Saul was after him. But is it the same for someone who has profited by his former power to rid himself treacherously of one of his most faithful servants so as to be able to steal his wife? Can one who has "despised Yahweh" (2 Sam 12:9–10), the God of faithfulness, still count on his help on the day when his son wishes to be rid of him so as to steal his kingdom? Nathan had indeed said to David, "Yahweh also has put away your sin; you shall not die" (12:13). As it happened, the child died, not David himself. But now for more than nine years (13:23, 38; 15:7) David has suffered in his sons and by them. Can he still count on God as he had in days past when God had chosen him because he was a man "after his own heart"? Is it not now Yahweh himself who is hunting him down?

"Would I had died instead of you, my son!"

David took refuge at Mahanaim in Transjordan, while Absalom, having made free with the king's harem, mobilized all the people against his father. Battle was joined in the forest of Ephraim. Joab, always faithful to David in spite of his hard heart of a grumbling old soldier, obliged the king to remain in the town during the battle. The excuse given for this was so that he should not be exposed to danger (2 Sam 18:3), but Joab's chief concern was fear lest the emotional state of David in a war against his son should discourage his followers. When the army set out, David, in front of all the people, gave the leaders a charge that reveals him utterly: "Deal gently for my sake with the young man Absalom" (18:5). Does not this rather suggest a king confiding his son to one of his captains when he is first going out to do battle? But Joab thinks he will best serve the king's real interests by putting his son to death with his own hands (18:11–14). Then followed the scene of the two runners who made for Mahanaim, thinking to bring David good news. Ahimaaz arrived first and reassured the king on the issue of the battle.

> "Is it well with the young man Absalom?"
> "When Joab sent your servant, I saw a great tumult, but I do not know what it was."
> "Turn aside, and stand here."
> Then the Cushite arrived in his turn.
> "Good tidings for my lord the king! For today Yahweh has done you justice in delivering you from the power of all who rose up against you."
> "Is it well with the young man Absalom?"
> "May the enemies of my lord the king, and all who rise up against you for evil, be dealt with like that young man." David was deeply moved, and went up to the chamber over the gate, and wept. Weeping and mourning he said, "O my son Absalom, my son, my son Absalom! Would I had died instead of you, O Absalom, my son, my son!" (see 18:29—19:1).

Beyond genius

David did not fully realize the import of what he was saying: Joab's lance that pierced Absalom dealt him also his deathblow. From now on we have to deal with a broken old man, battered by the turn of events, overreached by one after another of the partisans who were trying to possess themselves of his inheritance.

Let us dwell a little more on this last image of an old king breaking his heart over a rebel son. It is here that David reaches his summit. No more is there question of political genius. It is the heart alone that speaks, that old worn-out heart that has known how to love well and to love wickedly and that is now breaking for love of an enemy. We are a long way now from that inspired policy of refusing to take revenge that had gained David his kingdom. In Joab's eyes, David's weeping for the rebel proves that he is already broken. In the end, both Saul and the sons of Zeruiah were dull-witted brutes, like Ajax in Sophocles, but their destiny was not without its very special tragedy. Jonathan and David, on the other hand, were vulnerable beings who would never be understood by those hard-hearted folk who surrounded them and for whom they exercised so strange a fascination. In them is revealed something wholly new.

God speaks from a broken heart

In David, the heart of the father reveals to us its depths. We understand that not even the Savior of Israel has said his last word to his rebel son. *At the price of his sin, David had to attain to that utter breaking of his heart so that there might rise to his lips those words, "O my son, would I had died instead of you", that well up in God's heart when he sees his sons choose death by refusing his love.* The harp of the young musician who charmed both God and man cannot yet make that theme resound. It was necessary that the heart of the son of Adam should be crushed if it was truly to become "like the heart of God", so that it would be able to prophesy this reply that comes from God to David himself and to all rebel sons. Ezekiel would declare later on that God wills not the death of a sinner (see Ezek 18:23; 33:11). But Yahweh had already said, by the lips of his *alter ego* David, that he was ready to die in the place of his rebel sons. So true is it that

God uses as his mouthpiece the lips of sinners whose hearts have been broken and remolded by himself.

And so it is another heart tortured by jealousy and broken by love that God will make use of to give us a glimpse of the secret and indissoluble bond that binds him to his people.

7

The Jealous God and the Deceived Husband

If there is one thing that must not be forgotten, it is that all through (or almost all through) the Old Testament, we find this *leitmotif*, "Yahweh our God is a jealous god."[1] If we do not face up to this, we should have an Old Testament that was artificially sweetened. And when we have begun to see how God reveals himself through the hearts of men (which he uses rather like resonators), we meet with the shepherd's heart of Moses and the father's heart of David. But all this seemed to be converging in almost too direct a manner on God as the Father, while eluding many of the hazards and crossways in the development of religious thought in Israel.

Protected or consumed

Let us, therefore, now make a fresh start from the hard and difficult principle that Yahweh is a jealous god. This must mean that Yahweh is either a savior who delivers from agony of mind and despair and liberates all those who are in distress or else he is a consuming fire that burns up those who forget him and treat him otherwise than as the redoubtable, because living, God that he is. The destiny of the whole human race thus takes on, within that of Israel, a peculiarly

[1] See Ex 20:5; 34:14; Deut 4:24; 5:9; 6:15; Jos 24:19; Nah 1:2.

dramatic resonance. Henceforward, now that Israel has been chosen, only two attitudes are possible: either to be the object of God's favor and protection or else to risk being consumed and destroyed by him.

If man wishes to count on this protection and is anxious that the divine power should not turn to destruction, his fundamental attitude must be that of fear. To fear God,[2] yes, but in a sense that perhaps surprises us, because in the Bible trembling is something that has two almost contradictory meanings. Man trembles because he is afraid, and he trembles because he loves[3] and in that moment he does not even feel joy. In the fear of Yahweh both aspects are included at the same time. The fear of the Lord is for Israel the fact of taking seriously that he is what he is and of not forgetting who he is. The opposite of fear is not so much familiarity as forgetfulness.[4] Fear God or forget him, that is the alternative.

Sunk in forgetfulness

The generation that had passed through the Red Sea and had sung enthusiastically with Moses the song of deliverance on the edge of the desert had now long passed away. And even they, after all, had forgotten the power of their God only a few days later. Now, successive generations maintained the house of Israel, generations that had not experienced the initial wonders;[5] generations therefore that live in ignorance.

[2] References to the fear of God are too numerous to be cited here, but here are some from Deuteronomy: 4:10; 5:29; 6:2, 13, 24; 8:6; 10:12, 20; 13:5; 14:23; 17:19; 28:58; 31:12–13.

[3] See Hos 11:10–11.

[4] A few texts from Deuteronomy on forgetfulness: 4:9, 23; 6:12; 8:11, 14, 19; 9:7; 25:19; 32:18.

[5] See Deut 11:2.

They had forgotten this God who destroyed terribly and saved powerfully. The people no longer knew him. This was particularly the case during the time of the kings, a time when the people had become so socially organized that they no longer had that immediate contact with God which their forefathers had had at the time of their destitution and the holy war of salvation.[6]

So the people now no longer know who the God is that had opened up the sea for them. And so they forget, that is to say, they live in a world that has become secular, where the personality of God exists only as a sort of principle, but in which his presence is no longer vividly felt among the people. He no longer counts as he counted just after he had saved and created Israel. This forgetfulness of the people is described in the canticle in Deuteronomy (32:9–18):

> Yahweh's[7] portion is his people,
> Jacob his allotted heritage.

[6] For the holy war, see *AI*, pp. 258 ff.

[7] Yahweh's "portion", which is Israel, is contrasted with the other peoples, who are mentioned in the preceding verse as the portions of the "sons of God" (that is, members of the heavenly court of the Most High, characterized later in Israel's faith as "angels of God"). Toward the end of the second century B.C. the scribes of Israel were shocked to see Scripture assert that the "nations" were confided by the Most High to the "sons of God". Would there not be danger of such an affirmation being interpreted as a justification for the existence of pagan religions? So in the Hebrew text they changed "sons of *God*" into "sons of *Israel*", even though it was unsuitable in the context. The Septuagint was content to replace "*sons* of God" by "*angels* of God", so as to avoid any danger of a polytheistic interpretation. It has been necessary to wait until 1952 to rediscover on a fragment of the Dead Sea Scrolls the reading "sons of God", which is what the textual critics supposed it should be. Although the Vulgate of Jerome follows the corrected Hebrew text ("sons of Israel") Western scholars down to the end of the twelfth century reasoned on the basis of the Greek text (thus, Anselm of Canterbury, Hugh of St. Victor, Peter Lombard).

"He found him in a desert land,
  and in the howling waste of the wilderness;
he encircled him, he cared for him,
  he kept him as the apple of his eye.
Like an eagle that stirs up its nest,
  that flutters over its young,
spreading out its wings, catching them,
  bearing them on its pinions,
Yahweh alone did lead him,
  and there was no foreign god with him.
He made him ride on the high places of the earth,
  and he ate the produce of the field;
and he made him suck honey out of the rock,
  and oil out of the flinty rock.
Curds from the herd, and milk from the flock,
  with fat of lambs and rams,
  herds of Bashan and goats,
with the finest of the wheat—
  and of the blood of the grape you drank wine.
Jacob ate and was satisfied.

"But Jeshurun[8] waxed fat, and kicked;
  you waxed fat, you grew thick, you became sleek;
then he forsook God who made him,
  and scoffed at the Rock of his salvation.
They stirred him to jealousy with strange gods;
  with abominable practices they provoked him to anger.
They sacrificed to demons which were no gods,
  to gods they had never known,
to new gods that had come in of late,
  whom your fathers had never dreaded.
You were unmindful of the Rock that begot you,
  and you forgot the God who gave you birth."

[8] A surname of Israel.

The story is very well told. First of all, it was God who had saved and carried this people. It was God who protected it and later enriched it with all the gifts of the earth. Then the people became prosperous, self-confident and "waxed fat". Its very heart became fat, as is said elsewhere in the Bible.[9] After that, the people no longer understood, no longer had knowledge. Of the time of confusion, of the time when it had experienced salvation, it was utterly ignorant.

Cheap Gods

On the contrary, in a life that had become fundamentally secular, the people willingly offered incense to "cheap" gods that made no great demand on them, who were very amenable and to which they attributed the success of their harvests. For this there thundered the words of indignation, "You were unmindful of the Rock that begot you, and you forgot the God who gave you birth." The Book of Isaiah begins with the same complaint:

> The vision of Isaiah the son of Amoz, which he saw concerning Judah and Jerusalem in the days of Uzziah, Jotham, Ahaz, and Hezekiah, kings of Judah.
> Hear, O heavens, and give ear, O earth;
> for Yahweh has spoken:
> "Sons have I reared and brought up,
> but they have rebelled against me.
> The ox knows its owner,
> and the donkey its master's crib;
> but Israel does not know,
> my people does not understand."

[9] See Ps 119:70; 17:10.

The people no longer have that recognition, in the etymological sense of the word, that enables the domestic animal to know where to look for its food. Israel no longer knows from whom it draws its life. Henceforth, it attributes its life to myths, to images, to anything that has nothing in common with the living God. Because they have forgotten the power that saved them, they now confuse the living God with "vanities". All those things that man imagines as powers and gods—the violence of the storm, the fruitfulness of the earth, all this more or less personified in such an idol—these were the things to which incense was traditionally offered in the old pilgrimage places of Canaan;[10] these were the things to which worship was offered, and no longer to the savior. God's face had been entirely concealed by man's imagination, by everything that man made for himself in God's place.

A devouring fire

That is why, once the people had fallen into this ghastly confusion of values, confusing the one and only Absolute with all the lies that usurp the name of absolute, a fire came forth from the unknown God to destroy this people. At the moment of his death, Moses bore witness to this (Deut 4:22–31):

> "For I must die in this land, I must not go over the Jordan; but you shall go over and take possession of that good land. Take heed to yourselves, lest you forget the covenant of Yahweh your God, which he made with you, and make a graven image in the form of anything which Yahweh your God has forbidden you. For Yahweh your God is a devouring fire, a jealous God. When you beget children and

[10] For these "high places", see *AI*, pp. 248 ff.

children's children, and have grown old in the land, if you act corruptly by making a graven image in the form of anything, and by doing what is evil in the sight of Yahweh your God, so as to provoke him to anger, I call heaven and earth to witness against you this day, that you will soon utterly perish from the land which you are going over the Jordan to possess; you will not live long upon it, but will be utterly destroyed. And Yahweh will scatter you among the peoples, and you will be left few in number among the nations where Yahweh will drive you. And there you will serve gods of wood and stone, the work of men's hands, that neither see, nor hear, nor eat, nor smell. But from there you will seek Yahweh your God,[11] and you will find him, if you search after him with all your heart and with all your soul. When you are in tribulation, and all these things come upon you in the latter days, you will return to Yahweh your God and obey his voice, for Yahweh your God is a merciful God; he will not fail you or destroy you or forget the covenant with your fathers which he swore to them."

Through death toward a new life

There we have the two great truths between which all the faith of Israel abides: Yahweh is a jealous God, Yahweh is a merciful God.[12] Though they may appear contradictory, these two facts are absolute certainties. For if God's jealousy brings the

[11] This "seeking" for the forgotten God is evoked in 2 Sam 12:16; 21:1; 1 Chron 11:16; 20:4; 2 Chron 7:14; 15:15; Ezra 8:22; Ps 27:8; 40:17; 69:6; 70:4; 83:16; 105:3–4; Prov 28:5; Is 45:19; 51:1; Jer 29:13; 50:4; Hos 3:5; 5:6; 7:10; Zeph 1:6; 2:3; Zech 8:21–22; Mal 3:1.

[12] This idea occurs more often in the Bible than that of God's jealousy. It is expressed in two ways: (1) Yahweh is full of *ḥesed*, that is "piety" in the Latin sense of the word (which means essentially a man's fidelity to bonds of family and affection); (2) Yahweh is full of *raḥamīm*, a word that expresses the affective relationship binding the womb to what comes forth from it.

people to the brink of annihilation, his mercy gives them back life. For it is only by passing through death to a new life that this people to whom God speaks can become the definitive people of God, a people that does not forget and is able to abide in the hands of its savior. And, moreover, this idea does not make its first appearance in the New Testament; the prophets are obsessed with it. It is the conception of "the remnant of Israel", so fundamental in the Bible. "Only a remnant shall be converted." This is the hope, the "narrow door",[13] the hope of Isaiah: "Yes, I will destroy him down to the root, but like the great terebinths which, once felled, still enable shoots to spring from their stumps, so shall a remnant return."[14] This is the very core of Isaiah's message.

But Israel will not be converted[15] until the people as such have been reduced to nothing, because that false shell of prosperity and forgetfulness, of secular organization that they have built up around them, must be broken. It is the prison house of their hearts.[16] And it is only afterward, in confusion, in solitude, in the lack of all hope,[17] that Yahweh will once again interfere to save them. But this will not be like the first deliverance, which had been ratified by the law of Sinai.[18] The new deliverance will be a new creation. Not only a vocation, an appeal, as before, but a change of heart. Such are the prophecies of Ezekiel (Ezek 11:19; 36:26): ". . . I will take the stony heart out of their flesh and

[13] See Mt 7:13–14; Lk 13:24.

[14] Adapted from Is 6:13; 10:21.

[15] "Conversion" is a central biblical idea. See, among many other texts: Deut 30:2; Tob 13:6; Ps 80:3; Prov 1:23; Sir 17:25–26; Is 10:21; 45:22; Jer 3:14; 4:1; 31:18; 35:15; Lam 5:21; Bar 4:2; Hos 14:2; Joel 2:12–13; Zech 1:3–4; Mk 1:4, 15; Acts 3:19.

[16] Hos 13:8.

[17] Hos 3:4.

[18] Jer 31:32.

give them a heart of flesh" (that is to say, a penetrable, pliable heart). Such a heart will recognize its God, will remember and not forget, will not shrivel up in forgetfulness.

Impotence of the law

Here we have the major drama of Israel's history: this inability of Israel to remain in the hands of God. Why? Job gave us the real reason. It is because in reality the man whom God chose is still the old man, still the man who, taken in general and as a crowd, flies from God, and who, each time God lays his hand upon him, only waits for his terrified heart to calm down so as to be able to escape the hand of his Savior. Such a man must be re-created. But he can only be re-created once he has experienced his own impotence in God's hands.

The object of the law is to make Israel understand the extent to which mankind is given over to sin, the extent of man's need to die in order to be reborn. For if the law had not told me, "You must not do that", I should not have realized that sin was in me;[19] I should not have understood that I am really enslaved, estranged, and that my will to follow my God is the servant of another will that is foreign to my better self but which nevertheless tortures and encompasses me. This longing for a new birth that was to make its appearance in Israel at the time of the destruction of Jerusalem and the Exile, among prophets like Ezekiel[20] and Jeremiah,[21] or the second redactor of Deuteronomy[22] who produced an edition of this work during the Exile, could never have appeared if there had not first been the precept of holiness.

[19] See Rom 7:7, 14–23.
[20] See Ezek 36:26–28; 37:13.
[21] See Jer 31:31–34.
[22] See Deut 30:3–6.

Holiness calls for holiness

Let us go back for a moment to the jealousy of God and try to discover what the Bible puts forth most clearly as its motive. The most secret motive we will leave until the end of this chapter. The first motive to appear is most clearly indicated in Leviticus. See, for example, the motive God gives for all the legislation about worship. "And Yahweh said to Moses, 'Say to all the congregation of the sons of Israel, You shall be holy; for I, Yahweh your God, am holy'" (Lev 19:1–2). From this flow all the consequences: Every one of you shall revere his mother and his father, and you shall keep my Sabbaths; do not turn to idols. All these are inferences stemming from the basic precept, "You shall be holy; for I, Yahweh your God, am holy." Here we have the very foundation of the spirituality of Leviticus.

The same thing is strongly emphasized in Lev 11:44–54: "For I am Yahweh, your God; consecrate yourselves, therefore, and be holy, for I am holy. You shall not defile yourselves with any swarming thing that crawls upon the earth. For I am Yahweh who brought you up out of the land of Egypt, to be your God; you shall therefore be holy, for I am holy."[23] One cannot fail to see the insistence with which this motive is repeated. In this case it is simply a matter of what may or may not be eaten at table, this animal may be eaten, that animal may not. Yahweh declares his own holiness is sufficient motive for the people to abstain from unclean meats.

But we must not fail to recognize another deep implication of this formula. When God says, "You shall be holy; for I am holy; you must not therefore defile yourselves with

[23] For other references to the precept of holiness see Lev 20:7–8, 24–26; 21:6–8, 15, 22–23; 22:2–3, 9, 15–16, 32. It is always Yahweh's holiness that is the reason for that of his people.

any crawling creature of the earth", he establishes a radical difference between Israel and everything that moves on the earth, insect or man. This is because Israel alone knows who is the true God, and knows it not only theoretically, but by the experience of being in God's hands and of having been chosen by him. Consequently, the following question arises: Is Israel going to exchange this treasure for anything else whatsoever? Is it going to act in precisely the opposite way to the man who, having discovered treasure hidden in a field, goes and sells everything he has to buy that treasure?[24] Is the man whose birth has made him possessor of the treasure hidden in the field going to think of mortgaging it or trading it for something or other that men of this world think is desirable?

A treasure not to be sold

The drama is that the man who has just discovered the treasure is thrilled, his heart is full of it, he cannot rest, he dreams about it. On the other hand, the man who has inherited his treasure from his ancestors knows it too well; its sentimental value has diminished in his eyes. It requires only some other desire to come into his head to make him ready to exchange, to sell the thing whose true value he no longer recognizes. But God is certainly not some security to be quoted daily on the Stock Exchange. God is a secret and highly subtle security, always running the risk of being forgotten by whoever lets himself be obsessed by anything that comes within reach of his heart or desires. Israel's chosen destiny is to possess the glory of God.[25] But as St. Paul

[24] See Mt 13:44.

[25] For Yahweh's glory dwelling in Israel, see Ex 40:34–35; 1 Kings 8:11–13; 2 Chron 7:3; Ps 26:8; 85:10; Jer 14:21; Ezek 3:12; 43:2, 4–5; 44:4; Dan 3:53; Zech 2:9.

says, we carry this treasure of glory, which is the knowledge and possession of God, in earthen vessels,[26] and because these vessels are of earthenware they are fragile. That is why the whole law exists as an attempt to protect them, for fear that the treasure be scattered and lost.

The formula, "Be holy because I am holy", is best explained by its very implications: "Do not get yourselves mixed up with others who do not know me; you must not involve yourselves with them any more than I involve myself with what they worship." Between God and the things that men worship and think of as absolute, there is the antithesis of everything to nothing. Since that is the case, let there be the same antithesis, the same gulf between you, bearers of the heavenly treasure, and all those others who have no knowledge of that treasure. Why? In case you should be contaminated, in case you also should exchange your treasure for vanities.

Perhaps someone will think that this is just the opposite of the teaching of the New Testament, which tells us to spread abroad the seed that has been given us, to become as leaven in the midst of those with whom we live. True, it is just the opposite, but for a good reason. For at that time the Spirit had not been given,[27] man was not yet reborn,[28] the treasure was still contained in fragile vessels, the graft[29] had not yet established itself. It was then a matter of carefully protecting a life not yet possessed, a treasure not yet assured, a fire that had not yet set humanity ablaze.[30] In the New Testament, on the other hand, the trend is one of diffusion, of reaching out to others

[26] See 2 Cor 4:7.
[27] See Jn 7:39; Acts 2:33.
[28] See Jn 3:5–8; Tit 3:5.
[29] See Rom 11:17–24.
[30] See Lk 12:49.

and communicating to them the gifts received,[31] of bringing a vast people to birth.[32]

Building a ghetto

The important thing for the Israelites was that they should be centered once more on the one and only absolute. That is why they themselves built around them the walls of their ghetto. And this was done intentionally out of anxiety for their own fidelity. Israel had to be ready to sacrifice everything, every other contact insofar as those contacts threatened the possession of the treasure. So as to be able to keep its treasure safe, Israel had to renounce all pacts with the other people of the land of Canaan. For indeed, when a pact was made with another people, their gods were the sworn witnesses of it.[33] By indiscriminate mixing with other peoples, there was a risk of being drawn unconsciously to think of Yahweh as one god among others. A further prohibition was that of marriage with foreigners. One has only to look at Solomon to see how much the love of a foreign woman can change the principles of the man who loves her.

In Deuteronomy (7:1–16), these two demands are affirmed and the consequences of the first made explicit:

> "When Yahweh your God brings you into the land which you are entering to take possession of it, and clears away many nations before you, the Hittites, the Girgashites, the Amorites, the Canaanites, the Perizzites, the Hivites, and the Jebusites, seven nations greater and mightier than yourselves, and when Yahweh your God gives them over to you,

[31] See Mt 10:27; 28:19; Mk 16:15; Lk 24:47.

[32] See Rom 8; 29; Rev 7:9.

[33] See Ex 23:13; Jos 23:7; Jer 5:7.

> and you defeat them, then you must utterly destroy them; you shall make no covenant with them, and show no mercy to them.[34] You shall not make marriages with them, giving your daughters to their sons or taking their daughters for your sons.[35] For they would turn away your sons from following me, to serve other gods; then the anger of Yahweh would be kindled against you, and he would destroy you quickly. But thus shall you deal with them: you shall break down their altars, and dash in pieces their pillars, and hew down their Asherim, and burn their graven images with fire. For you are a people holy to Yahweh your God; Yahweh your God has chosen you to be a people for his own possession,[36] out of all the peoples that are on the face of the earth."

Not one survivor . . .

The Book of Joshua tells us how this order of God was carried out. Only the Gibeonites succeeded by means of a trick in signing a treaty with the Israelites (9:3–18). They pretended to be from a distant people, outside the promised land. And Joshua reckoned that he was not bound to destroy them. But Jericho (6:17–21), Ai (8:24–27), the cities of the south (10:28–40) and those of the north (11:10–15) were subjected to the anathema. The whole account re-echoes the sombre *leitmotif:* "They smote them with the edge of the sword, and utterly destroyed them; he left none remaining." It is true that the first chapter of the Book of Judges strikes a rather different note and suggests rather a gradual interpenetration of the Israelite and Canaanite

[34] For this prohibition, see Ex 23:32; Jos 9:7, 24.

[35] For prohibition of mixed marriages, see Ex 34:15–16; 1 Kings 11:1–4; Ezra 9:2–3, 12–14; 10:2–3, 10–14; Neh 10:31; 13:23–27; Mal 2:11–12.

[36] For choice of Israel as Yahweh's peculiar people, see Ex 19:5–6; Deut 4:20; 14:2; 26:19; 32:9; Ps 33:12; Amos 3:2.

peoples. But at the beginning of the following chapter, failure to observe the integral anathema is stigmatized as a grave sin in Israel (2:1–5).

The principle therefore is clearly established and, moreover, such a demand is absolutely logical. If the fact of possessing the true God is a treasure of inestimable value, the natural consequence is that everything else is secondary when compared with it. Therefore if any threat endangers the people's faith in the true God, it is better, as the Gospel will one day say, to pluck out one's eye[37] rather than risk losing one's faith in the true God. If you are in a place that is infected and full of contagion, the only thing to do is thoroughly to clean the place, so as to be able to live in good health. And these people who did not know the true God might, little by little, cause their own beliefs and superstitions to infiltrate into the hearts of the Israelites in place of the true faith. The Israelites must therefore thoroughly cleanse an infected and contagious place.

Sowing the seed of true faith

But is it not tragic that this place should be made up of men and that its disinfection must be achieved by means of massacres? Is one really going to protect a people's faith by destroying other people who might be a danger for that faith? Is not this to justify all wars of religion? Before being shocked, let us try to understand. The Israelites did not consider themselves as men among other men. They believed themselves to be the seed of the true faith in this world. It is not a question of knowing whether certain men should be preferred to others, but of knowing if the seed of the true faith in this world is to run the risk of being destroyed.

[37] Mt 5:29.

Israel is no more than the bearer of this seed of true faith. This is why Israel reckons that to destroy this seed is a much graver matter than destroying that part of the human race which surrounds them, if that is the price to be paid for cleansing the land in order that the flame of faith may be preserved, and the seed remain fruitful to transform eventually all of mankind.

Everything rests on the fact that we are dealing with a chosen people, not with just one group of men in the midst of other groups of men. And the chosen people is conscious of its vocation to be a light for the world.[38] But will not this mean that we shall fall from cold cruelty into a terrible paranoia that is the basis of all fanaticism? The whole question is posed: Paranoia or truth? Is it true that this people has been chosen to be the light of the world? If it is, then it is equally true that its continued existence as a shining light is of the first importance for the world, even if it has to begin by burning.

Progress in revelation

I should have been afraid of not doing justice to the Bible if I had not attempted this justification of fanaticism. The logic of it hardly convinces us completely. Perhaps that is because we live in the age of the New Testament and the divisions of Christendom still show the dreadful wounds of anachronistic anathemas. The existence of each man as an absolute and the prohibition of collective reprisals were truths that were revealed only at the time of Ezekiel,[39] in the sixth century before Christ. The anathema,[40] on the

[38] See Is 42:6; 49:6; 60:3.
[39] See *JB*, p. 1375, note on Ezek 14:12.
[40] See *AI*, pp. 260f.

other hand, was understood as a consequence of God's jealousy when the promised land was won, six centuries earlier.

It seems likely that God revealed certain values successively and that the people, thinking they understood what God wished to say at a particular moment, at once gave expression to it with such conviction and intensity that they gave to it a quasi-definitive value, whereas it certainly was not *all* that God had to say about the matter in question. And to call some line of action a general rule when it is not yet a general rule involves the risk of changing its shade of meaning. It is reasonable enough then to wonder if these affirmations, these overlogical consequences of God's jealousy, such as the anathema and the destruction of foreign peoples, were really willed by God. Although the Bible says that these orders came from the mouth of God, was not this the *manner in which Israel understood God*? Or was this truly *what God wished this people to understand* in its beginnings? Is it extremely difficult to give an answer to this. We might say that what God meant essentially was that he is the one true God, nothing must be preferred to him, and that all eventually passes away. This is true enough, but God does not proclaim platitudes! If we say that God really willed the destruction of the former inhabitants of Palestine because they were a threat to the faith of Israel, can we be sure of this? So much prejudice, so much hatred, so much resentment can show itself in actions of this sort.

A lesser evil

It is so natural for man to try and justify by absolute motives some hatred that happens to crop up. Is it not likely that this was already so for the period we are discussing? It is always the case that God who speaks to men, to sinful men, has accepted with full knowledge of the result that his words would be interpreted in that way; God has accepted, with full knowledge of the result that his word becomes a sword[41] that brings, at least for a moment, fanaticism on the earth. This is important. Perhaps God did not directly will this fanaticism, but he certainly permitted it as a lesser evil. For God, what counted was that the revelation of the unique absolute had been given, even if for a moment we derived from this revelation consequences that were biased and very incomplete.

This shows us that there is still for God an orderliness, even in the worst, and that even if destroying one's neighbor for motives of religion is not *good*, it is not the worst thing that can happen. Tepidity[42] and downright ignorance of the true light[43] are worse in God's eyes than the chaotic consequences of that light's first dawning. I think that one must remember at least this. Even if all these massacres were not good, in God's perspective they were a lesser evil in comparison with the state of ignorance, of the error of a humanity that was stagnating in ignorance of its creator.

Unhappy in love

However, this first discovery of the demands of God's jealousy is no more than an initiation into this mystery. Five centuries later God would reveal the secret of his jealousy to one of his confidants, Hosea, son of Beeri. This man

[41] This remains even in the New Testament. See Mt 10:34–36; Lk 12:51–53.

[42] For tepidity, see Rev 3:15–16; Mt 5:13.

[43] For spiritual blindness, see Mt 15:14; Lk 6:42; Jn 9:39–41; Rev 3:18.

had married a most attractive woman called Gomer, whom he loved devotedly. Unfortunately he was not alone in thinking her attractive, and she was not satisfied with the love that he lavished upon her. It was not long before she came to regard her home as no more than somewhere to stay, and to utilize her husband's countless favors to win other hearts for her pleasure. She had several children, and Hosea was not sure if they were his (Hos 1:3, 6, 8).[44] At last she deserted her home altogether and began to embark on one adventure after another, leaving Hosea humiliated but still heartbroken for love of her.

Nevertheless, it was on God's order that Hosea had chosen this woman, whose well-known wantonness was going to wreck his life utterly (1:2). And now that Hosea felt himself ridiculed and mad with jealousy, God remained silent. When she got older, his wife was not so successful. Finding she could no longer use so easily her worn-out charms, she began to find the authority of the casual master on whom she then depended a burden. She started to think wistfully of the years when Hosea's sincere love had cherished her. "I will go and return to my first husband, for it was better with me then than now" (2:7). There would be no doubt about his taking her back. He was so devoted to her that he would surely welcome her and guarantee her a peaceful old age. So she renewed contact with Hosea, told him of her good dispositions and discreetly added that her present companion would let her go for fifteen pieces of silver and "a bushel and a half of barley" (3:2).

[44] The author does not hold the note in *JB*, p. 1451, on Hos 1:2 to be well founded. There seems to be no serious reason for not taking literally the expression "children of harlotry" in 1:2.

The deceived husband prophesies

This news did not fill Hosea with unmixed joy. However, his love for her had not grown less. But in all justice, he had expected something better than this return to him as to a last resort. He had thought himself able to give more than an assurance against loneliness to a harlot worn out by years and adventures. On seeing her come back to him in such a state, defiled, aged and already wretched, Hosea was seized between his wounded honor and his spurned love. And it was at that precise moment that God spoke to him. For this was exactly the moment for which the jealous God had been waiting for centuries, just as God had so long awaited the day when David's lips would pour out those words, "My son, would I had died instead of you".

So it was in just that moment of hesitation that God spoke to the broken heart of the betrayed husband, and said to him, "Go again, love a woman who is beloved of a paramour and is an adulteress; even as Yahweh loves the people of Israel, though they turn to other gods and love cakes of raisins" (3:1). God is saying, For me, it is always the same story with Israel: the people are always fleeing away from me, they always squander whatever I give them and make little personal agreements with foreigners. Every day they go looking for new gods which they prefer to me, their own God, and go sneaking off after their lovers. And then, when everything goes badly, then the people return to me with their supplications and say, "You are the God of my Fathers, I am coming back to you, to you and only to you." But I know very well what this play-acting means. It simply means that at the moment they are threatened by some enemy, and they know very well that the wood and stone that they have worshipped cannot deliver them from danger. In the day when they really need deliverance, I am sorely tempted to leave them to wriggle out of their difficulties as best they can. If when all goes well they forget me and only remember me when they despair of other help, do you think I, your God, will accept that? Nevertheless, you see how it is; I take them back every time. And so do not hesitate, take back your wife.

Loving or compassionate?

Then it was that Hosea understood what had never been understood before him, the secret motives of God's jealousy. This jealousy was in fact the very reverse; it was the touchstone of a sentiment that one would never have imagined the Creator could have for his creature: *God is in love with his creature*, in love with something that draws its very life from him, was made by him, but has nothing to give him. However, it is not merely a matter of pity, compassion, or an inclination to save, but rather of loving. Now there is no love without admiration. I think that what distinguished pity from love most strikingly is that with pity there is an awareness that one is better placed than the other; in the case of pity one bends down to the other because the heart has been touched by the other's misery, whereas with real love there is always wonder, always admiration. And when God says that he loves, it is a very serious matter and means that he has wonder and admiration for the beloved.[45] It seems almost blasphemous to say that God can *love* his creature. How could such a crazy idea ever come

[45] See Is 43:3, where God says to Israel:

"I give Egypt as your ransom,
  Ethiopia and Seba in exchange for you.
Because you are precious in my eyes,
  and honored, and I love you,
I give men in return for you,
  peoples in exchange for your life."

forth from a human brain—that God loves his creature? We can imagine that his mercy should be poured out without limit, but that he *loves*. . . ?

God declares his love

Nevertheless, God's declaration of his love could not be more formal.[46] It wells up from the heart of Jeremiah from the moment of his calling: "The word of Yahweh came to me, saying, 'Go and proclaim in the hearing of Jerusalem, / Thus says Yahweh, I remember the devotion of your youth, your love as a bride, how you followed me in the wilderness, in a land not sown'" (Jer 2:1–2). And further on, in 31:20–22, it is alternately from the heart of a father and the heart of a bridegroom that there rises up the infinitely variable love of God:

> "Is Ephraim my dear son?
>   Is he my darling child?
> For as often as I speak against him,
>   I do remember him still.
> Therefore my heart yearns for him;
>   I will surely have mercy on him,
>   says Yahweh.
>
> "Set up waymarks for yourself,
>   make yourself guideposts;
> consider well the highway,
>   the road by which you went.

[46] In Hebrew, to love is *āhab*. Here are the Old Testament texts in which it is formally said that God "loves" men: Deut 4:37; 7:13; 10:15, 18; 23:6; 2 Sam 12:24; Neh 13:26; Ps 47:4; 146:8; Prov 3:12; 15:9; Is 43:4; 48:14; Jer 31:3; Hos 11:1; 14:5; Mal 1:2. To these may be added the texts in which the verb "to love" only appears in Greek, *agapān*: Hos 2:23; Deut 32:12; 2 Sam 7:18; Jud 9:4; Zech 10:6; Wis 4:10; 7:28; Sir 4:10, 14; 45:1; 46:13. Finally in Wis 11:24, it is said that God "loves all that exists" (here the perspective is no longer Hebraic but Hellenistic).

Return, O virgin of Israel,
return to these your cities.
How long will you waver,
O faithless daughter?
For Yahweh has created a new thing on the earth:
a woman protects a man."

It is usual for a husband who has been abandoned by his wife to go in search of her, since she is really subject to him (Judg 19:3). But Yahweh stirs up in the heart of the unfaithful wife a longing for the husband's love together with an agonizing fear of no longer being able to soften the heart of the angry husband. God gives the answer to this fear through the mouth of the author of the Book of Consolation:

"For Yahweh has called you
like a wife forsaken and grieved in spirit,
like a wife of his youth when she is cast off,
says your God.
For a brief moment I forsook you,
but with great compassion I will gather you.
In overflowing wrath for a moment
I hid my face from you,
but with everlasting mercy I will have compassion on you,
says Yahweh your Redeemer."

(Is 54:6–8)

Yahweh does not offer himself to Israel as a father and a husband only. He even borrows the features of a mother:

"Can a woman forget her sucking child,
that she should have no compassion on the son of her womb?
Even these may forget,
yet I will not forget you."

(Is 49:15)

A jealous passion

It is in the Song of Solomon (Canticle of Canticles) that the loving union that binds Yahweh to his people finds its most passionate expression. Here images of erotic love are sublimated and used to celebrate this union which is always so elusive and whose consummation will seal the reconciliation between God and mankind. As a lover, God concludes his song with these words:

> "Under the apple tree I awakened you.
> There your mother was in travail with you,
> there she who bore you was in travail.
>
> Set me as a seal upon your heart,
> as a seal upon your arm;
> for love is strong as death,
> jealousy is cruel as the grave.
> Its flashes are flashes of fire,
> a most vehement flame.
> Many waters cannot quench love,
> neither can floods drown it."
>
> (Song 8:5–7)

This unimaginable passion is, then, the secret of the jealousy with which God burns for men. God is only jealous of idols and false gods insofar as they exemplify that spirit of prostitution[47] which steals man's heart away from him. "O my people, what have I done to you? In what have I wearied you? Answer me!" (Mic 6:3). The passionate and pleading love with which he besieges hearts that will not know him provides the inmost motive force of his jealousy.

[47] It is because God's people is like a bethrothed virgin, whose love is consecrated to him who loves her, that religious infidelity borrows the vocabulary of prostitution and adultery. See, among other texts, Jer 2:23–25; Ezek 23.

The Old Testament strongly affirms the fact of God's love for men without allowing us to explain it. What can possibly make of this perverse and moribund humanity, barely worthy of pity, the object of such passion on the part of its creator?

The Well-beloved who is to be born

What is needed, then, is some new being born within the ranks of mankind, a divine fruit of which it knows nothing, but which it has been created to bear and yet is able to refuse: God's Son, for whose conception through the power of God's love mankind was made. *What, then, can God love in man if not God himself who is to be born man so as to make man divine?* This is the mysterious fruit that the hungry Messiah will look for in vain on the barren fig tree,[48] and that must be born of the divine graft that he himself will bring. This fruit has grace-filled pollen that brings the promise to the human flower. The bridegroom's love awakens the sleepy beloved, so that she may one day be able to place within the Father's arms the Son, which his love will have caused her to conceive.

What God loves in his people of old is this vocation to be mother of the new people, among whom his Son, conceived by that mother, will gradually attain to perfect stature.[49] It remains for us now, therefore, to see the saddened eyes of the prophets looking out for that birth in which God would take a human body.

[48] Mt 21:18–19; Mk 11:12–14.

[49] Eph 4:13, 16; Col 2:19. See *JB*, p. 335 (New Testament pagination), note j on Eph 4:13.

8

Preservation or Re-creation?

When the people of Israel were about to leave Sinai, Yahweh said to them (Ex 33:3): "Go up to a land flowing with milk and honey;[1] but I will not go up among you, lest I consume you in the way, for you are a stiff-necked people." And Moses replied (33:15–16), "If your presence will not go with me, do not carry us up from here. For how shall it be known that I have found favor in your sight, I and your people? Is it not in your going with us... ?" And later he added (34:9), "If now I have found favor in your sight, O Lord, let the Lord, I beg you, go in the midst of us, although it is a stiff-necked people; and pardon our iniquity and our sin, and take us for your inheritance."

Impossible intimacy

The primary intention of the covenant of Sinai was to establish the closest possible intimacy between the people and their God (Ex 19:5–6): "Now therefore, if you will obey my voice and keep my covenant, you shall be my own possession among all peoples . . . and you shall be to me a kingdom of priests and a holy nation." But the episode of the

[1] Traditional description of the promised land: Ex 3:8; 13:5; Lev 20:24; Num 13:27; 14:8; 16:13–14; Deut 6:3; 11:9; 26:9, 15; 27:3; 31:20; Jos 5:6; Jer 11:5; 32:22; Ezek 20:6, 15; Sir 46:8; Bar 1:20.

golden calf showed at once how impossible it was for this people, stained by original sin, to realize this plan of absolute intimacy with the Most High. The tables of the law were broken by Moses (32:19) and were replaced by other tables containing a new statute,[2] according to which the contact between God and his people is maintained, but no longer in the form of absolute intimacy, which for Israel was no longer possible under pain of death.

It is important to insist that God's plan remains the same. God wants to create direct intimacy between mankind and himself. But such direct intimacy is not possible with men who have been turned aside and blinded by sin. The most that is possible is for the old man branded by sin to be brought to a new birth, and so led to give place to the new man. In this old man the basis must be formed, little by little, of a new man who is to be born of him. And to this new man will correspond a new law, the "New Covenant", to which Jeremiah's hope ever looked forward.[3]

Substitutes

The New Covenant is not really something different from the covenant of Sinai. Already at Sinai God primarily wanted

[2] It is noteworthy that just after Yahweh's refusal to accompany Israel personally (Ex 33:1–5) we are told of Moses' plan to set up the Tabernacle *outside the camp* and at a good distance from it (33:7). Similarly when Moses came down from the mountain again with the second tables of the Law, the shining of his face kept the frightened people *at a distance*. These indications emphasize the fact that God's presence keeps the sinful people at a distance, whereas, at the time of the founding of the covenant, the leaders of the people had been able to *contemplate God*, eat and drink in his presence (24:11), and the Tabernacle had been primarily conceived as God's residence *in the midst of* his people (25:8; 29:45).

[3] Jer 31:31; 32:40.

close intimacy between his people and himself. From the time of the first setback, the making of the golden calf, a law of substitutes was established that first became explicit in Israel's whole system of cult. Later, after the Exile, it became explicit in extensive legalism, that is to say, the attempt to preserve a justice based on the observance of detailed and extremely concrete precepts derived more or less directly from Sinai. These types of holiness (based on cult or legalism) are types of holiness by substitution, stemming from the impossibility of realizing adequately, here and now, the original command, "Be you holy, because I am holy." From now on, the organization of worship will have as its aim the patient restoring of a fragile holiness that is constantly threatened. The priesthood will establish itself like a strict caste acting both as a screen and as a means of mediation between the infinitely holy God and the utterly degraded people. But God's ultimate eventual plan is certainly not to make permanent this system of substitution which is only suitable for a people still branded with original sin. On the contrary, God envisages as his final project the formation in this people of a seed that will grow into a new people. But the degraded people will be delivered up to death only when the seed they bear within them is alive, when there is born of them the new man, the new humanity in which the initial plan of union with God will be realized. This is how we must look upon the relationship that unites the "covenant of the second tables" with the "new and eternal covenant".

Consecration of the Levites

Let us now examine the setting-up of the system of substitutes that was to preserve the people of Israel while they waited for the ripening of the fruit they bore within them. In the eighth chapter of the Book of Numbers, the purpose of the Levites is explained to us. In verses 6 and 7, Yahweh speaks to Moses saying,

> "Take the Levites from among the sons of Israel, and cleanse them. And thus you shall do to them, to cleanse them: sprinkle the water of expiation upon them, and let them go with a razor over all their body, and wash their clothes and cleanse themselves."

Why this purification of the tribe of Levi, this consecration to God of a twelfth part of the people of Israel? Verses 10, 11 and 14 give us the reason:

> When you present the Levites before Yahweh, the sons of Israel shall lay their hands upon the Levites, and Aaron shall offer the Levites before Yahweh as a wave offering from the sons of Israel, that it may be theirs to do the service of Yahweh. . . . Thus you shall separate the Levites from among the sons of Israel, and the Levites shall be mine."

The motive of this consecration of Levites, therefore, is to represent the whole of Israel. This people has been destined to be set apart from the rest of humanity so as to belong to Yahweh. Since they have not succeeded in being faithful to this consecration, Yahweh chooses from among them a part to be exclusively his own. The Levites will thus realize in the midst of Israel the vocation that should be Israel's among the nations.[4] Why should the people place their hands upon them? We must not see here a kind of prototype of priestly ordination. This laying on of hands for the Levites has quite a different meaning. In priestly ordination, the laying-on of

[4] See Num 3:12, 45; 8:16–18.

hands indicates the transmission of priestly power,[5] whereas in the case of the Levites it is rather the transmission of culpability, for Israel is guilty.

Priest-victims

When an animal was offered as a sacrifice of expiation, the people, or rather the people's representatives, had to place their hands on the beast offered,[6] making this victim in some way a substitute for the sins of the people. The people would not be put to death, but the animal would. The people had deserved to be put to death, but this slaying of an animal would remind the people of their sin and be at the same time a pledge of expiation. Something analogous to this takes place in the case of the Levites. Israel was to have been consecrated to Yahweh but has been rendered unclean. But Israel delegates the tribe of Levi to represent them before Yahweh and in the future fulfills symbolically the vocation that should have been that of the whole people. Moreover, the expression "Aaron shall offer the Levites before Yahweh as a wave offering from the sons of Israel"[7] clearly shows that there is some sort of sacrifice here, since the gestures of sacrifice are made over the Levites. By making them sacred, they are made into a living sacrifice. It is to be regretted that in our priestly ordination the idea of sacrifice, the aspect of a victim, is less apparent. The Levites will be allowed to offer sacrifice only after they have

[5] This sense appears already in the Bible in such contexts as Num 27:18; Deut 34:9; Acts 6:6; 8:17; 13:3; 1 Tim 4:14; 2 Tim 1:6.

[6] See *BJ*, note on Lev 24:14.

[7] For this "wave offering" or *tenûphah*, see *JB*, note on Ex 29:24. The application of this rite to the consecration of Levites can be only symbolic, but it keeps its essential liturgical sense.

been symbolically sacrificed as victims themselves. Here is hidden a profound religious symbol that was not to pass away with the fulfillment of the old law.

A caste that screens

In verse 19 of the same chapter [Num 8], Moses indicates the precise role of those consecrated: "I have given the Levites ... to do the service for the sons of Israel at the tent of meeting, and to make atonement for the sons of Israel, that there may be no plague among the sons of Israel in case the sons of Israel should come near the sanctuary." [8] For indeed no member of an unclean people may approach the holy place. But in their place, the Levites will establish the bond with the Lord, will offer victims,[9] and will purify[10] the people in the Lord's name. In this manner they fulfill exactly the part of a caste[11] acting as a screen in a presence that is dangerous and, as it were, "radioactive". None but those who have given themselves entirely and been consecrated may approach that presence with impunity. Through them, a mediated contact is possible between the people and their Lord, even though this Lord hides his face[12] from the polluted people. This is why there was a priesthood, distinct from the laity. In other words, there is a distinction between

[8] Here are a few examples of nonconsecrated men being stricken for approaching holy things: Num 17:27–28; 2 Sam 6:6–7; 1 Chron 13:9–10; 2 Chron 26:16–20; 2 Mac 3.

[9] For the priest's duty in sacrifice, see *AI*, pp. 355ff.

[10] For rites of expiation and purification, see *AI*, pp. 418 ff., 460ff.

[11] The "screen" of the Levites is evident in Num 1:53.

[12] To "hide his face" means the suspension of freeing intimacy, abandonment to punishment. See Deut 31:17–18; 32:20; Job 13:24; Ps 10:11; 13:1–2; 22:24; 27:9; 30:7; 44:24; 69:17; 88:14; 102:2; 104:29; 143:7; Is 8:17; 54:8; 64:6; Jer 33:5; Ezek 7:22; 39:23, 24, 29; Mic 3:4.

those who handle things that are necessarily polluted and those who must remain absolutely pure, representing the others and taken from among them.

The lot of these intermediaries is explained also in the Book of Leviticus (10:3). On the occasion of a terrible chastisement, Moses said to Aaron, "This is what Yahweh has said, 'I will show myself holy among those who are near me, and before all the people I will be glorified.' " Moses had pondered deeply on these words which Yahweh had proclaimed to him before, but which he had neither remembered nor understood until now. These words affirm that among the descendants of Jacob and therefore of Adam, only certain souls, living closer to the Lord, can really live by his *holiness*; but their presence as consecrated beings among a polluted people will be a constant reminder to the latter of God's inaccessible *glory*, which only consecrated souls can penetrate.

A caste that mediates

In the sixteenth chapter of Leviticus, Yahweh reveals to Moses the rite of expiation that will constitute the supreme office of the priesthood as a mediating caste. "Tell Aaron your brother not to come at all times into the holy place within the veil, before the mercy seat which is upon the ark, lest he die; for I will appear in the cloud upon the mercy seat" (16:2b). Here we see God retiring as it were behind another screen. Even the priesthood consecrated to the Lord may not always, or without precaution,[13] approach the Lord. Even the priest must pay some sort of due if he would gain access. Holiness is always concealing itself.

[13] For the precautions that even the consecrated must take before touching holy things, see Num 4:4–20.

In verse 4, God prescribes the vestments for the priest performing the expiation: "He shall put on the holy linen coat, and shall have the linen breeches on his body, be girded with the linen sash, and wear the linen turban." A regular surgeon's outfit. "[T]hese are the holy garments.[14] He shall bathe his body in water, and then put them on." This all seems to insist on a state of complete asepsis; the priest must be totally aseptic in order to approach God, not through fear of contaminating him, but because if the priest himself is contaminated, God's holiness becomes destructive. For any pollution brings danger of destruction when it meets God's holiness.

Waves of expiation

Thus prepared then, the priest will receive the victims from the community. Then, as verse 11 tells us, "[He] shall present the bull as a sin offering for himself, and shall make atonement for himself and for his house." Verse 16 adds, "thus he shall make atonement for the holy place, because of the uncleannesses of the sons of Israel." The presence of the sanctuary in the midst of a polluted people renders the sanctuary[15] itself in a certain way unclean. The priest must therefore first make expiation for himself, as minister of holiness, then he must make expiation for the sanctuary that mediates God's presence. It is only after this that he can make expiation on behalf of the people. There are, then, "waves" of expiation. The priest must first renew his own contact with the Lord. Then he must renew the bond between the

[14] For precautions to be taken with sacred vestments, see Ezek 42:14; 44:19.

[15] The people's wickedness transforms the sacred rites into abominations: Is 1:15; Amos 2:8.

Lord and the sanctuary itself. After that, he can renew the bond that unites the Lord with his people. The purity of the people must thus be restored each year. But all this is no more than a feeble substitute for the profaned holiness. This very ritual emphasizes the fact that holiness is something that is always hiding itself. Man cannot reach holiness; he can only repair a polluted purity. He must repair it year by year so as at least to retain a semiremote contact with his Lord. Such is the ritual law of the Old Testament.

How transmit experience of God?

The task of restoring Israel's ancient values that have been profaned makes a profound mark on the priesthood. In their anxiety to maintain the people's first fidelity to their God, the priests must tirelessly fight against forgetfulness, and even more against any break in successive generations. In this connection, let us read the Book of Deuteronomy, a catechism in the true spirit of Moses. Here is what the dying Moses said to the desert generation (11:2–7):

> "And consider this day (since I am not speaking to your children who have not known or seen it), consider the discipline of Yahweh your God, his greatness, his mighty hand and his outstretched arm, his signs and his deeds which he did in Egypt to Pharaoh ... and to all his land; and what he did to the army of Egypt, to their horses and to their chariots; how he made the water of the Red Sea overflow them as they pursued after you, and how Yahweh has destroyed them to this day; and what he did to you in the wilderness, until you came to this place; and what he did to Dathan and Abiram the sons of Eliab, son of Reuben; how the earth opened its mouth and swallowed them up, with their households, their tents, and every living thing

> that followed them, in the midst of all Israel; for your eyes that have seen all the great work of Yahweh which he did."

All these experiences were firmly impressed on the minds of a single generation, but not on those of their children. What must be done to bridge the gulf of future generations?

Creating "us"

It is still in Deuteronomy that we read (6:20–25): "When your son asks you in time to come, 'What is the meaning of the decrees and the statutes and the ordinances which Yahweh our God has commanded you?' [One recognizes the child who finds that it is not normal to live a life that is so hemmed in by observances, and wants to know the reason for it.] [T]hen you shall say to your son, 'We were Pharaoh's slaves in Egypt'" [Note that "we" includes the father of a twentieth-century generation as well as past or future generations. This "we" and "us" is common to all generations of Jews who remember that "we were Pharaoh's slaves". The "we" refers to this same people who are actually alive now.]

> "*We* were Pharaoh's slaves in Egypt; and Yahweh brought *us* out of Egypt with a mighty hand; and Yahweh showed signs and wonders, great and grievous, against Egypt and against Pharaoh and all his household, before *our* eyes; and he brought *us* out from there, that he might bring *us* in and give us the land which he swore to give to our fathers. And Yahweh commanded *us* to do all these statutes, to fear Yahweh our God, for our good always, that he might preserve *us* alive, as at this day. And it will be righteousness for *us*" (emphasis added).

The traditional observances then are justified by trying to make the child realize as vividly as possible that it is *the people*, of which *he* is today a member, who were formerly saved, who then learned God's orders, who accepted them and who must keep the initial engagement all through succeeding generations.

Rereading the law

This periodic recalling of God's mighty deeds aims at presenting the law as a way of life for each generation of Israel, and assuring their genuine continuity. The priests are the ministers of the idea of "keeping the law", which sealed the covenant.[16] Their principal aim therefore is to represent the people in that state of mind in which the first generation had accepted what must be still observed today.

In Deuteronomy (31:9–13) a rereading of the law is prescribed to take place every seven years in the presence of the whole people, young and old, men and women, on the occasion of the Feast of Tabernacles. Its object is to keep alive that "fear" of God which springs from ardent zeal and reverence and is the fundamental preservative of the people's fidelity: "their children, who have not known it, will hear and learn to fear Yahweh your God, as long as you live . . ." The priests did not reckon that "no one is ignorant of the law". They judged it better to reread it periodically as a defense against forgetfulness. Granted the progressive succession of generations, there would be new people to hear it every time; and they counted on these long readings to make sure that this successsion of generations remained one and the same people.

[16] "Keeping the law" is a basic theme of Deuteronomy. Here the references are innumerable.

As for the king (Deut 17:18–19),

> "when he sits on the throne of his kingdom, he shall write for himself in a book a copy of this law, from that which is in the charge of the Levitical priests; and it shall be with him, and he shall read in it all the days of his life, that he may learn to fear Yahweh his God, by keeping all the words of this law."

To make sure that he rules his kingdom well, then, it is thought best that he should have for his own use a personal copy of the law. And although he may have many scribes to work for him, who no doubt could copy it out better than he could, it is prescribed that he shall copy it out himself in order to be the more deeply impregnated with it. This copy must be made to the dictation of the priests, the official guardians of the sacred text, and not from some copy that may be more or less corrupt. Finally, the king is ordered to make a daily practice of spiritual reading from this law, "that his heart may not be lifted up above his brethren, and that he may not turn aside from the commandment, either to the right hand or to the left". What an admirable priestly ambition! Trying to impose justice on kings by a daily lesson from Holy Scripture.

Rereading the commandments

But the king is not the only one who must know the commandments. Their perpetual presence in the mind of the Israelite is expressed in a very suggestive manner in the verses of Deuteronomy that follow the *š^{e}ma^{c}*, Israel's confession of faith (6:4–9):

> "Hear, O Israel: Yahweh our God is the one Yahweh; and you shall love Yahweh your God with all your heart, and

> with all your soul, and with all your might. And these words which I command you this day shall be upon your heart; and you shall teach them diligently to your children, and shall talk of them when you sit in your house, and when you walk by the way, and when you lie down, and when you rise. And you shall bind them as a sign upon your hand, and they shall be as frontlets between your eyes. And you shall write them on the doorposts of your house and on your gates."

At every moment the Israelites must be aware of Yahweh's precepts, and the recital of them must captivate their imagination and memory.

Priestly pessimism

This priestly perspective may appear optimistic, as though the priest said to himself: "But this people is not so utterly lost; no need to think that catastrophe is inevitable. They may very well be saved. It is only a matter of reminding them[17] of what they have forgotten; that's all there is to it! If they are told about God's mighty works and the daily practice of observances, they can soon be put on their feet again." The priest has boundless confidence in religious instruction as a remedy for forgetfulness. But all this conceals a most profound pessimism: the golden age was at the beginning, but since then there has been steady degeneration. The future can bring nothing but the danger of forgetfulness, against which one must be armed. "Since it is impossible to make the moment of betrothal between Israel and their God an everlasting one, let us try

[17] "Remember" is a constant theme of Deuteronomy: 5:15; 7:18; 8:2, 18; 9:7; 15:15; 16:3, 12; 24:9, 18, 22; 25:17; 32:7.

to patch it up from time to time." The priest consecrates all his strength to save from the usury of time a faithfulness that more or less sleeps. He is endlessly trying to pull against the current of emancipation and flight, and to bring the people back to their true condition, which is always visible in the background.

The restorations and policies of reform are always focused on the same point. The priest can define himself as a restorer.[18] Because of this he is filled with deep pessimism: things can only go from bad to worse. He must therefore swim courageously against the tide. It is a question of striving in complete faithfulness to restore the spontaneous and enthusiastic fidelity characteristic of Israel's beginnings; for the only spontaneous forces at work in this world are the forces of disintegration. "Let us, then, fight against them with our own fidelity."

Prophetic optimism

If the future has nothing to bring to the conjugal union between God and Israel except cooling off and loss of enthusiasm, then the priest is right. But if, on the contrary, this union is a mystery of life and fruitfulness, then one will think like the prophet: since the germ that must give life is there, the seed must die and rot so as to yield much more

[18] This appears most clearly at the end of the Exile. The priest Ezekiel (1:3) dreams during his exile of planning the restoration of the Temple (40–46). The priest Ezra (7:1–5) devoted himself to the restoration of observance of the law at the time of the return from the Exile (Ezra 9–10; Neh 8). Already before the Exile, it was the priest Jehoiada who had restored the legitimate Davidic line in the kingdom of Judah (2 Kings 11), and it was also the priest Hilkiah who started the religious restoration of Josiah (2 Kings 22:8).

fruit and multiply itself to infinity.[19] The prophet has no great aversion from the great misfortune that might hypnotize him, nor does he let go of the shaky supports of this world in case he should be drawn by the giddiness of the abyss. On the contrary, he is possessed by a secret optimism.[20] He knows perfectly well that what looks like death will really give birth to a new being. For the prophet, death means a new birth, and this people of today is destroyed only so as to let loose in the whole world the seed of a new people.

A prophet who did not convert

When Isaiah saw king Ahaz obstinately clinging to the idea of appealing to Assyria against the Syro-Ephraimite coalition, and when he saw him refuse to rely on Yahweh's help (Is 7:9–13; 8:6), he foretold an Assyrian invasion that would ravage Ahaz's kingdom (7:20; 8:7–8). It was then that Isaiah grasped the meaning of the mysterious word of God that he heard in the Temple on the day of his calling:

> "Make the heart of this people fat,
> and their ears heavy,
> and shut their eyes;
> lest they see with their eyes,
> and hear with their ears,
> and understand with their hearts,
> and turn and be healed."
>
> (Is 6:10)

On that day Isaiah, astounded by this divine command, asked:

[19] There is no better expression of prophetic insight than the words of Jesus to the Greeks in Jn 12:24.

[20] Even Jeremiah, the most heartbroken of all the prophets, knew the exaltation experienced by those who carry out the lofty works of God (15:16).

"How long, O Lord?"
And he said:
"Until cities lie waste
without inhabitant,
and houses without men,
and the land is utterly desolate,
and Yahweh removes men far away,
and the forsaken places are many in the midst of the land.
And though a tenth remain in it,
it will be burned again,
like a terebinth or an oak,
whose stump remains standing
when it is felled."

(Is 6:11–13)

When Isaiah saw that Ahaz took no notice of his words and of the threatened Assyrian invasion, he realized that his mission as an unheeded prophet was coming true. God did not intend a passing conversion, but the ruin of the people. He had not sent Isaiah as a preacher of some ephemeral "great return", but he had made him the herald of his mighty works. Why? Because the stump is holy seed (6:13). And this seed will not come to fruition unless the tree with all its branches is first felled.

The holy seed

And so God gave Ahaz a sign: a child will be born and will be called "God with us". His childhood will coincide with the devastating invasion (7:14–16; 8:8). It is he who is the holy seed, the pledge that "those who dwelt in a land of deep darkness, on them has light shined" (9:1). At the very time when the people "pass through the land, greatly distressed and hungry ... curs[ing] their king and their God" (8:21), the heart of Isaiah overflows with a hidden joy:

> For to us a child is born,
>   to us a son is given;
> and the government will be upon his shoulder,
>   and his name will be called
> "Wonderful Counselor, Mighty God,
>   Everlasting Father, Prince of Peace."
> Of the increase of his government and of peace
>   there will be no end,
> upon the throne of David, and over his kingdom,
>   to establish it, and to uphold it
> with justice and with righteousness
>   from this time forth and for evermore.
> The zeal of Yahweh of hosts will do this. (9:5–6)

Swift plunder

Isaiah learned from Yahweh that only "a remnant shall return" and with this in mind he named his first son Shear-jashub.[21] He grew dismayed at the "quick spoils, swift plunder", and hence named his second son Maher-shalal-hash-baz.[22] And it was this *plunder* that was to reduce the people to the state of a *remnant* over which the child "God with us" would be able to inaugurate his reign of peace. Impatience lessens the distance of the final reckoning in the heart of the prophets. And so Isaiah glimpses all this as something near at hand, whereas God is only beginning to initiate through him and for his people a process of regeneration that would stretch for thousands of years. Even if

[21] See *BJ*, note on Is 7:3.
[22] Is 8:1–4.

his haste makes him telescope further perspectives, Isaiah has been initiated into the mystery of regeneration for the fallen humanity to which he belongs.

Making the temporary eternal

Faced with this type of prophecy, what is the attitude of the priest who is unaware of the secret sloughing that is being prepared? With overly naïve confidence, he tries to make permanent a humanity that is in a merely provisional state. God's word, however, which is thundered by the prophets, breaks the chrysalis from which the larva must emerge to become a butterfly. This, then, is his role: to bring this provisional stage to an end and hasten the coming of the final stage.[23] Even if the prophet's word must seem to condemn the whole of the people's present life, it is by no means a word of despair. For this word is two-edged: on one side it puts to death the people of today, and on the other it opens the way for the people of the future. In the prophet's eyes, the only value in the people of his day is that they are the larva of a future people. What is left is a mass of rough sketches that have become caricatures, substitutes for holiness that are in danger of becoming permanent and so of slowing down the growth of what must be born.

Is it a robbers' den?

And so we find that organized cult became the object of violent attacks by the prophets. This organization of worship was the outcome of inspired laws that make up the

[23] Jeremiah was called "to pluck up and to overturn, to destroy and to break down" so as to be able to "build and plant" (1:10; cf. 31:28; 45:4).

greater part of Leviticus. Nevertheless, the prophets violently attacked what had actually resulted from those laws. Does this mean that God contradicts in some books what he has laid down in others? Before answering this delicate question that must not be evaded, let us listen to Jeremiah, the prophet who was excommunicated and forbidden to go in the Temple.[24] We shall see that there were serious reasons for the tension between him and the priests.

One day, before this ban was put on him, Jeremiah received from God an order to stand at the Temple gate (Jer 7:4–11). He was to tell all the people of Judah who entered by that gate to prostrate themselves before Yahweh:

> "Do not trust in these deceptive words: 'This is the temple of Yahweh, the temple of Yahweh, the temple of Yahweh.' For if you truly amend your ways and your doings, if you truly execute justice one with another, if you do not oppress the alien, the fatherless or the widow, or shed innocent blood in this place, and if you do not go after other gods to your own hurt, then I will let you dwell in this place, in the land that I gave of old to your fathers for ever. Behold, you trust in deceptive words to no avail. Will you steal, murder, commit adultery, swear falsely, burn incense to Baal, and go after other gods that you have not known, and then come and stand before me in this house, which is called by my name, and say, 'We are delivered!'—only to go on doing all these abominations? Has this house, which is called by my name, become a den of robbers in your eyes? Behold, I myself have seen it, says Yahweh."

Here we have the original context of these words, "Has this house, which is called by my name, become a den of

[24] See Jer 36:5.

robbers?"—words which our Lord would repeat[25] when he drove the merchants out of the Temple.

God wants to destroy the Temple

What does "den of robbers" mean in its original context? It signifies a refuge where one feels safe against justice. But can this ritual action, this means of being reconciled to the Lord at the price of a calf, without any change in one's way of life, give man security? Is it enough to say to oneself, "I can always go to confession and put things right", to be restored to the justice of God? Jeremiah does not speak of confession, but of the immolation of bulls. In confession, immolations are more limited and must be more personal.

But then God adds (vv. 12–14):

> "Go now to my place that was in Shiloh,[26] where I made my name dwell at first, and see what I did to it for the wickedness of my people Israel. And now, because you have done all these things, says Yahweh, and when I spoke to you persistently you did not listen, and when I called you, you did not answer, therefore I will do to this house which is called by my name, and in which you trust, and to the place which I gave to you and to your fathers, as I did to Shiloh."

In other words, God is going to destroy the Temple. Why? Not purely and simply to punish Israel, for this would just not be true. I would rather be inclined to say that it was to allow Israel time for this final shedding, so that they would

[25] Mt 21:13; Mk 11:15; Lk 19:46.

[26] Shiloh had been the place where the ark remained during the time of the young Samuel, before Jerusalem had been conquered. Since then, Shiloh had been utterly destroyed.

no longer have a place in which to seek false confidence that was facile, inexpensive and easily acquired by a few gestures and a little money.

Abuse of "tranquillizers"

What God wants is that the sin of his people may not be hidden by false hopes and false reconciliations. The people must at least be aware of the fact that they are a sinful people and stand in need of the Lord's pardon. Now the Temple and its worship, not as it had been instituted but as it had been lived and practiced, had become merely an easy way of quieting a bad conscience.[27] One could buy "tranquillizers" there for superficial hearts that had not recovered true peace but an abatement of remorse through forgetfulness. The sin was not forgiven, but the need for pardon was momentarily silenced by sacred rites. It is this that makes the Temple a thing to be abolished, not only for Jeremiah but for God who speaks to him.

As we shall see in the incident that follows, this condemnation does not only envisage the Temple (Jer 19:1–2, 10):

> Thus said Yahweh, "Go, buy a potter's earthen flask, and take some of the elders of the people and some of the senior priests [to be witnesses of the prophet's action], and go out to the valley of the son of Hinnom at the entry of the Potsherd Gate,[28] and proclaim there the words that I tell

[27] With Malachi, the last of the prophets, we find once again violent criticism of the way in which the priests directed the affairs of the restored Temple (1:6—2:9). Already the oldest of the prophets whose words we possess had been expelled by a priest from the sanctuary where he was prophesying (Amos 7:10–17).

[28] So called because of a refuse-heap where broken pots were thrown, which made it a suitable spot for the prophecy that was to follow.

> you ... Then you shall break the flask in the sight of the men who go with you, and shall say to them, 'Thus says Yahweh of hosts: So will I break this people and this city, as one breaks a potter's vessel, so that it can never be mended.' "

What does this condemnation mean? It means that in God's eyes, the existence of Judah as a kingdom and of the Temple in its midst are things to be destroyed. It is time for this people, or rather the remains of this people, to give birth to the "remnant", the germ that is to be raised up to give birth to another people. And this false security in the political sphere (the kingdom),[29] as also in the religious sphere (the Temple), must be wrenched away from Israel, so that Israel may understand that what matters is not the preservation of the idea of merit through substitution but the endurance of suffering in childbearing and in straining after the realities of the latter days that God is preparing. God wills to see the religious and political institutions of Israel destroyed, like the master builder who destroys the scaffolding that now does no more than conceal the definitive building: the new[30] and eternal[31] covenant at last established.

The prophet and the commissioner

But at the beginning of chapter twenty, we once again find Jeremiah absorbed by God's plan to which he has to bear witness, and which brings him nothing but derision and outrage from all sides. And now he comes up against an

[29] The prophets had often to call kings to task: Hos 13:10–11; Jer 13:18; 22:24; 22:30—23:2; Ezek 34:1–10.

[30] Jer 31:31; Lk 22:20; 1 Cor 11:25; 2 Cor 3:6; Heb 8:13; 9:15; 12:24.

[31] Jer 32:40; Bar 2:35; Is 55:3; 61:8; Heb 13:20.

official whose responsibilities are clear-cut and markedly distinct from his own:

> Now Pashhur the priest, the son of Immer, who was chief officer in the house of Yahweh [a conscientious commissioner of police], heard Jeremiah prophesying these things. Then Pashhur beat Jeremiah the prophet, and put him in the stocks that were in the upper Benjamin Gate of the house of Yahweh. On the next day, when Pashhur released Jeremiah from the stocks, Jeremiah said to him, "Yahweh does not call your name Pashhur, but Terror on every side. For thus says Yahweh: Behold, I will make you a terror to yourself and to all your friends. They shall fall by the sword of their enemies while you look on."

Here we have a chief of police who realizes that it is dangerous for the good order of the ceremonies and the profitable collection of funds to announce that the Temple will very soon be destroyed by God's order. And this poor priest has found himself in a distressing situation for having carried out what he believed to be his duty in the matter of this troublemaker called Jeremiah. The fact is he does not understand that all these actions, which are supposed to be directly addressed to Yahweh, are no more than a perpetual substitute for another kind of justice. This is why these actions are in danger of becoming an occasion of dissimulation and cause the absolute necessity of that other justice to be forgotten.

The priests defend their monopoly

And yet it was the Lord himself who had revealed these precepts of cult. How came it that the prophets could say in his name, "I did not speak to your fathers or command them concerning burnt offerings and sacrifices" (Jer 7:22)? This seems to contradict many statements in the Torah. The answer seems to me to be that God wills the Temple not as a means of salvation, but as a perpetual reminder of the distance that separates him from his corrupted people. He wills it to stir up in the hearts of this people the appeal of a new kind of justice.[32] In fact the Temple has become the monopoly of the priests who have made of it a means of financial gain[33] and hired their own "prophets" to oppose Jeremiah (Jer 28). These prophets in the pay of the Temple are full of optimism over the future of the Temple cult, and poor Jeremiah is derided by windbags who take God's name in vain,[34] prophesying in the interest of those who pay them, but not commissioned by God. Kings also have their false prophets at this time. It is essential for a kingdom to stand firm, and prophets are hired to preserve the people from becoming demoralized (Mic 3:5); they say that victory is sure (1 Kings 22:1–28), that the king is the best of kings, and so on. It is a real anticipation of a ministry of information.

[32] Such was the *raison d'être* of the law, according to St. Paul. See *JB*, p. 279 (New Testament pagination) note on Rom 7:7.

[33] The Temple treasure was said to be of unheard-of richness (2 Mac 3:6). Fearing the Seleucid greed, the priests pretended that it *only* contained four hundred talents of silver and two hundred of gold. This did not stop Antiochus Epiphanes from taking eighteen hundred talents of precious metal from the treasury. For earlier periods we have no records, but the priests at Jerusalem were always treasure collectors, often neglecting urgently needed repairs (2 Kings 12:5–17). The people loved rich utensils of silver and gold that made up the greater part of this treasure, as is seen by the importance attached to them at the time of the deportation and return from the Babylonian captivity (Jer 27:16–21; 28:3, 6; Dan 1:2; 5:2; Ezra 1:7–8; 5:14; 6:5).

[34] One "takes God's name in vain" when one says "Thus says Yahweh" to give weight to purely human assertions. See Jer 5:31; 14:14; 23:16–40; Ezek 13:1–16.

The worst of prophetic transactions

Faced with professionals such as these, Jeremiah suffered. He did not suffer simply because what he said caused him to be attacked on all sides; he suffered above all because he knew that the message he carried was for the destruction of a people he loved.[35] And God told him nothing about the outcome of that destruction. It was only later, when it was obvious that Israel was going to be destroyed, that God said secretly to Jeremiah (32:7), who had been imprisoned for corrupting the army's morale, "Listen, one of the fields of your uncle's legacy is for sale, buy it!" For the moment, that is all God said, but its meaning clearly was, "It is all right to make plans for the future; you will get over this catastrophe." This is how God gives back hope. In those days, deep theological truths were recognized in actions that were extremely simple and concrete. When God told Jeremiah that it was worth while buying that field, it was to open his heart to the prophecy of the New Covenant (Jer 32:37–41).

Two examples of God's jealousy

If we want to sum up the deep motives for the condradictory judgments given by the priests and the prophets about God's design for his people, we must go back to two ideas of God's jealousy.

For the old man who continues to look upon God as a despot whose jealousy is both dreadful and irrational, the first thing to do is to establish an efficacious ritual to cast in face of the devouring jealousy that threatens to consume

[35] See Jer 8:18–23; 13:17; 14:17; 17:16.

the unfaithful people. After that, one will do one's best to revive the people's faithfulness, hoping that the redoubtable "radioactivity" of the Most High will become well-disposed toward a converted people. Conversion is always understood as a return to beginnings, and the way to win God's favor seems somewhat like the industrious harnessing of nameless and terrifying energies.

For the new man who knows he is the beloved of God and who seeks to be born again out of the cruel remains of the old man, the perspective is wholly different. With an impatience that he keeps to himself he discerns in God's actions signs that the old man is about to be put to death. Yearning for the New Covenant, which is the norm for his perfection, he is impatient to see the old law, that chrysalis where he is formed as in the cloistered novitiate of a future butterfly, fall into disuse. Since he is as yet only in the state of gestation, it is a matter of being born to the light. And birth is the name of death for him who knows he is the beloved of the Almighty. For him, God's jealousy is nothing but impatience to see the old man's death and the restoration of the beloved for whom he has been waiting and who has been waiting for him.

The great midwives of man are called the Cross and the Spirit. It remains for us to put their work in the picture, beginning with the presentiments of the prophets.

9

Blood to Drink

The cry of blood

When two brothers, Cain and Abel, were born of the same womb, a new voice rose up from the earth: the voice of innocent blood poured out (Gen 4:10). This voice, inaudible to the ears of men, would never cease to beleaguer God's justice with its implacable cry. By jealousy, fallen man had sought to destroy his brother in whom the Creator's image could still be recognized.

The cry of blood poured out is a cry for vengeance: the blood of the murderer must atone for that of the victim.[1] In the wineskins of God, all innocent blood and all tears are stored up,[2] and he makes a bitter and poisonous mixture to fill the cups of his wrath[3] in the day of vengeance. Then those who have been glutted with blood will have to drain that cup to the dregs.[4] They will be seen writhing in agony,[5] and their cries will at last drown those of their victims.[6]

[1] See Exod 21:12, 23–25; Lev 24:17–21; Num 35:16–21, 31–34; Deut 19:11–13; 2 Sam 14:7.

[2] See Ps 56:8.

[3] See Rev 14:17–20; 19:15; see *JB*, p. 449 (New Testament pagination), note k, on Rev 19:15.

[4] See Rev 15:6; 16:19; 17:6; 18:6, 24.

[5] See Jer 48:26; Ezek 23:32–33.

[6] See Ex 11:6; 3:7.

The gate of tears

It is not necessary for a man to have wielded the sword to find himself spattered with innocent blood. When David delivered up Bathsheba's husband to the sword of the enemy, he drew down the sword on to his own family (2 Sam 12:9–10). When Jezebel saw that her husband, Ahab, had failed to buy Naboth's vineyard, she had Naboth unjustly accused by his fellow citizens of some capital offense. After he had been executed, Ahab, who had not been told about his wife's schemes, was happy to profit by Naboth's unjust death by taking possession of the vineyard he wanted. By so doing he became an accomplice in his death. Elijah accused him of murder and foretold the extermination of his descendants (1 Kings 21).

At the beginning of our era, Palestinian rabbis reckoned that one can empty a man of his blood, and so become guilty of murder, without a single drop of that blood being spilled. For this, it was enough to make a man turn pale because of public injuries heaped upon him. This kind of "murder" would not be avenged by human tribunals, but would be at the Last Judgment. These same rabbis taught that the destruction of the Temple had stopped up the "gateway of prayer". But if human prayers no longer have access to God, there is still one gateway that remains open: "the gateway of tears and oppression", for they go directly to God without passing by the Temple. The cry of innocent blood poured out and the moans of the downcast ceaselessly assail the throne of the Judge.[7]

[7] See Gen 18:20–21; 19:13; Ex 2:23; 22:22; 1 Sam 9:16, Neh 9:9; Job 16:18–20; 34:28; Ps 9:12; 18:6; Jas 5:4.

Meat allowed

Before Abel was murdered by his brother, the only blood poured out on the earth by man had been that of Abel's sacrifices. At the time of his creation, man had been given the cereals and fruits of the earth for food (Gen 1:29). Man had been created in the image of God, and his Creator delegated to him his authority over the animals.[8] Abel, who is presented to us as the first keeper of sheep, offered the firstborn of his flocks in sacrifice to God (Gen 4:3), in recognition of the authority of the sovereign Shepherd. For his own use, he took only the milk of his flock, as certain pastoral tribes in Mauritania still do today. This is suggested to us by the Bible when it places after the Flood the inauguration of new dietary laws for man. From then on God tolerated the survival of a human race whose heart was full of evil inclinations (Gen 8:21). But the presence on the earth of this corrupt race broke the harmony of creation, so that animals merely became frightened game for mankind to eat. Nevertheless, before eating the flesh of an animal, man was commanded first to empty out all its blood, for the blood is the life over which man has no right (Gen 9:2–4).

The forbidding of bloodshed

This precept holds for all mankind that escaped from the Flood, and the law of Sinai merely takes it up again: "Whoever eats any blood, that person shall be cut off from his people" (Lev 7:27). Man, then, must eat neither an animal killed by another wild beast (Ex 22:30), nor an animal that has died a natural death (Deut 14:21) because in such cases the blood that is the life has been stifled and not entirely poured out.

[8] Gen 1:26–28; Sir 17:3–4.

Ritual animal slaughter is not described in the law, but the fact that it is mentioned in Deuteronomy 12:21 allows Israelites to recognize an oral tradition coming from Sinai. It was done by quickly cutting the animal into sections by a simple sawing movement across the windpipe and the gullet. By this means the lifeblood was able to gush out in a strong jet. All meat slaughtered by a non-Israelite was considered not to have been slaughtered in the right way, and to eat such meat rendered a man unclean for three days.

These rabbinical regulations are intended merely to make clear the conditions of the covenant made by God with the descendants of Noah. This is why the apostles, meeting together in Jerusalem for the first council in the history of the Church (Acts 15:5–29), agreed not to oblige non-Jewish Christians to undergo circumcision, the condition of the covenant with Abraham, but commanded them to "abstain from blood and from what is strangled" (Acts 15:20, 29; 21:25).

"My blood is drink indeed"

Profoundly imbued with this absolute prohibition to partake of blood, the disciples must have been horrified when, one morning on the banks of the lake of Tiberias, they heard their master declare:

> "[U]nless you eat the flesh of the Son of man and drink his blood, you have no life in you.... For my flesh is food indeed, and my blood is drink indeed" (Jn 6:53, 55).

The evangelist adds:

> Many of his disciples, when they heard it, said, "This is a hard saying; who can listen to it?" ... After this many of his disciples drew back and no longer went about with him (Jn 6:60, 66).

If God had so strictly forbidden those saved from the Flood to drink blood, was it because he was reserving his own for them to drink?

God had reserved for his own all blood shed by man. The blood of innocents, as we have seen, he reserved as evidence for the conviction of their murderers. The blood of animals slaughtered by man must likewise be offered to him as a substitute for the life of sinful man (Lev 17:11), condemned to death, but nevertheless spared by God's patience without the penalty being juridically commuted. And if God, having refrained from carrying out, by means of the Flood (Gen 8:21–22), the death penalty due to mankind since the sin of Adam (Gen 2:17), has not commuted the sentence passed on humanity, and if, under the terms of the Sinai covenant, he keeps that humanity alive and contents himself with receiving at man's hands the life of animals as a ridiculous substitute for human life, is it not because he reserves to himself the right to give these immolators of beasts, suddenly turned into immolators of God, his own life as a real substitute for their condemned life? We see, therefore, how the substitution of animal blood, which maintains in life the moribund humanity of the Old Covenant, foreshadows the drinking of divine blood, which will feed humanity in its new birth under the New Covenant.

The slaying of the firstborn

The first animal blood to appear clearly in the Bible under the guise of a substitute for man's own is that of the paschal lamb.[9] Here, two questions arise: Why did God will the extermination of all the firstborn in Egypt, and why did Israel

[9] Ex 12:3–7, 13, 21–23.

need a vicarious victim so as to escape the extermination aimed at the Egyptians? If the firstborn of Egypt were condemned to extermination[10] it was because the Egyptians had condemned God's firstborn to extermination. No doubt Israel was a younger people than Egypt, but God had sufficiently shown to the patriarchs that in his eyes the firstborn, that is, the chosen inheritor of a father's blessing, is not necessarily either the oldest or the strongest (Cain, Ishmael, Esau, Reuben), but the one God chooses freely from among the weakest (Abel, Isaac, Jacob, Joseph). In the same way, Israel was chosen freely by God as his firstborn, although this people was no more than the seed carried by a wandering nomad among the powerful civilizations of ancient culture. This calling of firstborn was confirmed in the eyes of divine wisdom, but not in those of men, when Israel was merely a collection of slaves vowed to racial destruction by a people in the full strength of national renaissance. Egypt had commanded that no male child of Israel should be allowed to live.[11] But Egypt did not realize that by the very fact of cursing and wanting to exterminate this people, it affirmed in the eyes of eternal justice that blessing of Israel which God himself had planted. The destruction of the firstborn is a terrible retaliation intended to open the eyes of the persecutors; what you do to the defenseless whom you hate will rebound on the defenseless whom you cherish, for every blow that strikes a defenseless being strikes the almighty Judge in the apple of his eye.[12]

[10] Ex 11:5; 12:29.

[11] Ex 1:16–18, 22.

[12] In Zech. 2:8 the original biblical text has, "Who touches you, touches *me* in the apple of my eye." The scribes of Israel, shocked by the idea that sinners can wound God, corrected it to "touches *himself*", as in all Hebrew mss. now known. But Jewish tradition has traces of this correction, and the original text is still attested by some Greek witnesses.

Saved as a victim

So we come to the second question: Why should Israel, who is the victim, need a vicarious victim in order to escape from the chastisement that is to fall upon its executioner? It is to make it perfectly clear to Israel that if it escapes from this chastisement, it does so not as Israel but as a victim. The blood of the pashcal lamb marking their doorposts manifests their actual situation as victims, which provides the motive for their quick deliverance. Egypt's position as executioner gives the motive for inflicting on the Egyptian firstborn the same death penalty that had threatened, but not been inflicted on, Adam's descendants. Similarly, it is only Israel's condition as victim that exempts this part of the same stock from infliction of the death penalty and brings instead the pledge of possessing the promised land,[13] that is to say, a foretaste of the recovery of Adam's blessing.[14] Every member of the human race condemned to death, therefore, will escape the penalty only by sharing the mystery of the victim who fulfills among men the situation of God's firstborn.

Saved by his victim

Let us now pass on to the Temple sacrifices. The prophets repeated incessantly that this bloody butchery was incapable of justifying Israel. Only faith in Yahweh, expressed by the practice of the Decalogue, can justify his people. Why then have they bathed the steps of God's altar with torrents

[13] After the promise made to Abraham (Gen 15:13), God subjected his people to four hundred years of oppression before the entry into the promised land.

[14] The emphasis with which the Bible speaks of the modest natural riches of Palestine (Deut 8:7–10; 11:10–12; Ex 3:8; Jer 2:7) shows that the entry into the promised land is thought of as giving Israel a pledge of recovering the lost paradise.

of blood for a thousand years? It is in the very gesture of immolation that its meaning is revealed. A member of Adam's race, which is destined for death, slays an animal, in other words a creature that has not fallen under the condemnation that weighs on man himself. Man pours out before God the lifeblood of this creature as a substitute for his own life that has been condemned by God. The outpoured innocent blood mysteriously becomes an intercession for him who poured it out. Only the blood of a spotless victim[15] can intercede for guilty man. This was so that the future descendants of Adam might at least catch a glimpse of the gravity of that criminal and mysterious action they will have performed by putting to death a victim that was wholly exempt from the death penalty.[16]

"With his stripes we are healed"

Toward the end of the Exile, the Jewish people entered much more deeply into this mystery through the song of the suffering servant, where the author of the Book of the Consolation of Israel shows the kings of foreign peoples meditating on the lot of the "servant of Yahweh". The Exile had stricken down the kingdom of Judah in spite of the fact that serious efforts at religious reform had been made. In the judgment of the prophet, this event cannot be interpreted as God's punishment of his "servant Israel".[17] What then can it mean when God annihilates his people in this way, putting his servant to

[15] When 1 Pet 1:18–19 says we have been ransomed by the blood of Christ "like that of a lamb without blemish or spot", the emphasis on the requirements for a Temple victim to be acceptable is transferred to the moral sphere (Lev 22:20–25; Mal 1:8, 13–14).

[16] Cf. 1 Jn 3:5 with Rom 5:12.

[17] See Is 41:8; 44:1–2, 21; 48:20, which clearly assimilate the "servant" to Israel. There is no reason to think "Israel" is a gloss in 49:3.

death? When God has given back independence to his people, when the servant "shall prosper . . . shall be exalted and lifted up" (Is 52:13), then the kings of other nations will be astonished in witnessing this unprecedented triumph of a people they had thought to destroy (52:15). Then will they say to one another:

Who has believed what we have heard?
And to whom has the arm of Yahweh been revealed?
For he grew up before him like a young plant,
and like a root out of dry ground;
he had no form or comeliness that we should look at him,
and no beauty that we should desire him.
He was despised and rejected by men;
a man of sorrows, and acquainted with grief;
and as one from whom men hide their faces
he was despised, and we esteemed him not.

Surely he has borne our griefs
and carried our sorrows;
yet we esteemed him stricken,
struck down by God, and afflicted.
But he was wounded for our transgressions,
he was bruised for our iniquities;
upon him was the chastisement that made us whole,
and with his stripes we are healed.
All we like sheep have gone astray;
we have turned every one to his own way;
and Yahweh has laid on him
the iniquity of us all.

He was oppressed, and he was afflicted,
yet he opened not his mouth;
like a lamb that is led to the slaughter,
and like a sheep that before its shearers is silent,
so he opened not his mouth.

By oppression and judgment he was taken away;
and as for his generation, who considered
that he was cut off out of the land of the living,
stricken for the transgression of my people?
And they made his grave with the wicked
and with a rich man in his death,
although he had done no violence,
and there was no deceit in his mouth.

Yet it was the will of Yahweh to bruise him;
he has put him to grief;
when he makes himself an offspring for sin,
he shall see his offspring, he shall prolong his days;
the will of Yahweh shall prosper in his hand;
he shall see the fruit of the travail of his soul and be satisfied . . .

(Is 53:1–11a)

Then God himself takes up the word and so explains the meaning of his servant's passion:

[B]y his knowledge shall the righteous one, my servant,
make many to be accounted righteous;
and he shall bear their iniquities.
Therefore I will divide him a portion with the great,
and he shall divide the spoil with the strong;
because he poured out his soul to death,
and was numbered with the trangsressors;
yet he bore the sin of many,
and made intercession for the transgressors.

(Is 53:11b–12)

Acceptance of extermination

It was the misfortunes of the ruined kingdom of Judah that brought before the prophet's eye this mysterious figure of the "servant". In him the destiny of the paschal lamb as well as that of the victims of the Temple sacrifices find their full meaning. But a new step has been taken. Whereas when the Israelites came out of Egypt it was through their condition of victim that they were exempted from the plague that struck down their executioners, the Israel of the Exile disclaimed such an exemption. They voluntarily took upon themselves the extermination that ought to have punished their tormentors, and which was the punishment that weighed on rebel mankind but which the murderers drew upon themselves because of their plans for race extinction. A small number of Jews whose sufferings had brought home to them God's plan for the salvation of mankind accepted on behalf of their people the destiny of Temple victims, whose innocent expiation sufficed to defer execution of the sentence hanging over those who were immolating them.

The power of the last sigh

This new destiny, dimly perceived and freely accepted by a conscientious minority in Israel,[18] gives to this people's historic drama the value of a prophetic gesture in which is revealed, in its universal bearing, the mystery of the servant. For it is a mystery, an event capable of two opposite interpretations according to whether it is looked at by the old man or the new.

In the judgment of the old man, who cannot grasp God's designs, the power of injustice has triumphed when the

[18] Fairly clear parallels, quoted in the last note, seem to identify the servant with Israel. This does not mean every individual of the conquered and dispersed people; it means a "remnant" (see note in *JB* on Is 4:3) who by their conversion (Is 10:21) have consciously taken on the destiny of the chosen people. This regenerated minority (the "good figs" of Jer 24:5) will have a twofold mission to the whole people and to all nations (Is 49:6).

innocent victim breathes his last sigh. This last sigh is the proof that there is no such thing as almighty justice.

In the judgment of the new man, who is mindful of God's designs, the last sigh of the innocent is more powerful than the unjust verdict passed upon him. The tyrant thinks he can get rid of that living reproach, which the just man is,[19] by putting him to death. But God's verdict on the murderer depends entirely on the last sigh of his victim. If this last sigh is a cry for vengeance, nobody can prevent this appeal from reaching the highest tribunal. If the last sigh is a prayer of intercession for the murderer, divine justice yields to the victim's pardon.

A transparent figure

Ever since Adam rebelled against the source of his own life, his descendants, themselves condemned to death, kill one another. And God has left the imposition of the verdict on murderers or their forgiveness to the power of their victims. But can we say that in this world some people are murderers and the others victims? Would it not be truer to say that all men are both murderers and victims? Who can find among the whole of Adam's posterity a single really innocent victim, whose life has not first been nourished by the death or at least the decay of certain of his brethren, however distant or unknown? How many victims die only because they were not able to make away with their murderers! How many nations, social classes or religions pass successively from the state of being persecuted to that of being persecutor, with hate stirring up hate and blood covering blood, without the one who today is covered with wounds being able to dress the least of the wounds of yesterday!

[19] See Wis 2:14–20; Jn 3:19–20.

Among the Hebrew people as they were at the end of their exile in Egypt, among the Jewish people as they were at the end of their exile in Babylon, the mysterious figure of the suffering servant appeared twice. On the first occasion, God revealed the rite of the paschal lamb to those members of the human race who had become aware of his design. By this rite, repeated every year, he made them begin to realize that the state of a victim unjustly condemned to death by his brethren is the only one that can deliver a part of Adam's descendants from the death sentence that God holds over them. On the second occasion God revealed that the victim had power not only over his own forgiveness but over that of his murderers.

Refusal of a destiny

The figure of the one who will deliver mankind from its condemnation is now outlined. But in whom will it find its full realization? In Israel this figure has been able to appear only momentarily at two privileged moments of its history. But the vocation of the suffering servant will transfigure the destiny of an elite only at a critical moment. It never became the key to the full meaning of Israel's destiny. Doubtless it is still customary among the Jews of today to identify Israel with the suffering servant of the Book of Consolation, but all the rabbis I know resolutely refuse to interpret the sufferings of their people as a sacrifice of expiation offered for the *goyyim* who are the cause of these sufferings.[20] They are ready to go through all kinds of exegetical acrobatics in order to eliminate this aspect of the suffering servant's

[20] Nevertheless, such was the interpretation of Rashi, the most celebrated Jewish commentator of the Middle Ages. See his commentary on Is 53:4–5, 12.

destiny, reproaching André Schwarz-Bart with having allowed himself to be dangerously contaminated by Christian theories by giving prominence to this aspect of the destiny in his *The Last of the Just*.

The situation is therefore clear: once the crisis of the Exile is passed, the lot of the servant, as glimpsed by the most lucid of the prophets, has fallen into escheat. Israel failed to recognize in him the key to their mysterious destiny of being the sorrowful sufferers for the condemned descendants of Adam.

God takes on this destiny

But God does not speak in order to say nothing; he only speaks so as to say more than his mouthpieces. And the mysteries of which the prophets caught a glimpse are destined to find their fulfillment in a situation that is more crucial, more crucified than that which enabled the prophets to have their glimpse of them. God determined to take upon himself a destiny that the descendants of Adam were incapable of undertaking. This destiny was the unavoidable vocation of the faithful *remnant* of his people. God determined to become that *remnant* himself and to live out its lot to its complete fulfillment. Thus he would make it attainable for every member of Adam's descendants who would enter into the New Covenant sealed in his outpoured blood.

Yeshoua, remnant of Israel

Whether Israel wills it or not, its destiny of servant, which could not be undertaken by the whole of Jacob's descendants in the flesh but was disclosed by a few individuals among those descendants during the sufferings of the Exile, has been fully accomplished in the humanity that a Jewish virgin put at her God's disposal. Just as the whole of Israel's destiny had only been glimpsed during the confusion of the Exile by a few members of this people, so was it reserved for a certain Yeshoua, son of the Jewess Miryam, alone to live out the perfect accomplishment of that destiny, being condemned by the leaders of his people[21] and abandoned by his disciples.[22] During the Babylonian Exile the "remnant", in whom Israel's destiny was concentrated, was restricted to a few faithful members of the tribe of Judah. Under the procurator Pilate and the high priest Caiaphas, this "remnant" would be concentrated in a single individual, and his destiny as victim would place him under the ban not only of nations, as had been the case during the Exile, but of his own people.[23] The leaders of his people would take on, in the name of the whole of Adam's descendants, the role of executioner.[24] He himself would take on, in the name of his people who were blind to the mystery of their destiny, the role of victim.

By nature a murderer, by choice a victim

In thus fulfilling the vocation of the servant, Jesus does not monopolize it. In the name of Israel he assumes the destiny of all victims in order to transform it. And if he assumes

[21] Mt 26:65; 27:22–23; Mk 14:64; 15:11–14; Lk 23:1–2, 20–24; Jn 11:50; 19:6–7.

[22] Mt 26:31–34, 56; Mk 14:27–30, 50; Jn 16:32.

[23] See Gal 3:13.

[24] Peter said to the Jews about the condemnation of Jesus: "I know that you acted in ignorance, as did also your rulers. But what God foretold by the mouth of all the prophets, that his Christ should suffer, he thus fulfilled" (Acts 3:17–18). In the slaying of Jesus a drama is realized that far surpasses the time and place used as its setting, as well as the race and generation that passed the verdict of condemnation. It is a matter of darkness refusing "light": "the light has come into the world, and men loved darkness rather than light, because their deeds were evil" (Jn 3:19).

and transforms this destiny, it is to make it accessible to every murderer, whether Jew or gentile; for the blood that flowed from his crucified body is the only drink capable of giving back life to his moribund murderers. The destiny of all victims is accomplished in him, and by him is offered to all murderers as their sole hope. Every son of Adam is at once both victim and murderer, bound by indissoluble bonds to him who is the incarnation of the victim, as well as to him who is the incarnation of the murderer. The breath of those who survive is stolen from those who die. But man as victim can recognize himself and accept in Jesus the accomplishment of his destiny as intercessor for his murderers only if man as murderer recognizes himself as crucifying Jesus and prefers, when faced with this cross, to choose to be a victim.

It is not enough to say that every man holds the dual role of murderer and victim of his brethren. We have to add that every son of Adam is the victim of his destiny as murderer and murderer of his destiny as victim. In every man whose mind is not clear about this, these two destinies fail to recognize each other. Thinking he is a victim, man refuses to confess himself a murderer; and the murderous tendencies that he bears within him forbid him to choose as his destiny communion with his victims.

"He who came by water and blood"

Faced with Jesus crucified, man finds himself on the left of the sovereign judge. For, seeing the Son of God executed, the Spirit bears witness to man: "Every time you have put to death or have not succored one of these least of my brethren, it is me that you have put to death or failed to succor" (cf. Mt 25:31–46). So man discovers that every rejection of a beggar is a rejection of God. He finds himself repeating with his brethren, in whom he rejects God, the initial rebellion of Adam against God. When Adam discovered that he had rejected the Father, it was the death of his hope, but when the son of Adam discovers that he has rejected the Son of God in the persons of his brethren, it is the birth of his hope. For John saw water and blood coming forth from the body of Christ crucified: "He who saw it has borne witness—his testimony is true, and he knows that he tells the truth—that you also may believe" (Jn 19:34–35). Water is offered to the murderer for the baptism of repentance, when he has accepted the accusing testimony of the Spirit before the cross of his Lord. Blood is offered him in the New Covenant, so that he may enter into communion with the lot of the victim who was formerly unsuspected but is now omnipresent. For

> this is he who came by water and blood, Jesus Christ, not with the water only but with the water and the blood. And the Spirit is the witness, because the Spirit is the truth. There are three witnesses, the Spirit, the water, and the blood; and these three agree (1 Jn 5:6–8).

Robes made white in the blood

Those who, by the testimony of the Spirit at the "great judgment", are initiated before the cross into the mystery of the water and the blood will have "washed their robes and made them white in the blood of the Lamb" (Rev 7:14). Thereafter, their place is no more on the judge's left; now they are

> ". . . before the throne of God,
> and serve him day and night within his temple;
> and he who sits upon the throne will shelter them with his presence.

They shall hunger no more, neither thirst any more;
the sun shall not strike them, nor any scorching heat.
For the Lamb in the midst of the throne will be their shepherd,
and he will guide them to springs of living water;
and God will wipe away every tear from their eyes" (7:15–17).

A blood that speaks more graciously

How does the Lamb guide his disciples from the bath of the waters of repentance to the springs of life-giving water? It is the mystery of his outpoured blood that shows them the way. For "Jesus, the mediator of a new covenant, seals this alliance by the sprinkling of blood that speaks more graciously than the blood of Abel. See that you do not refuse him who is speaking" (Heb 12:24–25). The appeal that his blood sends out to men interprets the earnest cry that goes up to God. When Moses sealed the covenant of Sinai,

> he sent young men of the sons of Israel, who offered burnt offerings and sacrificed peace offerings of oxen to Yahweh. And Moses took half of the blood and put it in basins, and half the blood he threw against the altar. Then he took the book of the covenant, and read it in the hearing of the people; and they said, "All that Yahweh has spoken we will do, and we will be obedient." And Moses took the blood and threw it upon the people, and said, "Behold the blood of the covenant which Yahweh has made with you in accordance with all these words." (Ex 24:5–8)

The blood that sealed the covenant of Sinai therefore established a mysterious communion between the altar and the people. But it was the book of the law that contained the conditions of the covenant. The blood did not speak. Under the New Covenant, there is no book containing the conditions; it is the very blood of the victim of the covenant that speaks to those who are sprinkled with it.

Propitiation, victim and priest

What does this "blood that speaks graciously" say to those bound by the New Covenant? What they understand by it is an ardent cry rising up to God: "Father, forgive them; for they know not what they do" (Lk 23:34). This is a cry taken up by the first martyr: "Lord, do not hold this sin against them" (Acts 7:60)—a cry for pardon that eclipses the cry for vengeance that formerly rose up from the blood of Abel.[25] And the bleeding body of the crucified Son was no appeal for vengeance, but rather something put forward by God "as an expiation by his blood, to be received by faith" (Rom 3:25). Formerly each year in the Temple, on the day of expiation, the anointed priest went into the Holy of Holies with the blood of victims and sprinkled this blood (Lev 16:14–15) on a golden slab, measuring about four feet by two, which was placed on the ark of the covenant, between the two cherubim. This golden slab called the *kapporet* (propitiatory, that is to say, instrument of expiation) was looked upon as the throne of Yahweh invisibly present (Ex 25:17–22).

Under the New Covenant, the immolated Lamb is himself the instrument of expiation (the propitiatory); he is also the one in the midst of the throne (Rev 7:17) as a bleeding victim whose blood endlessly sprinkles the propitiatory of his crucified body. It is he also who is the anointed priest

[25] Gen 4:10. The last innocent victim of whose murder the Jewish Bible tells us is Zechariah the son of Jehoiada (2 Chron 24:22). And even he died crying out for vengeance: "May Yahweh see and avenge!"

(Messiah) who offers God the blood of expiation by sprinkling the propitiatory. Such is the ritual of expiation under the New Covenant. It is all found in the bloodstained body of this Yeshoua of Nazareth, nailed to the instrument of his execution. "For I decided to know nothing among you except Jesus Christ and him crucified" (1 Cor 2:2). For the exegete of the New Testament, it is not primarily a book that he has to study and explain, but the incessant cry that rises up from the outpoured blood with which this Testament is sealed.

A call to pardon

The cry of this blood is primarily a plea for pardon for those who shed it and by that very fact an appeal for their repentance. The first reply to this appeal, therefore, is the breaking of the "stony heart" (Ezek 36:26) of him who sees himself among those who shed it:

> "This Jesus, . . . you crucified and killed by the hands of lawless men". . . Now when they heard this they were cut to the heart, and said to Peter and the rest of the apostles, "Brethren, what shall we do?" And Peter said to them, "Repent, and be baptized every one of you in the name of Jesus Christ for the forgiveness of your sins" (Acts 2:23, 37–38).

It is not within the power of those who "killed the Author of life" (Acts 3:15) to give back life to their victim. The baptism of repentance received "in the name" of him they crucified will plunge them into the death of their victim:

> Do you not know that all of us who have been baptized [in other words, plunged] into Christ Jesus were baptized into his death? We were buried therefore with him by baptism

> into death ... For if we have been united with him in a death like his, we shall certainly be united with him in a resurrection like his. We know that our former man was crucified with him so that the sinful body might be destroyed, and we might no longer be enslaved to sin (Rom 6:3–6).

It is by plunging myself by baptism into the death of Christ that I slay within me the rebel and the murderer of his God (that is to say, the old man, the son of Adam) and become a victim with Christ who is Victim when I am plunged into his death and delivered from that death[26], which was the condemnation of the son of Adam.

A call to unity

All those who by baptism have become one with the Victim Christ have at the same time become one among themselves, thereby forming one body, immolated and freed from death: "we were all baptized into one body—Jews or Greeks, slaves or free" (1 Cor 12:13). "Here there cannot be Greek and Jew, circumcised and uncircumcised, barbarian, Scythian, slave, free man, but Christ is all, and in all" (Col 3:11). The second appeal of the blood shed on the cross is therefore a call for humanity to be at one with the destiny of the Crucified.[27]

A call to life

And the third appeal that rises up from this blood is a call to life. For death has no longer any power over the man

[26] Rom 6:8–9; Rev 1:18.

[27] The cross is a work of reconciliation, as Paul insists in the captivity Epistles (Eph 2:13, 16; Col 1:20–22.)

who in Christ is dead to his destiny as a son of Adam. Having cast aside the destiny of the old man in this baptismal death, he enters into possession of a new destiny, that of the new man over whom death has no more claim. And baptismal death has made it possible for one who was mortal to be absorbed by life. "[T]hen shall come to pass the saying that is written: 'Death is swallowed up in victory'" (1 Cor 15:54).

Blood forbidden under the Old Covenant

Now we can understand why those bound by the New Covenant must drink the blood of their covenant victim, whereas the blood of the Old Covenant victim was used to sprinkle the altar and the people but was not drunk. The key that enables us to interpret these two rites is the identification of blood and life. Since Adam's sin was to cut himself off from God as the source of his life,[28] the sons of Adam are born to a life destined to dry up quickly. The first reparation for the sin of Adam was in the pouring out of the life of man before God from whom it had been stolen. And God accepted the blood of man's victims as a symbol of reparation.[29] When the people of Israel received the sprinkling of a part of the victim's blood at Sinai, they were symbolically assimilated to the death of these victims. By sprinkling the altar with the other part of the victims' blood, Israel symbolically poured out before God the life stolen by Adam. But Israel had not the right to drink of that blood, because the sons of Adam could revive their moribund life by stealing in their turn the life given by God to other

[28] Jer 2:13.
[29] Lev 17:11.

creatures. All life *comes from* God and *goes to* God. In the intention of the creator this *coming* and *going* was to be a continuous cycle of living intimacy. If man cut off the source from which his life *came*, at least he must not cut off life (be it his own or that of other creatures) from the destination to which it *goes*. It is in this sense that he must not drink the blood of his victims but must sprinkle the altar with it as a symbol of his own life to which he consciously gives back its destination, since he is unable to drink from the source from which he has cut himself off.

Blood offered under the New Covenant

Under the New Covenant, baptism into the death of Jesus realizes this first stage in the restitution of the moral life of the "old man" to its true destination. But a *new* relationship between God and man is then inaugurated by communion in the blood of the victim.[30] This shows that the blood of Christ crucified not only gives back its true destination to the life of the sinner but reopens the source of that life. Indeed, the only blood that has not got to *go* to God is the blood of God that *comes* to men so as to open once again for them the springs of life-giving waters. Through communion in this blood, a new humanity finds life once more in the bosom of the old humanity slain by its own sin.

The closed door is opened

Here we see why the evangelist dwells on the opening by the soldier's lance of the source of water and blood (Jn

[30] See 1 Cor 11:25; Lk 22:20; Heb 10:19.

19:35) with all the enthusiasm of a man who has for so long bemoaned the flaming sword that closed all access to the tree of life (Gen 3:24). Yes, "They shall look on him whom they have pierced" (Zech 12:10 and Jn 19:37) and "they shall come trembling" (Hos 11:10) to drink from the side of their victim in whom they recognize their God.

But only the Spirit can bear witness to the mystery of the water and blood. It remains for us therefore to see how those who have died with Christ, and they alone, find in this death the work of the Spirit of resurrection in whom they can be born again.

10

The Breath of the Living God

Striving after the wind

The wisdom writers of Israel were obsessed by the thought of man's frailty, ever since the Exile had uprooted the kingdoms in which this people had tried to build up a history for itself. To express this frailty, the psalmists like to make use of the image of breath[1] that condenses for a second on meeting with cold air before being absorbed into it: "Surely every man stands as a mere breath . . . as nothing but turbulence of breath" (Ps 39:5–6). The most transparent and unstable of appearances, the vapor of breath was chosen by the author of the Book of Ecclesiastes to express the account of a life of striving: "Breath of breaths, the most fugitive of breath, all is nothing but breath!" (Eccles 1:2). Surrounded by a nature that renews itself each springtime, man knows that

[1] Another image is *shadow* (1 Chron 29:15; Job 8:9; 14:2; Ps 102:11; 109:23; 144:4; Eccles 6:12; 8:13; Wis 2:5; 5:9). Others are: morning mist or dew melted by the sun (Hos 6:4); light clouds that disappear in the midday sky (Wis 2:4); smoke (Hos 13:3); chaff before the wind (Zeph 2:2); a spark (Wis 2:2); the path of a boat (Wis 5:10) or a bird or an arrow (Wis 5:11–12); the memory of a one-day guest (Wis 5:14); the nightmare after waking (Ps 73:20); the locust that is gone at a bound (Ps 109:23); the grass or flower that withers in the east wind (Is 40:6–8); roses of a garland that die (Wis 2:8); froth dispersed by a storm (Wis 5:14). All these images, based on the same theme, show how much Israel was obsessed by the thought of the loss of sources of life.

in himself "dust returns to the earth as it was, and the spirit returns to God who gave it. The most fleeting of breaths, says the Preacher; all is mere breath." (Eccles 12:7–8). It is usually wrong to translate, in the Book of Ecclesiastes, the word "hevel" by "vanity". As the context of this last quotation shows, the word evokes for the author—as for the psalmists—that final clouding of a mirror which for a moment symbolizes the last breath of a dying person.

When your last breath has been blown away by the slightest current of air, are you going to "strive after wind", hoping it will give you back your vanished life? Where will you pursue the wind that has stolen away your last breath? "No man has power to retain the wind, or authority over the day of death" (Eccles 8:8). The expression "striving after the wind" is, according to Ecclesiastes,[2] the admission of defeat in an effort to endure. We should note also that in Hebrew the same word (*ṛūah*) means "wind" and "breath". This explains the constant interchange of the two meanings of the word. The man who tries to endure "strives after the wind" that escapes him in his last sigh. But man has no power "to master or to retain the breath" that animates him.

Breath and dust

According to Israelite tradition, man is thought of as made up of *dust* and *breath*. But this breath that gives him his being does not belong to man. The spirit of man is the breath of God breathed into the nostrils of a statuette modelled by him out of clay (Gen 2:7). As the flame of a match "catches" in a bundle of twigs, so the spirit of man is the breath of God that "catches" in man's lungs, and there sets

[2] 1:14,17; 2:11, 17, 26; 4:4, 6, 16; 6:9.

up the coming and going of breath, which is breathing. And man remains a living being so long as the source of breath is not cut off from his lungs; that is, as long as intake and output of breath keep the clockwork within him going. But if God "should take back his spirit to himself, and gather to himself his breath, all flesh would perish together, and man would return to dust" (Job 34:14–15). For it is only the breath of God that keeps man alive by animating the dust to which man will "return" when this breath leaves his lips in his last gasp (Gen 3:19).

Within the "human compound", the *dust* element[3] is therefore the symbol of despair: people used to cover their heads[4] when in mourning. On the other hand, the *breath* element expresses hope: a king is "[t]he breath of our nostrils" for his people (Lam 4:20) insofar as he is the incarnation of the nation's hope.

Breathe upon these slain!

If breath signifies life and its withdrawal death, the gift of a new breath to dead bodies will signify resurrection. In the Book of Revelation, the bodies of the two witnesses are left without burial in the street of the great city for all to see. Then "a breath of life from God entered them, and they stood up on their feet" (Rev 11:11). But it is in Ezekiel that the "breath" of resurrection is presented in the most striking manner (Ezek 37:1–10):

> The hand of Yahweh was upon me, and he brought me out by the breath of Yahweh, and set me down in the midst of the valley; it was full of bones. And he led me round among

[3] See Gen 18:27; Job 10:9; Ps 7:5; 22:15; 30:9; 44:26; 90:3; 103:14; 104:29; Eccles 3:20; Sir 16:30–17:1; Is 26:19; Dan 12:2.

[4] See Jos 7:6; 1 Sam 4:12; 2 Sam 1:2; Neh 9:1; Job 2:12; Lam 2:10; Ezek 27:30; Rev 18:19.

them; and behold, there were very many upon the valley; and behold, they were very dry. And he said to me, "Son of man, can these bones live?" And I answered, "O Lord Yahweh, you know." Again he said to me, "Prophesy to these bones, and say to them, O dry bones, hear the word of Yahweh. Thus says the Lord Yahweh to these bones: Behold I will cause breath to enter you, and you shall live. And I will lay sinews upon you, and will cause flesh to come upon you, and cover you with skin, and put breath in you, and you shall live; and you shall know that I am Yahweh." So I prophesied as I was commanded; and as I prophesied, there was a noise, and behold, a rattling; and the bones came together, bone to its bone. And as I looked, there were sinews on them, and flesh had come upon them, and skin covered them; but there was no breath in them. Then he said to me, "Prophesy to the breath, prophesy, son of man, and say to the breath, Thus says the Lord Yahweh: Come from the four winds, O breath, and breathe upon these slain, that they may live." So I prophesied as he commanded me, and the breath came into them, and they lived, and stood upon their feet, an exceedingly great host.

As an eagle swoops on its prey

Thus, on the command of God, Ezekiel succeeded in doing what appeared to the author of Ecclesiastes as the symbol of the impossible—the taming of the four winds and their breathing into the dead bodies as a breath of life to make them live again.

But is this not mere symbolism? Yes; just as "striving after the wind" symbolized for the Preacher the hopeless attempt to survive, so the taming of the wind signified for Ezekiel the rebirth of dead hope. God explained this to him:

"these bones are the whole house of Israel. Behold, they say, 'Our . . . hope is lost; we are clean cut off.' . . . But you

> shall know that I am Yahweh, when I open your graves, and raise you from your graves, O my people. And I will put my breath within you, and you shall live!" (Ezek 37:11, 13–14).

It is God who, in the person of the prophet, convokes the winds in which his breath moves, "blows to the south, and goes round to the north; round and round goes the wind, and on its circuits the wind returns" (Eccles 1:6). Led by the breath of Yahweh, Ezekiel himself first went here and there among the dry bones (37:1–2). Similarly, before the creation, "the breath of God was moving over the face of the waters" (Gen 1:2).

Then, by the mouth of his prophet, God commands his breath to stop its rapacious rounds over these dead bodies. Let it rather swoop on its prey like an eagle—but to give life.

Anointed by the breath of Yahweh

This divine eagle that soars over the world swoops not only on dead bodies to give them new life, but also on the living in order to possess them in a will (1 Sam 10:10; 19:20) or violent ecstasy (Judges 14:6, 19; 1 Sam 11:6). The one possessed by the breath of God is "turned into another man", because from now on "God is with [him]" (1 Sam 10:6–7), for his profit if he is docile to the inspiration (1 Sam 16:13; 18:14–16), for his hurt if he attempts to kick against the goad (1 Sam 16:14; 18:10; 19:9). When the oil runs down on the head of a man from a prophet's hand (1 Sam 10:1; 16:13; 1 Kings 1:34; 2 Kings 9:6), it transforms this son of Adam into "the Lord's anointed". This rite signifies essentially the gift of the "breath of Yahweh" as a new kind of power. At David's anointing this connection between the unction of Yahweh's anointed and the gift of Yahweh's breath is very striking: "Then Samuel took the horn of oil, and anointed him in the midst of his brothers; and the Spirit of Yahweh came mightily upon David from that day forward" (1 Sam 16:13).

As a dove comes to rest

A thousand years later, Yeshoua of Nazareth in the synagogue of his village received the scroll of the prophet Isaiah to read as the liturgical lesson in the village synagogue. He unrolled it as far as the place that we now call the beginning of the sixty-first chapter and read, "The Spirit of the Lord Yahweh is upon me, because Yahweh has anointed me...." The homily that he gave on this passage is very simple: "Today this scripture has been fulfilled in your hearing" (Lk 4:18, see 18–21). In fact, when he began to preach in Galilee, it was after his return from the Jordan, where he had been baptized by John and was "anointed with the Holy Spirit" (Acts 10:38).

When Jesus came up out of the water into which he had been plunged by the hand of the Baptist, the Breath came down upon him from heaven, not like an eagle swooping on to its prey, but like a dove coming to rest.[5] Possession by the Breath did not show itself in Jesus by the violent trances of a Saul,[6] but by the fullness of the gifts of God that are able to fill a human nature. As Isaiah had foreseen:

[5] Mt 3:16; Mk 1:10; Lk 3:22; Jn 1:32.

[6] On the contrary it was when Jesus expelled the "evil breath" from possessed people that it manifested itself in this manner (Mk 1:26; 9:26; cf. Lk 9:39).

There shall come forth a shoot from the stump of Jesse,
and a branch shall grow out of his roots.
And the Spirit of Yahweh shall rest upon him,
the spirit of wisdom and understanding,
the spirit of counsel and might,
the spirit of knowledge and the fear of Yahweh.
And his delight shall be in the fear of Yahweh.

(Is 11:1–3)

The Son gives life by his Breath

The "seven spirits of God" (Rev 1:4; 4:5), symbolized in the visual language of the Book of Revelation by the seven horns and seven eyes of the Lamb (5:6), signify the fullness of divine power and clear-sightedness. This power was not conferred on Jesus of Nazareth by some exterior source. The anointing by the Holy Spirit that John saw him receive was attested by the voice from on high: "This *is* my beloved Son, with whom I am well pleased" (Mt 3:17, emphasis added). "And John bore witness, 'I saw the Spirit descend as a dove from heaven and remain on him. I myself did not know him; but he who sent me to baptize with water said to me, "He on whom you see the Spirit descend and remain, *this is he* who baptizes with the Holy Spirit"' " (Jn 1:32–33, emphasis added). The solemn anointing of God's Anointed, his baptism in the Breath after being plunged into the Jordan, had therefore for its object the manifestation to the last prophet of the entry on the scene of the "well-beloved Son", anointed *as such* by the plenitude of the Breath of Yahweh and sent to baptize moribund humanity with that Breath which would restore life. And the life that the Anointed one will restore to humanity by the gift of his own Breath will be his own life as Son. In this way the reconciliation will be perfected, for only the Breath of the Son can breathe forth the name "Father". It is essential therefore that humanity be revived by the Breath of the Son so that man may be able to recognize God as his Father. Only thus can he finally escape from the haunting hallucination that disfigures the face in an unbearable way ever since the first disobedience. Paul bears witness to this: "God has sent the Spirit of his Son into our hearts, crying, 'Abba! Father!'" (Gal 4:6).[7] For Paul (2 Cor 1:21), as also for John (1 Jn 2:20, 27), the Breath communicated by Jesus to those baptized into his death is a participation in the Son's Anointing.

A matter of words

It must be obvious now that it is not out of idle fancy that I have so far used the word "Breath" instead of the more common "Spirit", and "Anointed" instead of "Messiah" or "Christ". Nowadays the word "spirit" evokes more the idea of the Greek *nous* (intellect) than the Greek *pneuma*, which designates primarily the breath of life. The word *spiritus* (from which came the English "spirit") has, in Latin, not lost its original sense of "breath" because of its obvious connection with the verb *spirare*. If one uses the word "spirit"

[7] In Aramaic, Jesus' language, *abba* means "father". Jesus used it at the beginning of his agony in Gethsemane (Mk 14:36). Mark, who uses this word heard by Peter when used by Jesus, was Paul's companion in his first missionary journey (Acts 12:24; 13:13; 15:37 and 39). When, a few years later, Paul wrote his epistle to the Galatians, why did he use an Aramaic word to express the filial supplication that the Breath of Jesus inspires in his disciples? Why does he use it again in Romans (8:15), when both Galatians and Romans did not know Aramaic, a language that Paul himself knew less well than Greek or Hebrew? Surely because the prayer of the Agony told him by Mark seemed the very type of filial supplication.

in English for Hebrew *rūah*, Greek *pneuma* or Latin *spiritus*, one immediately loses the association of images that these words suggest. It would no longer be seen why the "Spirit" gives life, or is called "from the four winds", nor why it is conferred by the Breath of Jesus (Jn 20:22) and calls out the name of Father. These things become more intelligible however if it is understood that this "spirit" is primarily a "breath". So it seems to me essential in biblical spirituality to sacrifice as little as possible the basic images underlying a whole conception of the world not yet formulated in a philosophical way.

It may be objected that in the Bible "breath" has gradually taken on many intellectual connotations that this word does not express satisfactorily, whereas the word "spirit" suggests them more readily. We can admit it and even point out that it is its maturing in biblical thought that has caused our word "spirit" to attach itself to the category of *nous*, whereas it sprang from the category of *pneuma*. But this transfer of meaning is an acquired fact. "Spirit" in English is a word that has been wholly uprooted. If we would recover its biblical roots, we must make use of the word "breath" and accept in advance the rich and subtle changes in meaning that the word assumed as its usage developed.

It is not my intention to reform the vocabulary of classical theology or of the catechism, but only to lay down certain basic demands for the vocabulary of biblical theology. This must remain embedded in a certain imagery. If it abandons this, it will merely be a speculative theology built up in an insufficiently rational way.

Similarly the words "Messiah", taken from the Hebrew, and "Christ", from the Greek, both mean "anointed". But this etymological value is no longer apparent to us in these words. I think therefore that biblical theology has everything to gain by keeping as far as possible to the image of anointing when speaking of Jesus.

Rebirth in the Breath

Having said this, let us return to the mystery of this Yeshoua who was anointed by the holy Breath. When John the Baptist saw the Breath descend and remain upon Jesus as he came up out of the Jordan, he understood that here was the one who had come to baptize, not like himself in water only, but in water and in the Breath.

Shortly after, when Jesus was talking by night with an influential Pharisee named Nicodemus, he opened up to him an unheard-of destiny:

> "Truly, truly, I say to you, unless one is born anew, he cannot see the kingdom of God."
> "How can a man be born when he is old? Can he enter a second time into his mother's womb and be born?"
> "Truly, truly, I say to you, unless one is born of water and the Breath, he cannot enter the kingdom of God. That which is born of the flesh is flesh, and that which is born of the Breath is breath. Do not marvel that I said to you, 'You must be born anew.' The breath breathes where it wills, and you hear the sound of it, but you do not know where it comes from or where it goes; so it is with every one who is born of the Breath" (Jn 3:3–8).

Just as the child drew in the breath of human life when he came into the world from his mother's womb, so it is reserved for him later to come to the Kingdom when he receives the Breath of a new life on coming forth from the womb of the baptismal waters.[8] Here we have a new Genesis

[8] For baptism as a new birth, see also Tit 3:5.

where the Breath that moves on the waters gives life to those that come forth from it. The mysterious happening that took place under the eyes of John the Baptist when he saw Jesus coming out of the Jordan thus takes on its full significance.

A Breath was only there . . .

But when Jesus was speaking to Nicodemus, this rebirth could not yet be accomplished, and John the Baptist was to die, leaving his disciples a baptism still incomplete. Nearly thirty years after the Baptist's death, Paul met some of these disciples at Ephesus and asked them:

> "Did you receive the holy Breath when you believed?"
> "No, we never even heard that there is a holy Breath."
> "Into what then were you baptized?"
> "Into John's baptism" (see Acts 19:2–3).

Then Paul had them baptized in the name of the Lord Jesus; the holy Breath came upon them,[9] and they began to speak with tongues[10] and to prophesy.[11]

. . . when Jesus had been glorified . . .

The ignorance of the disciples at Ephesus is explained by the evangelist John when he says that the holy Breath had not yet been given because Jesus was not yet glorified

[9] The gift of the holy Breath is intimately connected with baptism received in the Name of Jesus (Acts 2:38). Sometimes however it preceded it (Acts 10:44) or required the laying on of hands after it (Acts 8:15–17).

[10] For charisma of gift of tongues, see note in *JB* on Acts 2:4.

[11] On the charism of prohecy in the early Church see *JB*, p. 221 (New Testament pagination) note m on Acts 11:27.

(Jn 7:39). But to what event is the evangelist alluding when he speaks of the "glorification" of Jesus? One's first idea is that it must have been the Resurrection. Nevertheless, before his Passion, Jesus announced his immediate glorification to his disciples (Jn 12:23; 13:31; 17:1, 5), and this was on occasions when everything pointed toward his coming Passion (12:23–24; 13:30–31). The paradox of the cross, which one readily takes to be a characteristic of Paul (1 Cor 1:18–25), dwells as it were secretly in the Gospel of John. And so it was that on the first "Palm Sunday" Jesus declared, "Now is the judgment of this world, now shall the ruler of this world be cast out; and I, when I am lifted up from the earth, will draw all men to myself" (Jn 12:31–32).

. . . and lifted up from the earth . . .

This contrast between the fall of the prince of this world[12] and Jesus' exaltation makes of the latter a glorious occasion in which we should be tempted to see our Lord's coming forth from the tomb and his enthronement in heaven. To prevent our dreaming of resplendent glory, the evangelist comments on the words "lifted up from the earth": "He said this to show by what death he was to die" (12:33). The words already read in 3:14–16 have to be understood in the same sense: "And as Moses lifted up the serpent in the wilderness, so must the Son of man be *lifted up*, that whoever believes in him may have eternal life. For God so loved the world that he gave his only-begotten Son, that whoever believes in him should not perish but have eternal life."

[12] John speaks of "the prince of this world" in 16:11 (cf. 14:30). The meaning of "this world" is shown by the contexts where the expression occurs in his Gospel: 8:23; 12:25, 31; 13:1; 18:36; 1 Jn 4:17.

. . . like the bronze serpent . . .

The comparison between the "lifting up" of the Son of man and that of the bronze serpent is very enlightening. The people, lacking faith in their God, wished to rebel against Moses in the wilderness. God sent serpents against them with a deadly bite. Overcome by their punishment, the people acknowledged their sin and Moses prayed for them. God then commanded Moses to make a serpent of bronze and to set it on a pole, like the provincial standards of Egypt, "and if a serpent bit any man, he would look at the bronze serpent and live" (Num 21:9, see 4–9). This bronze serpent was preserved and later became the object of idolatry, so that King Hezekiah had to destroy it (2 Kings 18:4). These mixed memories, bound up with the bronze serpent, obliged the author of the Book of Wisdom to explain that those who turned toward the bronze serpent were not saved by the material object that they contemplated but by the "Savior of all" to whom they addressed their prayers. In the same manner as the phylacteries, the bronze serpent was supposed to remind people of "the commandment of the law" (Wis 16:6–7; cf. Ex 13:9).

. . . that saved believers who looked upon it

Just as it was necessary to look at the bronze serpent on its pole to be saved from the serpents, so it is necessary to look at the crucified one on his cross to be saved from death. And just as it was not enough to see that bronze object with bodily eyes but requiring instead the eyes of faith in the Savior of all, so it is not enough to gaze with bodily eyes at the crucified Christ nailed to the accursed wood, but glimpsing instead with eyes of faith the glory of

God's only Son manifested in that crucifixion. Furthermore, as the bronze serpent was a sign to remind people of the commandment of the law, so the crucified one is a sign to remind people of the commandment of the new law that is love.[13] "For God so loved the world that he gave his only-begotten Son" as a prey to the death that pursues his rebel children, "that whoever believes in him should not perish but have eternal life" (Jn 3:16).

The glorification of the Son nailed to the cross is not, then, the object of visible evidence but of faith. And so the Son requires an Advocate to plead his glory, which is mysteriously manifested only to the eyes of faith, and this Advocate (Paraclete) is none other than the Breath (Jn 14:26) of truth that bears witness to him (Jn 15:26).

The Breath bears witness to the Son . . .

> "Who is it that overcomes the world but he who believes that Jesus is the Son of God? This is he who came by water and blood, Jesus the Anointed, not with the water only but with the water and the blood. And the Breath is the witness, because the Breath is the truth. There are three witnesses, the Breath, the water, and the blood; and these three agree. If we receive the testimony of men, the testimony of God is greater; for this is the testimony of God that he has borne witness to his Son. . . . God gave us eternal life, and this life is in his Son. He who has the Son has life; he who has not the Son has not life. I write this to you who believe in the name of the Son of God, that you may know that you have eternal life.
>
> (1 Jn 5:5–13)

[13] The cross of Jesus is the supreme witness of God's love for men: Mt 20:28; Jn 10:11; 15:13; Rom 5:8; Eph 5:2 and 25; 1 Jn 3:16.

The fact that he who has come by the water of penitence and the blood of execution *is the Son of God*, forms the very substance of saving faith and is the first act of witness given by the Breath of truth. It is really a matter of believing "in the name of the only-begotten Son of God" (Jn 3:18), since "[he] who believes in the Son has eternal life;[14] he who does not obey the Son shall not see life" (3:36). But it is only when glorified by being lifted up on the cross that the Son becomes the object of faith for the gaze of "those who have pierced him" (Jn 19:37; Rev 1:7; cf. Zech 12:10). For this lifting up is really his enthronement. Here we have the unperceived meaning of the words "[w]hat I have written I have written" (Jn 19:22) uttered by Pilate concerning the title for Jesus' cross; he intended to ridicule the leading Jews in designating the crucified one as their king.

The glorification of Jesus on the cross is no more the conferring of a new privilege upon him than was the descent of the Breath on him at the moment of his baptism. The novelty is the opportunity that Jesus' Passion offers for believers to contemplate, in its glorious manifestation, his privilege as only Son (Jn 1:14), a privilege he holds from that love with which the Father loved him before the world was made (17:24 and verse 5).

The glory of the Son is to be "the only-begotten Son, who is in the bosom of the Father" (Jn 1:18), the "beloved Son with ... [whom the Father is] well pleased" (Mk 1:11),[15] the one who gives the Breath without measure, for "the

[14] For John, eternal life depends entirely on the faith that "Jesus is the Son of God". See texts already cited and Jn 6:40; 20:31.

[15] Jesus is said to be the "beloved Son" in Mt 3:17; 12:18; 17:5; Mk 1:11; 9:7; 12:6; Lk 3:22; 9:35; 20:13; 2 Pet 1:17.

Father loves the Son, and has given all things into his hand" (Jn 3:34–35).

... by the mouth of a centurion

But can it be that he who was condemned by the religious leaders of his people and hanged on the gibbet of the accursed (Gal 3:13), and who finally expired after crying out, "My God, my God, why have you forsaken me?"—can he be the Son? And yet it was a Roman centurion on guard before the cross who, on seeing the victim yield up his last breath, cried out, "Truly this man was a Son of God!" (Mk 15:34–39). Certainly this gentile knew as little of the motives for this condemnation as he did of the confidences given to the beloved disciple. He did not share in the disappointed hopes of those nationalist fanatics who had mistakenly expected that Jesus would restore national independence. But Jesus had said, "For judgment I came into this world, that those who do not see may see, and that those who see may become blind" (Jn 9:39). None of those who had every reason to see clearly knew how to confess in a loud voice before Christ crucified that he was the "Son of God". Neither the theologians of Israel, nor the nationalists waiting for their liberation by God's Anointed, nor even the disciples who had been brought up in intimacy with him, none of these confessed the Son at the precise moment of his glorification. It was a soldier of the occupying forces, carrying out a routine job of crucifixion, who alone lent his lips to the Breath of truth, to the Son's Advocate, for this solemn form of witness. For the Son had to be "a sign that is spoken against" (Lk 2:34) at the moment of his bloody enthronement on Calvary.

The Cross, glory of the Only-Begotten

Let us now listen to what the Breath of truth has to say before the dying Yeshoua of Nazareth. The Father's love for his only Son bursts forth in his sowing of his Son in a humanity that will now be able by faith to become unified in him. For the seed dies in the earth only so as to be able to yield its fruit. The Son only breathed forth his last breath as mortal man so as to be able to give the holy Breath to dying humanity. If it is his only Son whom the Father has chosen as victim, it is precisely because he is his well-beloved in whom he wills to perfect the destiny of a reborn humanity. His Son is his only true image, so it is according to this image that the divine sculptor wills to perfect his likeness in humanity. And the Son expresses most fully the image of the Father by dying on the cross. For God is Love (1 Jn 4:8, 16), and it is by giving his life for those he loves that the Son gives them the testimony of perfect love (Jn 15:13). By acting in this way, the Son raises up his love for men to the level of a perfect image of the love with which the Father loves him (Jn 15:9; 17:23). When the crucified one breathed his last sigh, the mystery of love that is God attained its full human transparency. In the innocent victim who dies so that his murderers may find life, love attains incandescence. And so the "name" of the Father (he who gives life by love) is perfectly glorified by the Son (12:28; 17:26), and at the same time the Son is glorified as he who comes in his Father's name (Jn 5:43).

But none can come by faith to the mystery of the Son in the brightness of his crucified glory unless the Father who sent the Son draws that Son's disciple (6:44) by the inward witness of the Breath of truth who inspires the confession of the faithful before the despised cross of their Savior.

Build a tomb for the Son of God?

From the moment that the Son was raised up on his throne of agony, there has existed a Breath (7:39) to plead as the Advocate of his glory. He pleads for the reversal of his sentence in the ears of those who pierce him and who contemplate him with amazement; a reversal that will work in their hearts, leading them to confess their sin and to condemn themselves as the murderers of their God just when they had thought they were just judges of a malefactor. And the divine Advocate does not make his pleading heard only before the crucified of Good Friday. He makes it heard before all those who are despised and rejected by their brethren in the image of him who is the Image of God. "No man has ever seen God" (1 Jn 4:12) and we did not see the Nazarene crucified to judge us for judging him, but we constantly have before our eyes those of whom he said, "Truly, I say to you, as you did it to one of the least of these my brethren, you did it to me" (Mt 25:40) and "as you did it not to one of the least of these, you did it not to me" (v. 45). It is, then, by our attitude toward those who, in his image, are despised and rejected that we can judge the sincerity of the confession of faith by which we pretend to hail as Son of God the one who was rejected by his brethren. In their presence we shall hear the Advocate become an accuser: "Woe to you, hypocrites! For you build tombs" for the Son of God, "saying, 'If we had lived in the days of our fathers, we would not have taken part with them in shedding the blood'" of the Son of God. "Thus you witness against yourselves, that you are the sons of those who murdered" the Son of God (cf. Mt 23:29–31). What kind of faith is it that "builds a tomb" for the Son of God? It is your own faith if you pretend to give thanks to him who died for love of you and at the same time stifle within you his Breath who dies of love for the most despised of his brethren.

The Breath, advocate or accuser

"The Father judges no one, but has given all judgment to the Son" (Jn 5:22). Before the face of the Son as judge stands the Breath as advocate. It was the pleading of this advocate that converted the executioners by making them recognize by faith the Son as judge in the features of the condemned criminal on Good Friday. Will they recognize out of love, every day, this same criminal in the features of every friendless pauper? If so, then they have in the Breath of truth an advocate before the judge, for the Breath of the Son who is Love is not cramped within them but has become their life. If not, then the Breath of truth will be their accuser before the judge, denouncing the hypocrisy of a faith that gave glory to the Son while refusing to be enkindled by the Breath of love that consumes him.

The baptismal gift of Breath

Now baptism is the very occasion on which the Breath of Jesus gives life to him who has chosen to plunge his own death into that of the Son of God. Baptism seals the confession of faith of those who have listened to the pleading of the Breath-Advocate. At the same time baptism animates with the Breath of the Son those sons of Adam who have chosen the cross of God's Son as the place for their death.

The last mortal breath of Jesus was the crowning work of the Breath of love and let loose on the world the tempest of this divine Breath. This was the Breath that rent the veil of the Temple and brought the dead to life (Mt 27:51–52) at the moment when he who is the Resurrection died (Jn 11:25). This was the Breath that raised up the crucified on the third day and established him in shining glory as Son of God (Rom 1:4) and Lord. This was the Breath with which, fifty days later, the Lord set his disciples on fire at Pentecost (Acts 2:2–4, 33). And this was the Breath who takes possession of those who are baptized in the name of the Lord Jesus (Acts 2:38; 8:17; 10:44–48; 19:5–6; 1 Cor 6:11; Titus 3:5) and born anew (Jn 3:5–6).

A covenant written on hearts with the Breath of God

But baptism as a sacrament is only the beginning of a destiny that is to be lived to the full under the sign of baptism as a mystery. What does this mean? It means that in him who has been baptized, the old man must be consumed by the same Breath of love that animates the new man. The docility to the Breath of love that was breathed forth by the crucified Son of God is the law of life for him who has been reborn as son of the Father in the Only-Begotten. The baptismal gift of Breath seals the New Covenant concluded by the Son of God, "written not with ink but with the Breath of the living God, not on tablets of stone but on tablets of human hearts" (2 Cor 3:3). Yahweh had foretold this by the mouth of Jeremiah:

> "Behold, the days are coming when . . . I will make a new covenant . . . I will put my law within them, and I will write it upon their hearts; and I will be their God, and they shall be my people. And no longer shall each man teach his neighbor and each his brother, saying, 'Know Yahweh,' for they shall all know me, from the least of them to the greatest, says Yahweh" (31:31–34).

And by the mouth of Ezekiel he explained:

> "I will sprinkle clean water upon you ... A new heart I will give you, and a new breath I will put within you; and I will take out of your flesh the heart of stone and give you a heart of flesh. And I will put my breath within you, and cause you to walk in my statutes and be careful to observe my ordinances" (36:25–27).

The Father will root out of the son of Adam what the degenerate call "love" and will plant within him instead what he himself calls love and what is his Breath. Then the life of man will take the form of the cross of his Lord in the eyes of his brethren. And the Father will recognize his Son in him whom the Breath will have regenerated in the image of the Only-Begotten.

INDEX

SCRIPTURE INDEX

OLD TESTAMENT

Genesis